2411

5.50

D1147694

This book is due for return o

FOR MY PARENTS

· MICHAEL DONNELLY ·

MANAGING
THE
MIND

A STUDY OF
MEDICAL PSYCHOLOGY
IN EARLY
NINETEENTH-CENTURY
BRITAIN

· TAVISTOCK PUBLICATIONS ·
LONDON AND NEW YORK

First published in 1983 by
Tavistock Publications Ltd
11, New Fetter Lane,
London EC4P 4EE

Published in the USA by
Tavistock Publications
in association with Methuen Inc.
733, Third Avenue, New York,
NY 10017

© 1983 Michael Donnelly

Typeset in Great Britain by
Scarborough Typesetting Services
and printed in the United States of America

British Library Cataloguing in
Publication Data

Donnelly, Michael
Managing the mind.
1. Psychology—History
I. Title
150'.9   BF81

ISBN 0–422–78370–6
ISBN 0–422–78380–3 Pbk.

Library of Congress Cataloging in
Publication Data

Donnelly, Michael, 1949–
Managing the mind.
Published in association with Methuen.
Bibliography: p.
Includes index.
1. Psychiatry—Great Britain—History.
I. Title.
[DNLM: 1. Psychiatry—History—
Great Britain.
2. Psychology, Medical—History—
Great Britain.   WM 11 FA1 D6m]
RC451.G7D66   1983   616.89' 00941
83–4748

ISBN 0–422–78370–6
ISBN 0–422–78380–3 (pbk.)

CONTENTS

PREFACE

This is a study of the formative period of medical psychology, the discipline which preceded and prepared the ground for modern psychiatry. It treats principally the decades between 1790 and 1850, and is based primarily on British materials, though much of what it relates pertains also to continental Europe and North America. From this vantage the study tries to reconstruct certain of the conditions, both institutional and ideological, under which new practices of psychological medicine emerged and developed.

The essay falls roughly into two parts. It describes firstly the historic shift in social policies which initiated the era of mental institutions. In the late eighteenth century there were few asylums in Britain, and few of the insane received medical attentions. By the late nineteenth century there was a national system of lunatic asylums, which catered for the great majority of insane patients and constituted the treatment of choice for many forms of insanity. Across the intervening decades the legal status of 'insane persons' changed dramatically; the state sponsored and funded an impressive programme to build 'fitting receptacles' for the insane; and mental institutions became a significant (and apparently permanent) part of social welfare. These were the great institutional changes initiated during the period.

The second part of the essay reconstitutes contemporary 'discourses' on insanity. It treats both the propositions of medical psychology itself, and also a set of more diffuse cultural representations of the insane and of madness. The ideological shifts in the period were equally dramatic and momentous. As against the earlier medicine of insanity medical psychology seemed to recuperate the insane as moral subjects: instead of brutes to be closely bound or beaten, they seemed individuals sensible of, and sensitive to, more gentle treatments, by moral means. 'Moral treatment' was indeed the reforming slogan to describe the new psychological techniques for managing the mind. This was the important ideological temper of the period.

The ground over which the essay moves has been charted frequently before. In histories of psychiatry and of social welfare the period 1790–1850 typically marks a watershed, or indeed a crucial turning point. This is the period of 'the birth of psychiatry' (see Zilboorg 1941), of 'the discovery of the asylum' (see Rothman 1971), of 'the nineteenth-century revolution in government', of 'the age of improvement'. By way of shorthand these labels are probably warranted. For the specific case of the mentally disordered the period marked a decisive change in their fate: institutional care became the first resort; and medical psychology produced the first recognizably modern knowledge and treatment of mental disorders.

How to reconstruct or account for these developments is a more difficult and controversial problem. The strategy adopted here is somewhat unusual, and requires a word of introduction. This essay does not offer a continuous narrative about 'the rise of medical psychology'; nor indeed does it advance a single comprehensive explanation of how, when, or why medical psychology rose as it did. The essay assembles and juxtaposes, rather, an array of disparate and dispersed materials – which it presents in a neutral, documentary tone – to suggest the different elements which constituted medical psychology. These elements range beyond what one would otherwise find in a history of psychiatric ideas or a history of provisions for the insane; and they are organized differently. The aim is to reconstruct a complex conjuncture of the varied elements which together made medical psychology possible. The underlying argument of the essay is that neither a history of psychiatric ideas nor a history of provisions for the insane is well-suited to represent this conjuncture.

Assembling and juxtaposing as the essay does may seem a cumbersome and inelegant procedure. It doubtless sacrifices many of the pleasures of the historical narrative which tells a story with dramatis personae, plot, denouement. . . . But it is a useful defence against certain risks to which the historiography of lunatic asylums and early psychiatry has been prone.

On the most common view the discovery of the asylum and the birth of psychiatry were works of 'reform'. This view has the virtue of being consistent with the rhetoric of contemporaries, who were self-styled 'reformers'. Furthermore, in an obvious sense, compared to the past these developments were reforms. They began with well-publicized disclosures about what the insane often suffered under the old system: frequent neglect, relieved only by haphazard individual charities; cruel, harsh, and uncomprehending repression which aggravated rather than treated their conditions. In place of haphazard relief, reform promised systematic provision of asylum care for 'all insane persons'; and in place of cruelty, an appropriate moral treatment based on kindness, sympathy, and psychological suasion. Against such a background the programme for lunacy reforms may well seem an historically appropriate or indeed necessary and inevitable response. It is hardly surprising (and doubtless apt) that historians should sympathize explicitly with such acts or intents of reform, and construct narratives accordingly.

The difficulty arises when sympathy for 'reform' swamps a proper sense of the past and its otherness. Then historians succumb or risk succumbing to a variety of anachronisms, collapsing the historical distance between themselves and their subjects, or reading present-day certainties and concerns back into a past where they did not (yet) exist. This is an evident problem with many histories of psychiatric ideas. In virtually all of the narratives there is a notable quickening of interest when the story reaches the late eighteenth or early nineteenth centuries. This is doubtless appropriate because of the importance of the period; but it happens also because historians recognize something 'modern' about that moment, and this quickens their sympathies. The figure of speech 'birth of psychiatry' so frequently applied to the period is a telling indicator. It contains a prediction of what is to come later, which was obviously denied to contemporaries; it defines phenomena from the aspect of their future destiny. What the historical accounts typically describe is how mad-doctors and alienists 'anticipated' later developments; how they were 'precursors' of later figures. The point of view for such statements is obviously the present. By virtue of hindsight historians know what has in fact happened – how the story is to end. The risk is that historians can be swayed by this knowledge in their selection and presentation of past events. Hence the lunacy reforms and reformers can seem interesting not only in themselves but because of what happened later; indeed later events in one way or another vindicated or endorsed retrospectively the 'vision' of the reformers. But the past cannot be represented as the future-in-embryo without distortion. Celebrating the lunacy reforms as the beginning of the modern era has thus had the effect of shrinking the real distance between early nineteenth-century medical psychology and the present. In assimilating past figures to the present historians have on many occasions lost their firm or sure grasp on the past – in its own terms. The result is that histories of the period at times evacuate much of the full content of contemporary thought – particularly those aspects which seem un-modern.

There is a second, related form of anachronism which stems from the questions that the historians typically pose themselves to answer. For writings about asylums and early psychiatry the over-arching questions are: how has society provided for the insane? and what is the history of ideas of madness? (or more specifically what is the history of psychiatric ideas?). These seem innocuous and straightforward questions. J. H. Plumb has suggested as plainly as anyone their rationale:

> 'Although human societies are capable of infinite variety in customs, morals, social organization and disposal of wealth and power, all breed individuals who are so aberrant − mad, if you wish − that they cannot be absorbed into the accepted patterns of living. And it was these − the idiots, the madmen, the mentally deficient − who, with the crippled at birth, created, perhaps, man's oldest social problem.
>
> (Plumb 1972: 25)

If it is taken in a loose way this statement is probably hard to fault. But it nonetheless betrays also a present-day point of view which is likely to mar historical writing. Most histories of asylums or of early psychiatry take for granted the present-day categories of mental disorder, and likewise the varied 'social problems' which these present. They then organize their inquiries in an implicitly functionalist fashion: taking these present-day categories (the mentally disordered as social problems) for universals, they ask, for example, how have other or previous societies 'coped' with the burden of the mentally disordered? What arrangements in other societies are/were the functional equivalents of modern mental hospitals? What ideas are/were the functional equivalents of modern psychiatric ideas? These are questions about historical or cultural variation, but they are posed only as the historian holds constant some category which, in essentials, is taken to be universal and naturalistic.

On this assumption it seems entirely appropriate and creditable that lunacy reformers of the nineteenth century should have created a univocal category, 'the insane', in law and social policy. This was a matter of discovering and acknowledging a class of unfortunates which already existed, and newly accepting responsibility for their care. Indeed the question which arises is, why did earlier societies fail to do this? In a similar way for histories of ideas the question arises, what obstacles prevented earlier societies from appreciating the real character of mental disorders (which scientific psychiatry has disclosed)?

If 'the insane' are taken, however, not as a naturalistic but as an historically constructed category, the questions to ask shift dramatically. On this second assumption it becomes itself an historical problem to account for the creation of a class of 'all insane persons'. In this instance at least it is the second assumption which is doubtless the more warranted and fruitful – and the one closer to the historical evidence. In the event 'the insane' was not an obvious, univocal category in the late eighteenth century. It emerged only against considerable odds, and probably only because of the unusual prestige accorded for several generations to medical psychology. It was not the social salience of insanity (nor the social problems the insane occasioned) which produced the category; in these respects the insane were quite heterogeneous. What was decisive were the *mental* characteristics (as perceived and defined by medical psychology) of the insane – which might have different and variable social consequences. Hence the early nineteenth-century category was literally conceivable only with the aid of psychological theories. The category was constructed at a particular, and historically contingent, conjuncture. This is a difficult point to grasp if one assumes from the beginning that the category 'the insane' is a stable referent – the constant in the equation. If the aim is to discover how societies have provided for a universal social problem – the insane – this prejudices the inquiry from the outset.

If the notion of the insane is problematic, then likewise the character of the lunacy reforms becomes more complicated to specify. The reforms were not simply a pragmatic accommodation to the self-evident 'social problems' the insane presented; nor simply a philanthropic or humanitarian response to the plight of unfortunates. These motives were doubtless significant, but they cannot suffice as an explanation. The creation of 'the insane' as a category in law and as an object of medical psychology has had in turn myriad and long-term consequences. Neither development was, however, foreordained or in any larger sense historically 'appropriate' or necessary. How these developments occurred was rather the effect of an historical conjuncture which needs to be reconstructed.

The intent of this essay is to work at cross-purposes against what are still commonly implicit assumptions in histories of the asylum and of early psychiatry. For this reason the study may be able to add something fresh to the growing specialist literature.

It may, more importantly, contribute something to an inquiry which is unlikely to have its own specialists. The larger aim of the essay is to begin reconstructing a more general contemporary notion of 'management', of which medical psychology supplies an exemplary, influential, and central instance, but only one special application. This is work which is just beginning. The links between lunacy reform and prison reform are now widely acknowledged. But there was in fact a much wider domain – what one can term loosely 'the social' – for which contemporary notions of 'management' were pertinent. Compared with the grander subjects of politics and economics, the contemporary discourses on 'the social' make an odd medley. They speak about domestic relationships in the family, between spouses and between parents and children; about training and discipline in the workshop; about education and the suasion of religious congregations; about managing institutional inmates; about 'taste', mores, and leisure habits; about the social psychology of the different classes; about the poor and how they might be moralized or made susceptible to the bite of economic incentives; and so forth. They speak, in sum, about 'character' and the exercise of moral influence or moral force by one party over another. These are more the humble concerns of day-to-day life than of great movements; and the discourses that speak of them are rarely grand or philosophic, but more given over to practical advice, anecdote, and the like.

These discourses – to which medical psychology provides an excellent introduction – reveal a good deal, despite their apparently humble character, about how contemporaries understood, and managed, their social relations. The formation of 'character', and hence of free-standing, competent individuals, was after all something that contemporary politics and economics presupposed but did not themselves account for. Before political society (before the society of juridical relations among contracting citizens), there were free-standing individuals; and likewise before civil society (before the society of market traders harmonized by an invisible hand), there were subjects capable of calculating their self-interest. How such individuals could be formed, and how their characters or personalities could be sustained, were in the end the burden of the social field. Even if inchoate, the social field was thus a necessary substratum for loftier discourses on political society and civil society. Reconstructing medical psychology makes at least a start in laying out the wider outlines of contemporary discourses on 'the social'.

This is the structure of the essay. Chapter 1 presents an overview of the legal and institutional changes which together created a social policy for the insane. It moves schematically across the major events of the lunacy reforms, and highlights one theme of the essay as a whole: the emergence of a class of 'insane persons' defined by their distinctive mental states.

Chapters 2 and 3, on representations of the model asylum and on the architecture of confinement, fill out certain aspects of the ideological temper or ethos of the reforms. They suggest that the programme to build 'fitting receptacles' for the insane was far more than a pragmatic or humanitarian measure to house and relieve distressed and disabled people. It involved rather more complicated notions of social relations and moral management within asylum practices.

Chapter 4 asks who were 'the insane' for whom these 'fitting receptacles' were designed. It reviews the medical, legal, and administrative classifications of the day, and the whole array of extant statistics about the insane. While these sources are very telling signs of the contemporary opinions about madness, they reveal little in a representative way about the contemporary character of 'madness' or the social characteristics of its victims. These remain difficult to infer.

The balance of the study considers 'medical psychology and allied discourses'. It passes in review a number of cultural themes – the 'problem of the irrational', the 'psychology of social classes', 'universal reason and individual differences', notions of 'moral influence' – which were pertinent to the understanding and definition of madness. Such perceptions of madness were hardly elaborated with scientific rigour; but they helped mark off the terrain on which medical psychology advanced and informed the practices which were established in the new lunatic asylums.

Once so established and institutionalized, as the study concludes, the discipline of medical psychology and the knowledge it produced became the authoritative discourse on madness and the source of rationales for its treatment.

A NOTE ON TERMINOLOGY

During the period on which this study focuses, there was no consistent or uniform set of terms for referring to the 'medical disorders'. The vocabulary of medical psychology became in time distinctive and specialized, and increasingly removed from lay terminology. The early terms were drawn particularly from Greek equivalents of words in popular use; they were in general not clearly or univocally defined. Although seemingly technical, they were in many cases rough-hewn and sometimes little more specific in their referents than their more colourful equivalents in the language of the street. As regards the general terms 'madness', 'insanity', 'lunacy', and 'idiocy', there was likewise little more precise usage among medical psychologists than among the general public. To suggest the full range and contemporary significance of these terms, their embellishments in popular speech and their more technical uses in medical discourse, would require a large-scale literary and linguistic analysis which is unfortunately beyond the scope of these pages.

Nonetheless, despite the strange impression of certain contemporary terms on modern ears attuned to a different psychiatric and psychological vocabulary, for the purpose of this study I have prefered the older usages even where these are likely to be somewhat obscure. Modern terms are not only inappropriate to represent the older categories, but more seriously would introduce all the risks of anachronism which this study, in its historical method, was conceived in part to avoid.

REFERENCES

A list of works cited is appended to the text. Where not otherwise noted in the references, the place of publication was London. For selective bibliographies in the subject and additional references readers should consult Hunter and Macalpine (1963), Jones (1972), Mora (1965), Scull (1979 and 1981), and Skultans (1975).

ACKNOWLEDGEMENTS

This essay was first completed in 1976, and then recently revised. A grant from the American Council of Learned Societies aided revisions. The essay took shape initially in discussions with Dr Susanne MacGregor and Professor Eric Hobsbawm. I would like to thank also friends, teachers, and colleagues who commented on parts on the manuscript, including Paul Hirst, Allen Adinolfi, Jim Mott, Michael Ignatieff, Stan Cohen, and Ed Hundert.

M.D.
1982

PART I
'FITTING RECEPTACLES'

· 1 ·

A SOCIAL POLICY FOR THE
INSANE

The practice of confining the mad is ancient; 'mental institutions' in the generic sense are, however, a relatively modern development. Before the eighteenth century the Bethlem Hospital was the only public institution for the insane in England, and one of very few in Europe. In the course of the next century several new lunatic asylums were put up in London and the provinces, and several civic infirmaries established separate wards specifically for the insane. The scale of even these establishments − the early varieties of separate confinement for the insane − was by modern standards tiny. The greater number of the insane who were confined were held under other arrangements, and generally outside medical auspices, in private 'madhouses', in gaols and bridewells, in poorhouses and work-houses, in back rooms or under the stairs. Confinement of the insane, whether vagrants, felons, the 'furiously mad' and dangerous, or the indigent and infirm, was largely expedient and often informal. Such was the customary fate of the insane until the state progressively established specific policies for confining 'insane persons', under a single jurisdiction, as a separate class.

The era of 'mental institutions' began in the early nineteenth century, although only fitfully. Parliament enacted a series of lunacy Bills drafted by a group of reformers, which redefined the legal status of the insane and encouraged a programme of building lunatic asylums. The early Acts were only partially effective; they remain of particular historical interest, how-ever, since they established the essential policies and programme which later Acts effectively carried into force. Thus the Lunacy Acts of 1845 made mandatory the building of county and borough asylums which the original County Asylums Act of 1808 had merely authorized and en-couraged. After 1845 the construction of asylums which lunacy reformers over several generations had urged accelerated sharply; soon after the mid-century the backbone of the modern system of mental hospitals (such as they were until very recently) was in place.

The state's capacity to confine the insane, separately, in 'fitting and proper' receptacles thus developed apace. At the end of the eighteenth century public asylums held probably no more than a thousand insane inmates. In 1844, of the more than 20,000 'insane persons' officially registered, a quarter were held in the purpose-built county asylums, a further quarter were confined in other public asylums or in private licensed madhouses, and half were still in workhouses, at home, or farmed out privately. From the 1850s the rate of committals to asylums and the numbers in confinement grew rapidly. By 1890 the lunatic population was more than 90,000, the greater number of whom were housed in the county and borough asylums. The trend to large-scale institutionalization was by then well established; and the fate of the insane was largely to pass the course of their disorders in mental institutions – in those great establishments which bulk prominently among the products of Victorian philanthropy.[1]

Before 1845 the fate of the insane was less certain or predictable, less uniform and less well regulated. Those who found their way to the early asylums and lunatic hospitals, which afforded the first separate confinement and a degree of medical attentions, were relatively few; they were probably only a small proportion of the insane. In addition, from the mid-eighteenth century the private 'madhouses' which began to spring up held an uncertain number of fee-paying inmates (see Parry-Jones 1972). But the majority of those confined were still held under more general confinement, amid other classes of the dependent, deviant, or criminal, in bridewells, workhouses, and common gaols. Some of the insane wandered, or otherwise fended for themselves as mendicants or magicians.[2] A large number no doubt were protected and sheltered by their families within the household, or were boarded out locally with neighbours.

The history of such provisions for the insane, in all their variety, is obscure before the era of mental institutions. Of the early varieties of separate confinement, the oldest and most celebrated English asylum, Bethlem, is familiar if not infamous largely from literary references. Bethlem was in fact more important by far for its reputation than for the actual dimensions of its charity. In 1403 a Royal Commission investigating the hospital found only *sex viri mente capti* and a somewhat larger inventory of manacles and chains apparently used to restrain them. In the mid-seventeenth century Bethlem housed at most forty 'distracted persons' yet was famous across Europe. Its corrupted name 'bedlam' already suggested by extension 'a scene of mad confusion or uproar' (OED). 'Bedlamite' and 'Tom o' Bedlam' were commonly known and widely used descriptions, although few of the insane actually enjoyed Bethlem's charity or even the ruder protection of a local 'bedlam-house'.[3]

St Mary of Bethlehem was founded in the thirteenth century, and like other medieval monastic houses probably on occasion relieved individual lunatics or idiots. The priory had acquired a particular association with the insane by perhaps the fourteenth century, and subsequently received a number of bequests and legacies given specifically to relieve those 'distress'd in their wits'. In the mid-sixteenth century Bethlem was rechartered as one of the five original Royal Hospitals of the City of London, and reserved for lunatics; it was later annexed by the Governors of the original Bridewell Hospital and managed as an adjunct, or perhaps fitting complement, to the Bridewell which was founded to correct the strumpet and the idle rogue (Clay 1909: 31ff., and Copeland 1888).

An official inquiry 'into the affairs of Bethlem Hospital' in 1633 established that most of the inmates were poor and from London and environs. The Governors, who were in most cases themselves substantial contributors to the hospital, decided the admissions policies and left the actual management to the janitor. The hospital apparently admitted in general on the basis of petitions and recommendations from the local aldermen, church wardens, or overseers of the poor. There were at times some well-born or notable cases among the inmates, including Oliver Cromwell's porter Daniel, who was a religious maniac; Nat Lee, the drunken poet and playwright; and the troublesome Richard Stafford, who was confined by order of the Board of the Green Cloth for dispersing 'many Scandalous Pamphlets and libells filled with Enthusiasm and Sedition' (Wheatley 1891: I, 175). Such notable inmates frequently became the butts of popular satirists or furnished object-lessons for moral preachers, and they are thus more a part of the remarkable fund of legend, folklore, and anecdote which Bethlem generated from its early days, than representative of its real history.

The hospital was reconstructed in 1675–76 on a prominent site in Moorfields, by the Ditch; the siting of Bedlam there no doubt further enriched the already 'colourful' reputation of the district.[4] It was by all accounts an impressive and conspicuous building among London's landmarks, with a frontage of over 500 feet, although it was shoddily built and decayed in little over a hundred years. The new hospital could accommodate 120 inmates, who were admitted then somewhat selectively. The hospital would accept inmates for only a maximum twelve-month period, and required the parish or relatives of the lunatic to make a bond agreement to remove him if he remained 'uncured' (or bury him if he died in the meanwhile).

Bethlem had as well other specific policies toward admissions, and like other later asylums refused entry to pregnant women, the venereally diseased, and often to epileptics, as well as 'incurables'. In the words of a contemporary account:

> 'Now those are judged the fittest Objects for this Hospital that are raving and furious, and capable of Cure; or if not, yet are likely to do mischief to themselves or others; and are Poor, and cannot be otherwise provided for. But those that are only Melancholik, or Ideots, and judged not capable of Cure, these the Governors think the House ought not to be burthened with.'   (Strype 1720: I, 192f.)

The hospital was indeed 'burthened' with too many petitions for relief even in the seventeenth century; hence the specific conditions defining the proper objects of its charity. The actual practices of admitting to Bethlem are, however, in general unclear. By reputation (perhaps simply on the strength of their association with Bedlam) the Bedlamites were the most outrageous and extravagant of madmen.

In the mid-eighteenth century two wings for 'Incurable Lunaticks' were appended to the hospital building, as a result of a large bequest in 1733 for this purpose. These wings provided for perhaps another hundred inmates, which nearly doubled Bethlem's capacity. A ward for chronic lunatics was likewise opened at Guy's Hospital, London, in 1728, in accordance with the conditions of Guy's will. Despite these bequests a considerable number of charitable appeals continued to urge the relief of lunatics and to put forward, as in a Spital Sermon of 1759, 'the Case of Incurable Lunaticks, and the Charity due to them'.

Bethlem was a large establishment by eighteenth-century standards, holding at times as many as 300 inmates. But it could accommodate only a portion of the London insane who were then confined. In 1751 a rival institution to Bethlem, St Luke's Hospital for Lunaticks, was founded in London and sited in Upper Moorfields opposite Bethlem. It was established as a subscription hospital, and supported largely by London merchants (like the contemporary lying-in hospitals and foundling homes). St Luke's was designed to accommodate people of some means, at a time when Bethlem was suffering particular criticisms from within the medical professions about its standards of treatment, and when Bedlamites still suffered the notoriety which open public visiting in Bethlem on Sundays occasioned. The original appeal for funds argued that 'the Principal End' in establishing another 'Hospitall for *Lunaticks*' was plain:

> 'not only as [lunaticks] are incapable of providing for themselves and Families, are not admitted into other Hospitalls or capable of being relieved (as in other Diseases) by private Charity: but also as there must be Servants peculiarly qualified, and every Patient must have a separate Room, and Diet, most of them, equal to Persons in Health. From hence it appears, that the Expences necessarily attending the Confinement and other means of Cure, are such as People even in middling Circumstances cannot bear, it generally requiring several Months, and often a whole Year before a Cure is compleated.'
>
> (*Reasons for the Establishing and Further Encouragement of St Luke's Hospitall for Lunaticks* 1772)

By 1772 St Luke's housed about eighty patients, some of whom were admitted as 'uncurables', and it provided a modicum of clinical training for mad-doctors and other physicians and apothecaries. When the hospital was rebuilt in Old Street in 1786 it was greatly expanded, and by the turn of the century housed about 250 patients, roughly comparable in size to Bethlem.

Outside London, lunatics were sometimes sent up from the Home Counties, or in a few cases from as far afield as York, and received into Bethlem; but Bethlem, and later St Luke's, were principally London institutions. The first subscription hospitals and asylums for lunatics in the provinces were founded in the eighteenth century in several of the principal towns. The Bethel Hospital opened in 1724 in Norwich, although for a handful of patients only; in 1753 it housed something less than thirty (Bateman and Rye 1906). In 1767 the asylum opened at Newcastle upon Tyne (Hall 1767); in 1777 at York (Grey 1815); in 1792 at Liverpool (Bickerton 1936). The most well-known and best run of the provincial hospitals, the Manchester Lunatick Hospital, opened in 1766 with twenty-two 'cells'. It was sited with the Lying-in Hospital and the Lock Hospital (for the venereally diseased) next to the general Infirmary. The Lunatick Hospital was established by public subscription, primarily for those whose families could pay for their confinement, or for those paupers whose parishes would meet the (rather high) fees. A statement of the Hospital's trustees argued the need for local charity in 'the Case of poor Lunaticks', 'upon Account chiefly of their being denied Admission into all other Infirmaries, and their being in Common at too great a distance from London to receive any benefit from the two noble Hospitals established there'. The trustees' appeal also suggested that a charitable asylum in Manchester would spare those in middling circumstances the 'Impositions of Private Madhouses', providing in their stead a more discreet and secure place of confinement.

The provincial hospitals were in most cases well funded, although they depended in part on income from fees. At the Manchester Lunatick Hospital the scale of charges from the beginning differentiated between paupers, and 'Persons of middling Fortune', for whom the weekly charges were twice as great. The charges for paupers were later further reduced, although they were not insignificant, and moves to admit paupers gratis were several times defeated; the charges were never competitive with the costs of provisioning a pauper lunatic in the workhouse. In addition to the fees charged the Lunatick Hospital apparently spent considerable sums from its subscription fund, and this probably maintained a relatively high standard of treatment and provision (Brockbank 1934; Jones 1972: 45).

The charter of the Manchester Lunatick Hospital voiced little concern with the pauper insane as objects of its charity, and probably the Hospital held relatively few paupers before the years of the early nineteenth century. The Hospital was in this respect comparable in character to the contemporary specialist hospitals run privately by physicians. Other subscription hospitals and the provincial asylums were probably more like Poor Law institutions, and maintained similar standards, although the character and salubrity of the asylums varied considerably.

The famous Retreat at York, which was so widely admired by philanthropists, was founded in 1792, not by public subscription but privately by the Society of Friends, to serve primarily its own members. It was built for about thirty persons, with some degree of comforts and a 'domestic' atmosphere. Unlike the subscription hospitals, it was not initially established under medical auspices; it styled itself a Christian and philanthropic refuge, rather than 'hospital'. During the great 1815–16 Parliamentary investigations into madhouses, the Retreat was taken as an exemplar of sorts for the well-run asylum, against which the failures of Bethlem and the public asylum at York could be measured, although the institutions were of course of very different character (Tuke 1813; Hunt 1932).

This was the array of asylums and lunatic hospitals in England at the end of the eighteenth century. During the lunacy reforms after the turn of the century these older asylums were naturally the focus of considerable interest; they were broadly criticized by reformers, and occasionally praised for 'progressive' experiments. The early asylums were of course the most visible centres of confinement of the insane (and by reason of their scandals the most publicized); they were the only varieties which afforded consistent medical attentions. They constitute in this sense the background and ancestry of Victorian mental institutions. But in the actual numbers they accommodated the lunatic asylums were less significant, even at the end of the eighteenth century. Of the insane somehow confined, the greater number were doubtless held outside asylums, and probably beyond medical attentions. The larger background to the development of separate mental institutions included as well private 'madhouses', older varieties of general confinement, and a range of less well-defined or formal provisions for the insane. Together these were, practically, more significant for the fate of the insane than asylums or lunatic hospitals.

The privately run 'madhouses' spread more extensively than asylums and hospitals, and probably had at least a similar capacity by the end of the eighteenth century. There were an uncertain number of these 'houses' across the country and concentrated in certain districts of London. They were specifically houses for the insane, in a few cases as large as formally established lunatic hospitals, although they often lacked any medical personnel (Parry-Jones 1972: 29ff.).

The madhouses discharged different and usually distinct functions. Some received the wealthy insane and accommodated them appropriately in comfort, or if meanly nonetheless discreetly enough to preserve the family from scandal. Most were more humble, often simply households in a locale which across generations acquired a reputation for taking in insane boarders; some of the notable nineteenth-century private establishments apparently grew out of such informal circumstances. A number of mad-doctors established their own houses to service private practices; clergymen were also notably prominent among keepers, perhaps because of the older customary practice of entrusting a madman to the care of the local vicar. Certain of the houses, especially those in London, were frankly commercial ventures, and served the requirements of mad-doctors, of families seeking to confine one of their number, and of magistrates and parish officers seeking to farm out local lunatics and idiots.

A great number of the madhouses were probably conveniences of this sort. A so-called 'trade in lunacy' in fact grew up, with the demand for secure places of lock-up, and as a means of relief. Across a century or more, there was considerable scope for a 'trade in lunacy': madhouses commonly were established before there were lunatic hospitals or asylums in a locale, and they remained important in places where public hospitals or asylums were only latterly put up. Even in places where public hospitals or asylums were established and richly endowed, these functioned as selective charities which necessarily or as a matter of policy limited their admissions and relief-giving. It was such restrictive policies of the early asylums which provided at least part of the rationale and explanation for the spread of private mad-houses. The houses actually increased in their number and capacity in the first half of the nineteenth century, and declined (sometimes surviving as 'rest-homes') only when the state-run county asylums increasingly absorbed the bulk of pauper lunatics (Paternoster 1841; Parry-Jones 1972: 32).

After 1774 many of the private madhouses were officially licensed, as a result of the Act for Regulating Mad-houses, and were required to return the numbers of their inmates. There is hence some evidence about the extent of confinement in private madhouses. How the houses actually accepted their inmates is, however, less easy to understand. Many mad-houses clearly depended on the 'trade' with official bodies. The boarding-out of the pauper insane by parishes was frequently their most important source of support; and in some places a madhouse served by agreement as a secure lock-up for the dangerously insane. But before the mid-eighteenth century there were in general no statutory procedures and rarely explicit policies for confining and provisioning the insane, and thus the official uses of madhouses (and of common gaols, bridewells, and workhouses, in respect of the insane) were rarely uniform and regulated, or documented, but simply followed after the informal local arrangements.

Under common law, as Blackstone wrote in the *Commentaries*, 'persons deprived of their reason might be confined until they recovered their senses, without waiting for . . . special authority from the crown' (Blackstone 1765–69: Book IV, ch. 2). Although by the time of Blackstone's writing there was a statutory procedure 'chalked out for imprisoning, chaining and sending them to their proper homes', this hardly disturbed the local practices of relying as ever on such provisions for confinement, including private madhouses, as existed. Few 'proper homes' or 'fitting receptacles' for the insane had been purpose-built in Blackstone's day. The insane were thus confined expediently, sometimes specifically for reason of their insanity; or were held otherwise among felons, vagrants, or paupers without special distinguishing treatment, when they were offenders or indigent. The specific policies for segregating the insane in their 'proper homes' were not broadly in practice before the early nineteenth century;

this was indeed a practical impossibility until the construction of new asylums ultimately made separate confinement a realistic policy.

It was only slowly that the special status of the insane in social policy emerged. The Poor Laws, and notably the 1601 Act, made no special mention of the insane, and set down no particular provisions until after 1834. This was despite the fact that many insane paupers received outdoor relief and others were noted (often as troublesome figures) among workhouse inmates.

The Vagrancy Acts mentioned the insane explicitly in 1714 for the first time, and then again in 1744, when an Act authorized funds for 'keeping, maintaining and curing such Persons'; this Act established the statutory procedure for holding the insane in their 'proper homes' to which Blackstone referred.

Before the 1714 and 1744 Vagrancy Acts there were on occasion extraordinary directives pertaining explicitly to the insane, like the Privy Council's order in 1630 to the Justices of the Peace in Westminster, concerning three lunatics at-large:

> 'Whereas there are certaine persons who run up and downe the streets and doe much harme, being either distracted or els counterfeites, and therefore not to be suffered to have their liberties to range, as now they doe; of which persons one is called King Robert, another Doctor Owen, and the third Mistris Vaughan: we doe hereby will and require you to see them all sent to Bedlam, there to be kept, ordered and looked unto, to which purpose wee sende you herewith a warrant directed to the Master and Matrone of Bedlame, for the receiving of them.'
>
> (Acts of the Privy Council of England 1630)

The insane were of course always subject to apprehension as 'idle and disorderly', and lunatics were very likely found often among the 'idle and disorderly', whether acknowledged in charge sheets and the like as lunatics or not.

Beyond such *ad hoc* or customary arrangements, the Vagrancy Acts provided more general powers, or sanctioned explicitly broader existing practices; the 1744 Act distinguished impoverished lunatics from 'Rogues, Vagabonds, Sturdy Beggars and Vagrants', ordering town or parish officers to apprehend those 'furiously mad, and dangerous' and confine them, 'safely locked up, in such secure place . . . as such justices shall . . . direct and appoint'.

The law did not, however, specify these 'secure places'; in certain cases they doubtless included private madhouses and, where they existed, public asylums, but more usually the secure places in a locale were common gaols or workhouses.[5] John Howard incidentally discovered some lunatics and idiots in his visits to prisons, although the numbers of lunatics he recorded were relatively small. They were, however, a particular nuisance, since as Howard suggested prisons were not at all appropriate to them. These 'confined idiots and *Lunatics*', he wrote:

> 'serve for sport to idle visitants at assizes, and other times of general resort. Many of the bridewells are crowded and offensive, because the rooms which were designed for prisoners are occupied by the insane. Where these are not kept separate they disturb and terrify other prisoners. No care is taken of them, although it is probable that by medicine, and proper regimen, some of them might be restored to their senses, and to usefulness in life.'   (Howard 1792: 8)

An Act of 1763 had in fact ordered the segregation of 'persons of insane mind and outrageous behaviour' from other prisoners. Few eighteenth-century prison buildings allowed such separate accommodation, however, and there was probably little separation in practice.

Some of the insane in common gaols were doubtless themselves felons or lesser offenders; but it is difficult even to estimate the numbers of the criminal insane.[6] Bethlem was used at times, with questionable legality, as a place of safe custody for criminal lunatics or those acquitted of crimes by reason of insanity, but the practice was never systematic. In 1800 an Act for the safe Custody of insane Persons charged with Offences established the first specific policies towards insane offenders, and allowed them to be detained and held securely 'at His Majesty's pleasure'. Under the provisions of this Act several criminal lunatics were transferred to Bethlem. Later, with the completion in 1814–16 of the new Bethlem at St George's Fields in Lambeth, the Government secured a special separate wing to accommodate up to sixty criminal lunatics. In 1837 a national survey revealed that Bethlem held somewhat less than one-third of the 178 criminal lunatics, while county asylums held about an equal number (Official Publications 1837: XLIV). By 1856, seven years before the Criminal Lunatic Asylum opened at Broadmoor, Bethlem held only a small proportion of the 596 criminal lunatics; but well into the 1870s the county asylums, private madhouses, and some gaols still commonly held criminal lunatics, under specially secure conditions (see the Annual Reports of the Commissioners in Lunacy, Official Publications 1845).

The insane were held in workhouses, in uncertain numbers, at least until early in the twentieth century. Madmen had long been prominent in the folklore which surrounded the places; Crabbe appropriately ended his catalogue of the inmates of the old general workhouse enumerating:

'The lame, the blind, and far the happiest they!
The moping idiot and the madman gay.'

But in terms of the official records the insane were effectively invisible as a separate class in workhouses. Surveys like *An Account of Several Workhouses in Great Britain* (1732), which was based on official returns, rarely mentioned the insane explicitly, except by way of noting the problems occasioned by 'troublesome lunatics and idiots'.

Howard and other prison visitors discovered lunatics chained in workhouse cellars, and noted the small lunatic huts located in some exercise yards. But beyond such anecdotal or general references, there is little evidence about the fate of the insane under the Old Poor Law. It is clear simply that workhouses held appreciable numbers of insane inmates, and that many insane paupers (the greater number) were farmed out or relieved outdoors. When the Poor Law officials began ultimately to enumerate the 'pauper insane' separately, the returns for the early nineteenth century, which were highly defective and partial, nonetheless showed upwards of three-quarters of all persons of 'unsound mind', officially so recorded, as falling under the Poor Law authorities.[7] The absolute numbers were considerable, and this was evidently not a recent phenomenon, although many contemporaries believed that the prevalence and incidence of insanity were increasing dramatically.

There was rarely any separate accommodation for the insane in eighteenth-century workhouses; nor were there generally any particular provisions, except for those lunatics and idiots who proved refractory and unmanageable, and probably suffered the sort of special attentions to which the outdoor lunatic huts provide mute testimony. Exceptionally, some of the larger metropolitan workhouses provided separate infirmary wards for the insane, as they sometimes segregated the infectious and venereally diseased. St Peter's Workhouse in Bristol was a notable and famous example which apparently released the insane from the rigours of discipline in its 'model manufactory' and from the workhouse test. St Peter's accommodated the insane among the 'impotent sick' in a separate infirmary building, established in 1696, which later became the city's general asylum.

Until 1828 there was no requirement of 'certifying' the pauper insane as part of the orders for their detention. After 1828 certification was more common, at least for the grosser varieties of lunatics. But the confinement of many pauper lunatics and idiots continued to go unrecorded; workhouses often held the 'insane' indiscriminately with the other disabled classes inevitably and naturally found among paupers. For the pauper insane workhouse confinement was a method of relief, as well as a safeguard of public security and propriety. The particular mental states of the insane were not necessarily pertinent to their confinement, nor likely of interest to Poor Law officials, except where these states of mind were overtly dangerous or threatening. The insane thus merged into other categories.

The numbers of insane inmates in workhouses, and their variety, are accordingly uncertain before the end of the eighteenth century and indeed for long after. The numbers held in workhouses probably increased progressively, particularly after 1834 (see Hodgkinson 1966). The Poor Law Commissioners in fact frequently complained about the accumulation of the insane in workhouses, and on many occasions repeated their avowed policy of transferring pauper lunatics, particularly 'curables', to asylums. The Commissioners wrote, for instance, in 1844, after receiving a series of complaints regarding insane paupers from the Commissioners in Lunacy: 'We are deeply convinced that the paupers of insane mind should, where there is a chance of cure, be sent to an asylum as soon as possible after the commencement of the malady' (Official Publications 1844b). The customary practices were, however, less consistent. County asylums were in most cases overcrowded, and in any event the costs of maintaining a lunatic or idiot in an asylum or private madhouse were often prohibitive for local authorities.

Some of the pauper insane continued to receive outdoor relief after 1834, although probably at reduced levels. But as workhouses increasingly became great sick wards, and effectively Poor Law hospitals *avant la lettre*, the insane accumulated there noticeably often with troublesome and noisy consequences. They took a place among the other classes of the sickly and diseased whom voluntary hospitals refused: sick children, those with skin diseases, the tubercular, epileptics, the venereally diseased, the infectious, the chronically ill.

The presence of the insane, in numbers, prompted the Commissioners on several occasions to propose building separate Poor Law Union lunatic asylums, to siphon off these workhouse insane. Such initiatives were refused (and strongly opposed by the Commissioners in Lunacy), although they clearly acknowledged the principle of classification and separate accommodation which the New Poor Law in theory had enacted, and in which Nassau Senior and Chadwick firmly believed.

There was probably little consistent segregation within the sick wards of workhouses. Nor was there much prospect of transferring the pauper insane *en masse* from workhouses to asylums, until late in the century. The Poor Law officials and Commissioners in Lunacy tried simply to devise pragmatic policies for distributing particular classes of the insane as 'appropriately' as possible between workhouse and asylum. The 1844 Report of the Metropolitan Commissioners in Lunacy acknowledged the overcrowding of asylums; it urged accordingly that asylum superintendents try to preserve the medical or ostensibly 'curative' functions of their establishments by discharging the chronic insane and 'incurables' into other, custodial confinement, which could of course be provided more cheaply.[8] The Lunacy Act of 1862 likewise promoted the transfer of insane inmates, where appropriate, from workhouses to asylums, and vice versa.

The obvious rationale for these directives was an effort to preserve or establish asylums as 'curative' institutions which could receive acute cases and secure the dangerously insane, while releasing chronic cases and 'incurables' to other, less specialized varieties of confinement. In practice, however, few asylums were ever entirely 'curable' institutions; and conversely workhouses often held 'curables'. Particularly in rural areas workhouses might hold the varieties of the insane indiscriminately, occasioning at times alarm about the confinement of dangerous lunatics and idiots under poor security. Among the workhouse insane in general, the greater proportion were no doubt 'harmless' or chronically disordered.[9] The workhouses would also commonly receive syphilitics and epileptics, on the grounds that other institutions often refused them. But the apportioning of the insane between workhouse and asylum was never entirely consistent, and both asylums and workhouses remained in some measure general institutions which received the insane in all their variety. The county and borough asylums indeed shared in part the character of workhouse sick wards, and were more akin to general welfare institutions than to contemporary specialist hospitals.

The institutional confinement of the insane in the period before 1845 thus depended on a range of provisions and often expedient policies. Before the spread of a comprehensive system of lunatic asylums the insane commonly fell under the jurisdiction of the Poor Laws, or under the keepers of common gaols, bridewells, and private madhouses. The law bore upon lunatics and idiots through a variety of statutes which concerned poor relief, the repression of vagrancy and begging, and the protection of the King's peace. The statutes did not relate particularly to the insane and hardly acknowledged their mental states. Even where special or separate treatment of the insane was judged appropriate, there were often not the physical resources to deal with them. Before 1845 the 'insane' in general simply did not exist as a clear and distinct category for practical social policy or in law.

The enacting of a comprehensive lunacy law, which also established a statutory authority responsible for 'insane persons' as a class, was one of the works of early nineteenth-century reform. Previously the major provisions specifically concerning lunacy under law were limited in their practical scope to the insane of property, those well-to-do who were born idiots or grew unsound in mind and were thus incapable of managing their estates. From an early time the law provided for the protection of such estates, and for the wardship, and if necessary the confinement, of their insane owners. The early statute De Praerogativa Regis, which dated probably from the late thirteenth century, ruled that:

'The King has the custody of the lands of natural fools [*fatuorum naturalium*], taking their profits without waste, finding them their necessaries . . . and after their death must return them to the rightful heirs. . . . He must also see to it that when anyone who formerly had memory and understanding is not longer in his right mind [*compos mentis suae*] – as some may be between lucid intervals – their lands and tenements are safely kept without waste or destruction; that they and their families live and are maintained from the profits; and that what is left from maintaining them is reasonably kept for their use when they have recovered their memories. . . . The king shall take nothing to his own use, and if the person dies in that state shall distribute the remainder for his soul by the advice of the ordinary.'

(Holdsworth 1903: I, 473)

Such cases set in motion the procedures of 'inquisition' which the law required before depriving a lunatic or idiot of the management of his own affairs and placing him and his estates in wardship. These procedures, and the similar investigations formally required to place an idiot or lunatic of property under restraint and in confinement, were the only formal legal expression and equivalent of 'certification' and committal proceedings, until late in the eighteenth century. The procedures for inquisition did not apply broadly, and even within their narrow scope doubtless did not constitute secure protection, or provide legal recourse, against wrongful detention.[10]

16

'Certification' was not principally a medical affair, although physicians and apothecaries often gave testimonies to the investigators. The contemporary medicine of insanity in any case hardly allowed subtle distinctions and definitions of the varied states or even extremes of madness. In courts and in legal theory, the dispositions of the law with regard to the insane of property or to insane offenders were thoroughly pragmatic. For centuries the law acknowledged the peculiarities of the insane, classing them as brutes or innocents, 'without understanding', and thus in liberal parlance outside civil society; they were denied full legal responsibilities or status. But the category 'insanity' was itself grossly applied, and judgements of sanity were within the competence of ordinary laymen. The legal name *non compos mentis* was primarily a way of registering in a practical sense an individual's irrationality and incapacity, whatever their basis. The law was indeed not concerned with the mental aspects of insanity *per se*, but with their likely or possible social consequences. Similarly the fate of the insane who were vagrants or paupers, or among the 'idle and disorderly', did not depend on their particular mental states and their peculiarities, in which authorities were hardly interested. If in practice the insane sometimes received special charities and suffered special repressions, this was not by and large due to any specific legal status.

Against this general background of diverse and unspecific provisions for the insane before the end of the eighteenth century, the Lunacy Acts of 1845 marked the codification of a comprehensive lunacy law – a law which established the 'insane' as a separate class defined by their mental disorders and disabilities. The Acts empowered an inspectorate of Commissioners in Lunacy with general jurisdiction over the insane, wherever they were held; this created a single statutory authority responsible for the insane, where before lunatics and idiots had been subject to their immediate keepers (under the Poor Law; in gaols, in private madhouses, infirmaries, or lunatic hospitals); or where before, if they were secretly confined, they had been beyond any legal jurisdiction. The Commissioners' jurisdiction extended also to the matters of managing and curing the insane within confinement; the inspectorates in turn tried to establish norms for the proper treatment of lunatics, and thus came to regulate and enforce the types of treatment judged appropriate to the special character and conditions of the insane.

The 1845 Acts were the culmination of several decades of lunacy reforms which had prepared the ground. With the extension through the inspectorate of state control over the confinement of the insane, and the remarkable expansion in the number and capacity of asylums, the programme which lunacy reformers had conceived at the beginning of the century was largely achieved. The separate confinement of the insane, in specially designed 'fitting receptacles', was increasingly possible, and where possible, was strongly encouraged by law. The probable fate of individual lunatics changed accordingly, especially in the second third of the nineteenth century.

The success of the nineteenth-century lunacy reforms has long been associated with the careers of particular reformers, from the philanthropists who became interested in lunacy early in the century, to Shaftesbury who remained at the centre of lunacy reform activity for decades, and for whom the subject was an *idée fixe*. The actual timetable of reforms was indeed closely related to the periodic bursts of energy and indignation which characterized the reform campaigns and their agitations.

The background to the reforms actually stretches, however, into the eighteenth century. From the beginning of the century, and even at odd moments before, there were across several decades periodic waves of indignation about the conditions of madhouses, and the dangers of wrongful confinement of sane people within them. With the rise of the novel and a middle-class reading public the threat to sane people of being forcibly locked-up with and mixed among the insane became indeed a common literary theme, as confinement was later a widespread motif in 'gothic' novels. There were in fact several well-publicized contemporary scandals involving the questionable confinement by greedy heirs of a wealthy relation; and likewise cases such as those from which Richardson derived the materials for his novel *Clarissa*, of fathers having their marriageable daughters put away for refusing a proper match.

In 1706 Daniel Defoe took up the case of a particular young girl, and publicized in his review her allegedly improper detention in a private madhouse under the care of Dr Edward Tyson, then physician to Bethlem. 'I know no greater Grievance in the present distribution of Civil Authority', Defoe claimed, 'than that such People as those, are not brought under some public Regulation.' He suggested accordingly reforms to end 'Treating them as Criminals', which would extend the range of legal procedures and protection that the Chancery lunatics enjoyed, and establish certain legal safeguards against wrongful confinement of the sane or the 'cured' (Defoe 1706: 327, 353–56). Twenty odd years later Defoe published more elaborate proposals for the licensing and official inspection of private madhouses, in the better interests of their fee-paying inmates. He argued for the suppression of 'pretended madhouses, where many of the fair sex are unjustly confin'd, while their husbands keep mistresses, etc., and many widows are lock'd up for the sake of their jointure' (Defoe 1728: 30–4). Such abuses of madhouses drew comment through the century, although the calls for reform met little official response.

It was not until 1763 that the first public investigation into madhouses was started. The immediate pretext for this investigation was a famous anonymous article published by the *Gentlemen's Magazine* entitled 'A Case Humbly Offered to the Consideration of Parliament'; it sketched in dramatic and impassioned terms the predicament of some sane and honourable person 'forcibly taken or artfully decoyed into a private madhouse' for mercenary reasons, and there 'seized upon by a set of inhuman ruffians trained up to this barbarous profession, stripped naked, and conveyed to a dark-room' (1763: 25–6).

Shortly after the piece appeared Parliament duly appointed a Select Committee 'to enquire into the State of the private Madhouses in this Kingdom'. The Committee in fact conducted a very limited investigation into two madhouses only (the matter was evidently somewhat delicate because of the interests involved), but nonetheless concluded that the present state of madhouses required 'the Interposition of the Legislature'.

The Act for Regulating Madhouses was not actually passed until 1774, partly because of the opposition which the idea of such regulation immediately aroused. When the Act came into force, it required the licensing and yearly inspection of many private madhouses (although it provided no mechanism for withdrawing or revoking a license), and set down a number of strictures regarding the admission of fee-paying private inmates and their examination by physicians. The Act was in the event very unevenly put into effect, depending on the zeal of the respective local Justices or the Metropolitan Commissioners in Lunacy in London which the legislation created. The scope of the Act was limited in any event to private patients, and it was primarily concerned to prevent improper detention, which had likewise been the goal of critics like Defoe. The provisions of the Act were designed to protect the sane, but not in the main to control or regulate the conditions in confinement of the genuinely insane. As later lunacy reformers charged, the Act did not interfere with the running of private madhouses, however defective; it required nothing, and recommended nothing in the way of medical attentions, diet, use of physical restraints, or other matters of management in the houses. The purposes of inspection were rather precautionary than regulatory. The Act moreover not only neglected, but specifically excluded from its provisions the public subscription hospitals and asylums, and insane paupers; this was the more remarkable since many paupers were boarded out through the arrangements of their parishes, often forming the majority of inmates in private madhouses. Pauper lunatics were, however, exempted from the requirements and protections of inspection and certification, and this remained broadly the state of affairs until more than half a century later.

The lunacy Bills brought by later reformers in the early nineteenth century were far wider in their proposals; and they suggested more sweeping reforms than the Bill finally enacted in 1774 after the madhouse scandals and investigations. For several generations around the turn of the century lunacy was, as many contemporaries insisted, uncommonly prominent as a topic in public discussions. Some attributed the interest in the topic to the King's periodic insanities at the time, or to the several attempts on the King's life by crazed assassins, and later the assassination of the Prime Minister Spencer Perceval by a lunatic. The 1800 Act relating to criminal lunatics did in fact probably owe its timing to one of the attempts on George III; and the quickening interest in lunacy undoubtedly reflected at a remove the political uncertainties which the King's disorder caused. But the contemporary interest in lunacy and the concern with lunacy reforms had as well a greater and more enduring basis.

Towards the end of the eighteenth century the well-publicized expansion of Bethlem and St Luke's, and the founding of several provincial asylums (notably the Retreat which was established shortly after scandalous reports of the conditions at the York Asylum), initiated a broad discussion of provisions for the insane which came to interest many philanthropists. The condition of the insane and their confinement became indeed emblematic of several wider philanthropic currents – in particular, those that bore on what some contemporaries termed the 'institutional question'. Reformers of the late eighteenth century and after had to cope self-consciously with the 'residential establishments' which were more and more the recourse in different domains of 'police' or social policy. How to organize – or how to justify – such establishments was the common theme which ran through much contemporary discussion: Howard's reports of prisons and hospitals, the debates on Gilbert's Act for workhouses, the reform of gaols and the proposals for a model national penitentiary, Bentham's Panopticon scheme, the Nottinghamshire reforms in workhouses, and the general studies of mortality and morbidity in institutions. For all these areas of social policy the design and management of 'institutions' or 'residential establishments' were immediate concerns; and for future planning the 'institutional question' was becoming ever more significant. The construction of asylums, which advanced contemporaneously with the building of new workhouses and gaols, provided a special focus for the vogue of institutional experiments, not simply in the matters of ventilation and drainage, but also in 'moral architecture', and in the use of institutions for the reform of character.

Lunacy reform became indeed a characteristic and exemplary, if in some cases minor, concern of early nineteenth-century philanthropists; the proposals for lunacy reform accordingly grew more sweeping, and took on some aspects of the wider reform currents. They were less local and *ad hoc* in character than an integral part of a greater reforming programme, which sought to rationalize and reconstruct the whole array and direction of social policy. From limited proposals to protect the sane from contact with the genuinely insane, lunacy reform became during the generations at the turn of the century the means of enacting a general programme to house and cure, and otherwise regulate the confinement of the insane of all types. It sought a national system of asylums for separate confinement, and the reformed medical and psychological care of inmates.

The first of the great Parliamentary investigations, which were the motor of lunacy reforms, began in 1807 with the appointment of a Select Committee 'to enquire into the state of criminal and pauper lunatics, in England and Wales, and of the laws relating thereto'. The immediate pretext for the enquiry was a petition from the High Sheriff of Gloucestershire, Sir G. O. Paul, who was notably active in both prison and asylum reform; this petition raised the awkward problem of criminal lunatics, and in particular those detained under the 1800 Act 'at His Majesty's pleasure'. The Act had set down no specific provisions regarding the secure confinement of criminal lunatics, beyond the general proviso that they should be held in 'a secure place'. *Ad hoc* provisions were evidently not always adequate. Paul's petition described with considerable effect the case of one Aaron Bywater, acquitted of murder by reason of insanity, who had recently killed a fellow prisoner in the county gaol where he was being kept. There were other similar cases as well, and the petition raised the matter in general terms. 'To confine a madman together with criminals', Paul wrote arguing against present expedients, 'would be dangerous to those with whom he was confined, and pregnant with disturbance'. Prison orders for the criminal mad were indeed 'wholly inconsistent with their situation, unless it were intended to heighten not repress the symptoms of their disorder'; thus Paul urged separate accommodation for lunatics, appropriate to their condition (Official Publications 1807).

The Committee, which met under the general direction of Charles Wynn and George Rose, and included Romilly and Whitbread, Wilberforce and

G. O. Paul, interpreted its brief widely and took a broad range of testimony, not simply relating to the criminal insane. It heard Dr John Willis, Thomas Dunston, the Master of St Luke's, and the architect John Nash, among others, as well as assembling returns of the numbers of pauper and criminal lunatics on a national basis as far as was possible.

When the Committee reported, its recommendations went well beyond the elaboration of procedures for dealing with criminal lunatics. In answer to the general question posed in Paul's petition, 'cannot we unite the police intention with the efforts of humanity and provincial economy, and by that union create a mutual support?', the Committee recommended constructing a network of secure new asylums which could accommodate together the criminal and pauper lunatics, who were then still dispersed among many diverse institutions. The new asylums which the reforms proposed were to be separate, and 'appropriate' to the insane as a class in themselves; and thus the reformers began to develop and advance the rationales for separate confinement of the insane, and for a corresponding univocal category 'insanity' under law.

The passing of the County Asylums Act of 1808, an Act for the better Care and Maintenance of Lunatics, being Paupers or Criminals in England, shortly followed after the Committee's Report. This Act provided 'for the erecting of proper Houses for their reception', and in the meanwhile urged the better custody of criminal lunatics, in Bethlem or in the new county asylums as they were completed. The Select Committee had recommended the building of sixteen new asylums, each to serve districts or unions of about 500,000 persons, and each with a capacity for up to 300 inmates, which the Committee regarded as the most economic size. 'It may be sufficient for the Legislature, at least in the first instance, rather to recommend and assist, than to enforce the execution of such a plan', as the Committee wrote in politic tones, designed to encourage and not to alarm local powers. This was despite the fact that certain of the Committee members acknowledged from the outset that local charity to the criminal and pauper insane was less likely to find support than had earlier subscription hospitals and asylums.

The Act of 1808 in the event allowed for an asylum in each county, or among several, to be built on the county rates and with subscription funds. The asylums were to receive some criminal and all the pauper insane (on pain of fines), at the expense of their respective parishes. The terms of the Act were left, however, lax and permissive, doubtless again for politic reasons of respecting local control; a Bill with compulsory provisions would certainly have failed. As a result many counties responded slowly to the new provisions, on account of the expenses involved, and many not at all. By 1828 only nine counties had constructed new asylums under the operation of the 1808 Act, although other asylums were established and otherwise funded.

When the first county asylums opened, beginning with Nottinghamshire's in 1810, they were in most cases crowded with admissions. The statutory requirement written into the 1808 Act that Justices send all pauper lunatics to the county asylum proved impossible to implement and was quickly relaxed in a series of amendments.

In 1811 the Justices were allowed discretionary powers 'as to issuing or not issuing warrants' for confinement of paupers so that 'the number of applications on behalf of persons having just cause to be admitted would not at any time exceed the number of those who can be properly accommodated in such an asylum, with a view to cure, comfort and safe custody'. The effect of such discretion was probably to sanction the local authorities' prior customary reliance on the cheaper policies of boarding out the insane privately or by arrangement with pauper institutions.

The 1808 Act and later amendments had, however, the practical effect of weakening somewhat the control of Poor Law officials over the fate of the pauper insane. The law bound parish overseers to provide information on all insane persons under their jurisdiction on pain of fines; and it progressively shifted the effective authority and responsibility for admissions to county asylums into the hands of the magistrates rather than parish overseers. An amendment in 1819 'for making provision for the better care of pauper lunatics' vested the Justices with the power to order the pauper insane to asylums irrespective of the dispositions or wishes of local parish officers. This was not widespread in practice, but nonetheless significantly established the principle of statutory control over pauper lunatics outside the Poor Law.

After the 1807 Parliamentary investigations, the course of lunacy reforms progressed unevenly and patchily. The 1808 Act was not noticeably effective in its early years, except apparently where local philanthropists persuaded officials to take its lax terms seriously. Despite the poor results of the Act, it was not until 1845 that important provisions concerning the construction of county asylums became mandatory. In the interim there were several other Parliamentary inquiries, spaced at intervals across four decades, and several lunacy Bills were enacted out of the considerable number proposed. The timing and staging of the investigations and Bills depended still on the energies and the continuing interest of a relatively small number of active lunacy reformers. But the general political climate was still more important for the prospects of reform, and the course of lunacy legislation in fact paralleled the course of other contemporary social reforms and administrative reorganizations, which were also characteristically spread and codified by generally discreet, small-scale campaigns behind the scenes at Westminster.

In 1813–14 the widespread publicity surrounding two notorious asylum scandals, at the York Asylum and at Bethlem, served as the occasion for Parliament again to appoint a Select Committee to investigate the situation of lunatics and their confinement. The Committee investigated the two scandals in some depth, and drew pointed contrasts between the general conduct of the York Asylum and Bethlem, and the more salubrious Retreat near York and St Luke's. But the Committee also took evidence concerning other subscription hospitals and asylums, the new county asylums at Nottingham, Bedford, and Thorpe in Norfolk, the naval lunatics' asylum, workhouses around the country, and a number of private licensed madhouses. The *Minutes of Evidence*, which the Committee had printed in several large folio volumes in 1815–16, were as a result the first systematic and comprehensive survey of the varieties of confinement under which the insane were held, and are now the major documentary source about the contemporary conditions of confinement.

On the basis of the evidence collected, the Committee reported that their inquiries had

'convinced them that there are not in the Country a set of Beings more immediately requiring the protection of the Legislature than the persons in this state. . . . If the treatment of those in the middling or in the lower classes of life, shut up in hospitals, private madhouses, or parish workhouses, is looked at, your Committee are persuaded that a case cannot be found where the necessity for a remedy is more urgent.'
(Official Publications 1816: 3–4)

The Committee urged with 'the utmost confidence from the Evidence', that 'some new provision of law is indispensably necessary for insuring better care being taken of Insane Persons'. Beyond recommending further safeguards against wrongful detention and further elaboration of the insane's separate legal status, the Committee also advanced a series of specific points of criticism and advice about the proper conduct of asylums and madhouses, which it regarded as within the concern of legislation and state regulation. The conclusions of the Report thus recommended certain norms of care and treatment, and criticized in the present-day conditions, *inter alia*:

> 'the insufficiency of the number of Keepers, in proportion to the number of persons intrusted to their care, which unavoidably leads to a greater degree of restraint than the Patients would otherwise be under;
>
> restraint of persons much beyond what is necessary, certainly retarding recovery;
>
> the mixing Patients who are outrageous, with those who are quiet and inoffensive;
>
> the want of medical assistance, as applied to the malady for which the persons are confined; a point worthy of the most serious attention, as the practice very generally is to confine medical aid to corporal complaints;
>
> the situation of the parish paupers . . . in houses for Insane Persons and in parochial workhouses;
>
> the defective visitation of Private Madhouses;
>
> insufficiency of certificates on which Patients are received into the madhouses; etc.'   (Official Publications 1816: 3–4)

Although the Committee made accordingly broad recommendations, and advanced the proposal for a comprehensive lunacy law and provisions relevant to 'all Insane Persons', the series of Bills which followed the Report were in the event rather modest, and aimed simply at an improved inspectorate with better jurisdiction over private madhouses. Despite their modesty, lunacy Bills failed by turns in 1816, 1817, and 1819, largely because of opposition from the House of Lords to these among other works of philanthropy.

The 1815–16 Report was nevertheless significant, and made a landmark in the lunacy reforms. What later lunacy Bills would effectively enact – a comprehensive lunacy law, and the centralized inspectorate (with powers over private madhouses, public asylums and hospitals, and the insane in workhouses) – came in a form close to what the Report had initially proposed. Later Bills not only extended the regulations and provisions of the 1774 Act to cover the insane poor as well, but more significantly established – after the example of the 1815–16 Report – specific norms of treatment and institutional standards geared to the condition of the insane, and enforced by a new statutory body responsible for them as a class. Lunacy reforms thus ostensibly concerned 'all Insane Persons' defined by their mental conditions, not principally by their indigence or social incapacity; and the reformed laws accordingly began to regulate the conditions of confinement in order to provide 'fitting' environments, appropriate to the apparently special and distinctive mental conditions of the insane.

After another successful amendment to the 1808 Act passed in 1819, 'making provision for the better care of the pauper lunatics', a further Select Committee was established in 1827 to investigate 'the state of pauper lunatics from the metropolitan parishes'. This Committee examined in particular several private madhouses in London which together held more than 1000 inmates, most of them parish paupers; like the 1815–16 investigations it tried to document in detail not merely the general conditions of the places, but the character of their physical and moral treatments. The Committee indeed took the view that madhouses should be not merely well run, clean, and open to official inspection, but 'fitting' to their inmates and more than receptacles to confine them.

The new 1828 Madhouse Act in the event enlarged the inspectorate for private madhouses, the Metropolitan Commissioners, and required for the first time a medical certificate of insanity as well as a Justice's order for the detention of pauper lunatics. For private patients it required two medical certificates. An associated Bill, the new County Asylums Act, required annual returns from asylum officials of admissions, discharges, and deaths, as part of a new and more systematic style of planning and regulating; and it allowed the Secretary of State for the Home Department to send inspectors, at his discretion, around the country.

Between 1828 and 1842 the Metropolitan Commissioners in Lunacy filed periodic reports on their asylum and madhouse visits, and thus continued to a degree the investigative work of earlier Parliamentary Committees. In the decade after 1828 eight further county asylums were built, including the Middlesex Asylum at Hanwell (whose planning was part of the rationale for the 1827 investigation) to accommodate 1000 inmates, the Kent Asylum for 300 inmates, the Norfolk for 500, and the Suffolk for 600. By contemporary standards these were large establishments indeed, and were financed only with considerable state expenditures. The average size of asylums continued to rise through the century, and despite regional variations the new asylums were of a broad general type, whose specifications were widely accepted.[11]

The spread of the network of asylums nationally was nonetheless only partial, and the coverage of asylums was widely judged inadequate. In

1842 Shaftesbury, who was chairman of the Metropolitan Commissioners in Lunacy, ordered a national tour of inspection and despatched visitors to all asylums and madhouses in the country. The purpose of the comprehensive inspection was in part to provide a statistical account of the capacities and actual uses of asylums. The reports of the inspectors formed the basis of the great 1844 Report of the Metropolitan Commissioners in Lunacy, which was written largely by Shaftesbury and published for wide distribution with all the weight of fact and detail that the numerous inspectors' returns allowed. D. H. Tuke later called this document, which was one of the notable products of early Victorian 'improvement', a 'Doomsday Book of all that concerns institutions for the insane at that time' (Tuke, D. H. 1882: 178); compared with the Parliamentary Report of thirty years earlier, it was indeed far more comprehensive and still more detailed and specific in its recommendations.

The Commissioners suggested most importantly making the building of county and borough asylums mandatory, where these did not already exist. The 1845 Act 'to amend the Laws for the Provision and Regulation of Lunatic Asylums for Counties and Boroughs, and for the Maintenance and Care of Pauper Lunatics' carried this recommendation into force and required all counties and the principal boroughs to make special provisions for the insane and in particular for the insane poor; the county asylum programme conceived by an earlier generation of lunacy reformers was as a result virtually complete within the next decade.

An Act for the Regulation and Treatment of Lunatics put into effect other of the Commissioners' recommendations, and most notably established a new body of Commissioners in Lunacy who became a full-time centralized inspectorate over all institutions housing the insane. The Act required all such institutions to keep 'Registers and Medical Records' on the insane, according to a specified, uniform protocol. This was the first requirement of systematic record-taking on individual patients in asylums; and as a result the asylum records after 1845 provided the basis for more meaningful statistics. They were more scientifically interesting to alienists and physicians, as well as allowing in some measure evaluation of asylums and their treatments by means of general and uniform norms. A range of bureaucratic controls increasingly supplanted the more informal arrangements of local charity and personal supervision.

The lunacy reforms of the early nineteenth century, culminating with the Lunacy Acts of 1845, marked the several stages in law and policy through which early 'mental institutions' passed. By the mid-century asylums formed a national system, and the historic division of hospital services into separate general, chronic, and mental institutions, which persisted until the mid-twentieth century, was established. The programme to build 'fitting receptacles' for the insane was in part directed against the generally informal (and non-medical) provisions under which many lunatics and idiots were confined; but it was also focused specifically against the neglect of the insane by the medical professions, and their effective exclusion from the voluntary hospitals. When the state established separate lunatic asylums, and likewise the Poor Law and other municipal hospitals, they were designed appropriately to service the great classes of the disordered and diseased refused by other medical institutions. Voluntary hospitals admitted selectively, according to various restrictive policies, and usually only for the short term; and thus hospital practice was primarily based on relatively brief admissions which ended in patients' discharge or death. Because of their long-term indigence and often because of the character of their complaints, the insane, like the tubercular, the venereally diseased, the aged and infirm, and other chronically ill, rarely received the charities of the early general or specialist hospitals, although these classes suffered from what were undoubtedly the gravest and most widespread public health problems. Their exclusion from voluntary hospitals was the rationale for the separate development of public hospitals in Britain designed principally for the insane, the infectious, and the destitute chronically ill.

With hindsight it seems plain that there was indeed scope in the early nineteenth century for a social policy toward the insane. As a group the insane were generally incapacitated. They were, however, mostly excluded from voluntary hospitals, and hence languished without proper or appropriate care. Different works of 'reform' then recovered them, as objects of systematic (medical) attentions, rather than of occasional and inadequate charities. This is, from hindsight, a straightforward way of presenting the development of mental institutions.

It is, however, only a small starting point for an account of 'fitting receptacles'. In at least two respects it is, further, a mistaken starting point, which seriously prejudges the historical problem:

1 The 'fitness' of model asylums was in fact a quite complicated quality. Making 'fitting receptacles' was not simply a matter of humanitarianism or pragmatic accommodation to the 'social problems' the insane presented. Explanation of the programme for 'fitting

receptacles' hence requires closer study of the contemporary ideological notions which informed it. These are complicated, elaborate, and in certain respects strange for modern readers. They require in any event to be reconstructed, in so far as possible without the benefit of hindsight.

2 The 'insane' for whom these new works were intended were a heterogeneous group indeed. It is perilous to assume they presented the array of conditions (or of social problems) which modern psychiatry (and sociology) now recognize. Who were the 'insane'? and what were 'lunacy', 'idiocy', and 'madness'? are indeed historical questions which must be approached directly, again as if their answers were not obvious. In fact the contemporary contours of these categories were likewise complicated – and strange.

· 2 ·

REPRESENTATIONS OF THE ASYLUM

'Conceive a spacious building resembling the palace of a peer, airy, and elevated, and elegant, surrounded by extensive and swelling grounds and gardens. The interior is fitted up with galleries, and workshops, and music-rooms. The sun and the air are allowed to enter at every window, the view of the shrubberies and fields, and groups of labourers, is unobstructed by shutters or bars; all is clean, quiet, and attractive. The inmates all seem to be actuated by the common impulse of enjoyment, all are busy, and delighted by being so. The house and all around appears a hive of industry. When you pass the lodge, it is as if you had entered the precincts of some vast emporium of manufacture; labour is divided, so that it may be easy and well performed, and so apportioned, that it may suit the tastes and powers of each labourer. You meet the gardener, the common agriculturist, the mower, the weeder, all intent on their several occupations, and loud in their merriment. The flowers are tended, and trained, and watered by one, the humbler task of preparing the vegetables for table, is committed to another. Some of the inhabitants act as domestic servants, some as artizans, some rise to the rank of overseers. The bakehouse, the laundry, the kitchen, are all well supplied with indefatigable workers. In one part of the edifice are companies of straw-plaiters, basket-makers, knitters, spinners, among the women; in another, weavers, tailors, saddlers, and shoemakers, among the men. For those who are ignorant of these gentle crafts, but are strong and steady, there are loads to carry, water to draw, wood to cut, and for those who are both ignorant and weakly, there is oakum to tease and yarn to wind.' (Browne 1837: 229)

The most visible effect of the lunacy reforms was the spread of purpose-built asylums across the landscape. The building programme was indeed so successful that by mid-century it had laid the groundwork for a national system of asylums. The reformers' principal aim was not, however,

30

simply to construct new receptacles. Extending and rationalizing confinement were indeed important, and prerequisites for any sweeping reform, as were improvements in sanitation, ventilation, and diet within asylums. On such practical matters the reforms accomplished a good deal; and their example was quite pertinent to others burdened with managing what contemporaries called 'residential establishments' (hospitals, prisons, schools, etc.). But creating a regime of confinement 'fitting' to the insane, and an appropriate context for their moral treatment, was the reformers' important ideological spur. It is only this which accounts for the remarkable energy and ingenuity reformers devoted to devising asylum plans, in all the details of their physical and human organization.

A special 'ethos' of confinement pervaded the new model asylum, and distinguished it dramatically from the pandemonium and disorder of Bedlam. The reformers' descriptions of confinement conscientiously severed the older associations of asylums with the apparatus of prisons (and their gloomy, barred spaces, their clanking chains, their stench, their rude keepers, and so on); and they likewise distinguished the model asylum from the representations of Bedlam, which, like Hogarth's famous print of 'The Rake in Bedlam', celebrated the extravagant insane energies, the chaos, the terror, and the melancholy of the place. The new model asylum was to be at once less forbidding and less chaotic.

Dr Browne's account of 'what asylums ought to be' provides an admirable and largely representative example. It describes an imaginary asylum colony, conceived as a hierarchical rural society in miniature. The colony is of course fancifully drawn, even indeed sentimentalized. It is peopled by the *insane*, and yet apparently lacking any repressive apparatus, and without notable disease or disorder, or indeed personal unhappiness, among its inmates. But the description is nonetheless serious. However exaggerated for rhetorical purposes it well represents the ideological programme which the reformers advanced, and to a degree accomplished. Each phrase is resonant in contradicting the older associations of confinement.

A 'SPACIOUS BUILDING' (whose purpose is nonetheless to confine), 'AIRY AND ELEVATED', 'surrounded by extensive and swelling grounds', the sun and the air 'allowed to enter at every window'.

It was official policy to site asylums in the countryside, or in 'retiring' places near towns. Outside the towns land was more readily available, and cheaper, and appropriate sites more plentiful. The lunacy officials had long recommended elevated sites, if possible above rivers or near streams, to aid the disposal of wastes. Elevated and airy sites were more salubrious, since low-lying or swampy grounds produced the 'miasma' which bred and circulated fevers through the atmosphere. In Parliamentary investigations the most persistent criticisms of asylum planning were directed at poorly-situated asylums which took too little care to protect inmates from infections.

A situation in the countryside also allowed extensive grounds bounded by distant perimeter fences, which could serve as a buffer between the asylum buildings and the surrounding area, and as the basis of the asylum's internal economy. A large number of the new county asylums ran farms in their grounds, which provided to a greater or lesser degree all their own necessities.

Less tangibly, the reformers' characteristic siting of the model asylum in the countryside – open to the air – removed confinement from its familiar place and reputation in the towns, with their unhealthy, 'vitiated', and often disease-ridden atmosphere. De la Rive, one of the first continental visitors to the Retreat, admired it 'située à un mille de York, au milieu d'une campagne fertile et riante; ce n'est point l'idée d'une prison qu'elle fait naître, mais plutôt celle d'une grande ferme rustique; elle est entourée d'un jardin fermé' (de la Rive 1798: 5–6). Other contemporary descriptions of the Retreat represented it more explicitly in a rural idyll, and drew on the full range of values, moral and physical, which ideas of the countryside could evoke.[1] As if, by the antidote of fresh country air, the new model asylum escaped in its countrified setting the long-standing and immediate association of 'confinement' with close spaces, fetid and noxious air, filth, contagion, and disease.

The bases of these associations were multiple, and in large part realistic. The earliest varieties of confinement were quarantine houses and lazarettos (notably leper compounds), whose purpose was to enclose the diseased. Most early modern houses of confinement (and many hospices) were unrelievedly nasty and infamous. 'Gaol fever' and 'hospital fever' (typhus) were endemic in institutions throughout the eighteenth century, and indeed until the mid-nineteenth century in places, and were at times epidemic. The death-rate in prisons and other houses of confinement was notoriously high; at the end of the eighteenth century John Howard argued that far more prisoners died as a result of their confinement than were executed (Howard 1792: 8). There were also well-publicized cases of judges dying from contact with prisoners in their courts; in the 'Black

Sessions' of 1750 in London several judges, and forty others, died. Prisoners from Newgate were henceforth bathed with vinegar before their entrance into court (Hammond and Hammond 1933: 319).

During outbreaks of plague and later epidemics of infectious disease, inmates in confinement sometimes died *en masse* and generally suffered far more casualties than the population at large. With some justice institutions of confinement were popularly suspect as the breeding-grounds of plague – which threatened to spread beyond the bounds.

The miasmatic theory of contagion, and the evidence in its support, disposed contemporaries to fear the spaces of confinement and the foul and 'corrupting' air which hung about them.[2] In the social geography of towns, and especially in the great cities of London and Paris, the neighbourhoods of confinement acquired a particular reputation which, like the contiguity of slaughterhouses and tanneries, marked whole quarters (see Chevalier 1973: 86ff.). With the accumulated miseries of overcrowding, poor diet, bad sanitation, infection, and idleness, confinement marked the inmates themselves in their demeanour and attitude, most visible in daily experience in the persons of debtors who emerged from gaols in broken health. Howard remembered from his first contact with prisoners during his inspection tours their peculiar 'fallow meagre countenances', which spoke without words of their distress, and as he wryly remarked, grounded the expression 'to rot in prison' in a literal sense. Lunatics and idiots, whose heads were often shaved, were rendered more bizarre by their distinctive and alarming paleness, or yellowed skin; many apparently passed wholly subterranean lives, and some lived in total darkness. In the 1815 Parliamentary investigations one physician described the slow, halting movement toward the light of a barely-sighted, albino-like creature whom he and other asylum inspectors had disturbed in his cell during a visit (Dr Richard Fowler, in Official Publications 1815–16: 46).

The commonly weakened condition of the insane, their frequent incontinence, and the 'depleting' remedies of bleeding, purges, and restrictive diets, reduced them in confinement to a further degraded state, to which frequent asylum scandals amply testify. During the 1815–16 investigations many asylum visitors recorded their shock (and repulsion) at discovering scarcely human-looking creatures in dungeons, close cells, or lunatic huts where they were locked for weeks at a time, amid other lunatics and idiots.

After the disclosures and scandals during the lunacy reform proceedings, which forcibly renewed the long-established impressions of confinement and its connection with disease, debility, and filth, the new model asylum, elevated, airy, spacious, and open to the sun and breeze, was the inevitable emblem of reform. In the event, the county asylums which were often (if only for reasons of economy) sited amid fields were undoubtedly in time more salubrious, but largely owing to the measures of practical public health rather than to the symbolic efficacy of air, sun, and open spaces.

Windows 'UNOBSTRUCTED BY SHUTTERS OR BARS'.

Of the Retreat, de la Rive noted approvingly, 'point de barreau, point de grillages aux fenêtres'. Tuke had designed the windows in the Retreat specially to appear like ordinary windows, with their iron sashes even painted to look like wood. This was to spare the inmates unfortunate associations, and to visitors seemed a telling sign of the character of restraint in the place. By contrast, Dance's massive façade for the rebuilt Newgate (and many later prison designs) had no windows at all.

Tuke's design for the Retreat tried to make it appear an ordinary, if outsize, house, which would suggest the proper surroundings for the domestic atmosphere within he hoped to foster. The windows appeared ordinary because confinement in the Retreat depended on *moral* restraint. The whole panoply of mechanical restraints was hidden; chaining inmates was forbidden, and strait-waistcoats were available only in the last instance.

The domestic régime of moral restraint which Tuke established was, with Citizen Pinel's contemporaneous unchaining of the inmates at Bicêtre, the founding gesture of the model asylum movement. Removing mechanical restraints from the insane was the most dramatic single sign of the reform and the reforming 'spirit', which through several decades advanced to the point of urging complete abolition of mechanical restraints on the insane (see especially Hill 1839).

The practice of chaining madmen was ancient, and indeed seemed a natural consequence of their fury. At the end of the eighteenth century asylums were routinely equipped and fitted out with chains and other restraints, although their actual use was selective, and not the only method for managing inmates. In rural areas, and where solitary lunatics were confined, chaining was more general, since lunatics, when secured, could be left unattended. In asylums with few keepers chaining was likewise no doubt a more common resort. During the investigations into Bethlem in 1815, the Quaker Edward Wakefield testified that during his visit two keepers and an assistant were supervising about seventy-five men patients (with about an equal number of women in the other wing); when one inmate 'arose naked from his bed, and had deliberately and quietly walked a few paces from his cell door along the gallery', Wakefield recalled, he was 'instantly seized by the keepers, thrown into his bed, and leg-locked, without enquiry or observation: chains are universally substituted for the strait-waistcoat' (Official Publications 1815: 46).

The most alarming use of chains was, however, not for such temporary restraint (which indeed was commonly used to contain outbreaks of furious madness until they passed); it was in cases such as William Norris, a Bethlem inmate who, for more than ten years, was apparently never out of irons until discovered by the Parliamentary investigators. Wakefield described him, sitting immobile,

> 'a stout iron ring . . . rivetted round his neck, from which a short chain passed to a ring made to slide upwards or downwards on an upright massive iron bar, more than six feet high, inserted into the wall. Round his body a strong iron bar about two inches wide was rivetted; on each side of the bar was a circular projection, which being fastened to and inclosing each of his arms, pinioned them close to his sides. The waist bar was secured by two similar bars, which, passing over his shoulders, were rivetted to the waist bar both before and behind. The iron ring round his neck was connected to bars on his shoulders, by a double link. . . .'   (Official Publications 1815: 47)

Norris was fifty-five years of age, and in poor health, although he had once been violent.

Such cases did much to discredit the old 'terrific' system of asylum management, and gave reformers a certain moral leverage against established keepers. Although alienists were generally enthusiastic and partisan about the new 'therapy of kindness', many continued to rely, however, on mechanical restraints (usually fashioned of leather or strong canvas); in many places and particularly in isolated areas, madmen were commonly still closely bound.[3] William Tuke's claim that a domestic regime of moral treatment and moral restraint was not simply more humane but more efficacious in managing madmen, however important in the ideological programme of lunacy reforms, was not so widely honoured in practice. The design of asylums, which were places of *secure* confinement, in the event borrowed often from the 'terrific' features of prisons; and, further considering their scale, few asylums could afford to appear as Tuke styled the Retreat, like ordinary households.

'THE HOUSE AND ALL AROUND APPEARS A HIVE OF INDUSTRY';
'SOME VAST EMPORIUM OF MANUFACTURE'.

For an asylum which sought to be self-sufficient (a drive clearly reflected in Dr Browne's exhaustive catalogue of the full range of activities and occupations in his colony), the labour of inmates was its essential resource. In all but the best endowed asylums the labour of inmates was economically important and in most it was critical. But the lunacy reformers developed the *therapeutic* rationales of labour and continuous occupation at great length, for labour was the logical antidote to the idleness and dissipation on which so much of Bedlam's disorder and anarchy were based.

Although Bedlam had afforded secure confinement, and indeed was replete with chains and mechanical contrivances for restraining madmen, in the reformers' view it nonetheless left the mad too free at rein, and often in outright riot. When Hogarth pictured a Bedlam ward (in thoroughly conventional fashion), he represented not merely the pity and terror of the place, but its insane energies and chaos, and its comic and mischievous sidelights. In the company he assembled, each figure represents a stereotypic variant of the madman. Each in the narrow and crowded space is moreover entirely insulated in his own insane preoccupations; one poor gentleman, sitting in a cluster of figures, 'craz'd with care, and cross'd by hopeless love', is so 'absorbed in thought' and 'his whole soul so engrossed by the charms of his *Dulcinea*' that

> 'neither the discordant sounds of the fiddler, whose trembling strings
>
> "Grate harshly on the nerve auricular",
>
> nor the roar of the pope, who is furiously denouncing destruction of all heretics, nor the *ear-piercing noise* of a barking cur, can awake him from his reverie.' (Ireland 1791–98: I, 66)

Amid this cacophony the keeper is chaining the figure of Rakewell, oblivious to surrounding events, representing 'Moody Madness laughing wild/Amid severest woe'. No other authority in the scene interferes with the mad antics and displays; nothing channels or restricts the overflow and random discharge of insane energies; no one rouses lethargy or comforts terror. There is no hint of medical apparatus.

The scene indeed well represents the lunacy reformers' principal complaint against older asylums: behind thick walls and barred windows the asylums failed to classify and segregate the insane within the wards themselves, and left the inmates to their own devices and idleness. The different classes of the insane – the rabid and furious, the melancholic, the frantic, the idle, the vacuous, the convalescent and quiet – mixed together indiscriminately in general license and neglect, 'expending their effervescent excitement in antics and motions of various kinds, without utility or object, or plunged in profound melancholy, inertia and stupor' (Pinel 1806: 217).

The older asylums hence permitted an 'unrestrained indulgence of the natural propensities to indolence, to unproductive activity, or to depressing meditations, [which would] in a high degree contribute to aggravate the existing evil'; whereas, as Pinel argued, a regime of 'labourious employment, on the other hand, is not a little calculated to divert the thoughts of lunatics from their morbid channel, to fix their attention upon more pleasing objects, and by exercise to strengthen the functions of the understanding' (Pinel 1806: 217).

Labour allowed a discipline through its regularity; it detached the suffering madman from the freedom and anarchy of his thoughts, and from the insistent tyranny of his insane preoccupations, and occupied him otherwise by fixing him with the responsibility for a task and its associated demands on his attention. The regularity of labour, and its distinctive rhythms, enforced habits on the madman. On the premises of an associational psychology, the sheer weight of habitual sensations and associations could by their pressure of familiarity eventually impose new trains of thought on the mind of the madman; properly controlled, such new habits as were enforced by the routines of disciplined labour could be therapeutic and indeed, as the lunacy reformers argued, could become a powerful instrument for restoring the madman's disturbed and agitated life to its 'natural rhythms'.

In the popular representations of Bedlam there was no central sane influence disposing the behaviour of inmates, who accordingly ran wild or vegetated. Against the meaningless energies and indolence of Bedlamites, the lunacy reformers contraposed the image of concerted, orderly, and purposive behaviour, which was the very emblem of rationality. In the 'hive of industry' Dr Browne described, 'all are so busy as to overlook, or all are so contented as to forget their misery' (Browne 1837: 231). All are indeed taken over by the repetition of physical tasks which direct and channel their energies. Labour was thus a therapeutic resource of the new model asylum, and one of the instruments which extended the alienist's power to control and manipulate an inmate's physical world, and hence all the 'impressions' which struck his mind from the outside.

'LABOUR IS DIVIDED . . . and so apportioned, that it may suit the tastes and powers of each labourer.'

This is the first hint in Dr Browne's description of the complex classification of inmates, which was a major principle of reform. The programme for separate confinement of the insane was itself based on a form of classification, which separated inmates in the broad sense by type, and led to specialized and distinctive varieties of confinement appropriate to their inmates (notably the penitentiary, the juvenile home, the reformed asylum, specialist and fever hospitals, and so on). Within asylums, classification remedied the promiscuous mixing of madmen of all sorts which, reformers argued, further maddened the inmates. In the historic Bedlam men and women were segregated, and there were to a degree differences in treatment 'appropriate' to the different social classes; 'gentlemen', for instance, were unlikely to be chained. To these policies the reformers added a far more elaborated classification and separation of inmates by their social class, variety ('species') of disorder, and demeanour.

The complex social division of labour in Dr Browne's colony, supported by labourers of different 'tastes and powers', suggests this principle of classification, although it is the divisions by social class which appear most clearly in his text. For educated lunatics there are separate employments and 'diversions', in the form of leisured pursuits: for ladies reading, playing the harp, riding, walking in the country; for gentlemen intellectual pursuits, including news-rooms for 'politicians', or 'agreeable trifling' like landscape-painting. The educated lunatics also associate socially with the governor and physician rather than with the pauper inmates, since in the case of an educated lunatic 'his loss of caste may be fatal' if he were placed at the grade of paupers. For the rest, labourers are apportioned according to the requirements of production; 'some rise to the rank of overseers'; the unskilled are available as hewers of wood and drawers of water.

The 'mixing' of ranks which reformers criticized was more common in private madhouses and voluntary subscription hospitals than in the early public asylums, where the inmates were overwhelmingly paupers. The subscription hospitals owed their existence in most cases to the people of 'middling sort' who supported them, and for whom such lunatic hospitals catered to a degree, although they depended also on their income from parishes for keeping pauper lunatics. The charges for private inmates in the subscription hospitals were generally higher than for parish paupers, and the type of accommodation and comforts varied accordingly; but the social separation was rarely rigid.

In the new model asylum, which was planned for the insane of all ranks, the problem of division was naturally more extensive, and often influenced the physical plan of the asylum building. The asylum architect William Stark voiced a typical complaint at the mixing of classes in the 'common receptacles', where

'persons of liberal education, and of respectable rank in society, are unavoidably mixed with those of the lowest rank, of the most brutal manners, and of the most profligate habits; almost every possible state of disease is, in like manner, exhibited within the same ward, as if mental derangement, like the hand of death, levelled all distinctions.'

(Stark 1807: 10)

His own most widely publicized plan accordingly built in isolation of the classes, so that 'it may be put completely out of their power to go beyond their own boundary, or to meet with, or even see, any individual belonging to the other classes'; 'in this way, each class may be formed into a society inaccessible to all others' (Stark 1807: 15).

William Tuke and his associates had planned a similar segregation at the Retreat, which was founded after the death of a Quaker from their community in the public asylum at York. As Samuel Tuke later reported,

'It was thought that the indiscriminate mixture, which must occur in large public establishments, of persons of opposite religious sentiments and practices; of the profligate and the virtuous; the profane and the serious; was calculated to check the progress of returning reason, and to fix, still deeper, the melancholy and misanthropic train of ideas, which, in some descriptions of insanity, impresses the mind.'

(Tuke, S. 1813: 23)

The mixing of social classes, of religious communions, or of people of diverse habits and mores, was one pertinent aspect of a more general problem; in close confinement the inmates were suggestible and excited. They influenced each other, often malignly, and this tended to interfere with their therapeutic 'connection' to the alienist. Classifying and separating inmates afforded, on the other hand, means of interdicting certain influences of inmates over each other, and of opening them more to the contact and sanative influence of the alienist.

Contemporary attacks on prisons and gaols similarly often focused on the lack of 'classification' inside, which allowed hardened criminals to profit from the opportunity of confinement and recruit to their trade the young and as yet inexperienced offenders who were often locked up pell-mell with them, and fell under their sway. In close confinement in asylums, it was madness itself which seemed communicable from one to another; thus, for example,

> 'the religious despair of a patient in the next apartment brings back and confirms the religious despondency of his neighbour in this: the passions and violence of those who are parading in the airing ground revive the passions and ravings of those who are becoming more tranquil.'   (Conolly 1830: 28–9)

'So long as one lunatic associates with another lunatic, supposing the cases to be curable', as John Conolly claimed, 'so long must the chances of restoration to sanity be very materially diminished' (Conolly 1830: 29). The model asylum policies thus ideally barred the melancholic from contact with the maniac, and the convalescent from one who was still furious. The insane required not insane fellows to commiserate, but on the contrary, frequent communication with people of sound mind.

The separation of inmates depended in large measure on the architecture of asylums, and architects and alienists frequently collaborated on the actual plans. In aesthetic terms certain architects claimed, perhaps fancifully, to produce buildings and interior spaces fitting to the 'moods' and various psychological states of the mad. For his part, Pinel, who stressed the importance of perfect isolation of the different 'species' of insanity from each other, tried to apportion the 'species' through a given building according to their 'affinities' to the different sections of the place; to the melancholics he would allot a section facing out over cheerful scenery and adjoining a garden so that this class could exercise its affinity towards horticulture; the most 'furious and extravagant' maniacs he would sequester in the most secluded part of the building, so that their cries and howlings could never reach beyond the 'gloom and secrecy' of the place; similarly, 'the spectacle of degradation and nullity, presented by dementia and ideotism, ought never to be exposed to the observance of the other classes of maniacs'; etc. (Pinel 1806: 176).

In contrast to the undivided space in the Bedlam ward Hogarth depicted, where the varieties of madmen infect each other freely, the plans of the new model asylum raised walls to segregate the insane; the intent was to individualize the moral treatment of different classes to suit the 'tastes and powers' and needs of each. Moral treatment of the insane hence depended in principle on their complex classification, and the individualized approaches to inmates such classing ideally allowed. But classification also had the happy result of suppressing the 'sub-culture' of inmates and their mutually contagious influences, which if not repressed invariably erupted in the antics for which the mad crew of Bedlamites were traditionally famous.

Confinement in the new model asylum was, in pointed contrast to Bedlam, decorous, and not an object of shame. Hogarth had chosen a Bedlam ward as the appropriate setting to conclude his moral tale, to symbolize his hero's ultimate (and merited) reduction to an animal-like insensibility, at the nadir of human society. The barest allusion to 'Bedlam' would no doubt have sufficed Hogarth, since the associations he drew upon as the background for the last stage in 'The Rake's Progress' were commonplace. When the lunacy reformers in the early nineteenth century described the new model asylum, characteristically set in an open and elevated spot amid fields, with unbarred windows and no clanking of chains, animated by the industrious and orderly labour of its contented inmates, the images and their sentimental tones were carefully modulated against the echoes of 'Bedlam', which the lunacy inquiries and scandals had so recently renewed. Dr Browne imagined accompanying a visitor on a tour of his asylum colony, to look upon 'such fair and fertile scenes as harmonize with the tranquillity which reigns within, and tend to conjure up images of beauty and serenity in the mind which are akin to happiness' (Browne 1837: 230).

'Tranquillity' was the logical antipode to the pandemonium of Bedlam, and the tone judged suitable for the practices of a more sentimental charity than the insane had earlier received.

What produced these happy effects in the reformers' plan was the new system of management in asylums based on 'moral treatment'. The absent cause behind the 'hive of industry' Dr Browne described was the enlightened 'governor' himself, who coordinated the whole and represented its rational design. His humane and magisterial figure, which apparently often stood for the concrete ambitions of the reformers themselves in running asylums, was the organizing centre of the lunacy reform and the basis of the new régime.

The post of 'keeper' in madhouses was traditionally held in low repute – perhaps with justice since keepers were often venal and grasping, and the places they ran unwholesome. Within the medical professions the apothecaries and 'mad-doctors' who serviced public asylums and lunatic hospitals similarly earned in general little respect from colleagues, for what was humble work in a lowly branch of medicine. With some honourable exceptions mad-doctors and keepers were frequently brutish and callous, or neglected their duties outright. Against this background the lunacy reformers held out quite another image of the 'governor'. They were concerned to attract as superintendents and physicians men of the highest 'moral standing', who could carry out fitly the philanthropic tasks of medical psychology. The asylum governor appeared indeed as an ideal practitioner and exemplar of the new 'science of man' which medicine was becoming. From a disreputable task, managing the insane became for philanthropic circles work at the advancing edge of the human sciences.

By its design moral treatment in the model asylum thus depended upon the sympathies and personal qualities of its 'governor', who was by parts physician, medical superintendent, keeper, and attendant: a composite figure representing the best principles of treatment and 'healing' in all the social relations of the asylum, and on whose judicious management the whole depended. This 'healer' was not essentially a physician by qualifications, since knowledge of physic and the pharmacopoeia was not his requisite skill. Mad-doctors were naturally loath to surrender their prerogatives in treating the insane; but it is nonetheless striking how much a philanthropic temper came to be the principal recommendation in an individual for working with the insane.

With the onset of the lunacy reforms the medicine of insanity itself acquired a novel autonomy, which detached it from its former status as a peripheral and residual chapter in medical science, usually classed with other 'diseases of the head' or in the residuum of other poorly defined complaints. Moral treatment made a strikingly new departure; it was a therapeutics which depended not on the received array of medical interventions (which many alienists largely neglected) but rather on the character of the governor himself, and the relations he developed with each inmate under care. It was a regime of psychological techniques.

The first physician at the Retreat 'entered on his office with the anxiety and ardour of a *feeling mind*, upon the exertion of whose skill, depended the dearest interest of many of his fellow creatures' (Tuke, S. 1813: 110–11). His evident humanity, 'indefatigable perseverance' and optimism, were his most important recommendations, and these were indeed qualities commonly enumerated by the reformers in their descriptions of the ideal governor or physician. As John Haslam wrote,

'It should be the great object of the superintendent to gain the confidence of the patient, and to awaken in him respect and obedience . . . [which] can only be procured by superiority of talents, discipline of temper, and dignity of manners. Imbecility, misconduct, and empty consequence, although enforced with the most tyrannical severity, may excite fear, but this will always be mingled with contempt.'

(Haslam 1809: 278)

In very similar terms Pinel drew a simple contrast between the enlightened model governor and a less humane keeper:

'A coarse and unenlightened mind considers the violent expressions, vociferations and riotous demeanour of maniacs as malicious and intentional insults.'

'A man of better feeling and consideration, sees in those effervescences of a maniac but the impulses of an automaton, or rather the necessary effects of nervous excitement, no more calculated to excite anger than a blow or a crush from a stone propelled by its specific gravity.'

(Pinel 1806: 185)

The 'man of better feeling and consideration' would accordingly not return blows or stripes, which could further enrage and madden the lunatic, but practice a kindlier management, by 'moral' means. Pinel's own reputation in histories of psychiatry still owes largely to his gesture of unchaining maniacs at Bicêtre and reasoning with them; 'the lucid firmness of Pinel, who masters in a word and a gesture . . . animal frenzies that roar against him' constitutes, as Foucault has suggested, one of the founding myths of psychiatry and the original image of the magisterial psychiatrist calming the furies of mad outbreaks (Foucault 1965: 242).

The Quaker William Tuke's reputation in histories of psychiatry is similar, although more tinged with domestic overtones befitting the atmosphere of the institution where he presided with paternal airs. Samuel Tuke's *Description of the Retreat* records the case of a young maniac brought to William, bound in chains and still furious; although the young man's rages frightened even the guards who attended him, once at the Retreat his shackles were removed, he was presented and introduced formally to his new keepers, ate with them, and was taken finally to his room. A keeper explained to him there the regime and practices of the house. As the author moralizes the tale: 'The maniac was sensible of the kindness of his treatment. He promised to restrain himself'; and when later rages seized him, 'he would listen with attention to the persuasions and arguments of his friendly visiter. After such conversations the patient was generally better for some days or a week'. Four months later he was released cured, having been 'mastered by kindness' (Tuke, S. 1813: 146–47).

43

Tuke regarded the course of moral treatment as an education of sorts, like the upbringing of a child, albeit one with special attributes. The inmates were treated indeed 'as children who have an overabundance of strength and make dangerous use of it'; as de la Rive wrote of the inmates under Tuke's management:

> 'il leur faut des peines et des récompenses présentes: tout ce qui est un peu éloigné n'a point d'effet sur eux. Il faut leur appliquer un nouveau système d'éducation, donner un nouveau cours à leurs idées, les subjuger d'abord, les encourager ensuite, les appliquer au travail, leur rendre ce travail agréable par des moyens attrayans.'
>
> (de la Rive 1798: 29–30)

Such treatment required a physician of commanding presence, someone who could modulate his temper 'according to the exigency of the case', at one moment 'to be placid and accommodating in his manners, and the next, angry and absolute', much after the fashion of a parent with a capricious child. By reputation many of the famed mad-doctors were indeed awesome and imposing figures, although not so often as kindly or paternal in their manner as the reformers' ideal governor. On his first meeting a new patient, a French observer remarked of the clerical mad-doctor Francis Willis:

> 'his usually friendly and smiling countenance changed its expression. He suddenly became a different figure commanding the respect even of maniacs. His piercing eye seemed to read their hearts and divine their thoughts as they formed and before they were even uttered. In this way he gained control over them which he used as a means of cure.'
>
> ('Details sur l'établissement du Docteur Willis' 1796: 759)

Even the gentle Tuke apparently had a similar disarming power in his stare, and like others at the Retreat relied on the technique of moral control which contemporaries referred to as 'catching them with the eye'. A famous anecdote in Samuel Tuke's account of the Retreat records an incident in the grounds which occurred during a superintendent's walk alone with a patient; the maniac, who was subject to fits of violence, suddenly 'retired a few paces, and seized a large stone, which he immediately held up, as in the act of throwing at his companion. The superintendent, in no degree ruffled, fixed his eye upon the patient, and in a resolute tone of voice, at the same time advancing, commanded him to lay down the stone.' Chastened by the stern look, the maniac dropped the stone and 'submitted to be quietly led to his apartment' (Tuke, S. 1813: 172–73).

The 'power of the eye' was a widely evoked and admired symbol of the alienists' power over maniacs. It was an image which easily recalled the taming of wild beasts, or the 'fascination' of the snake-charmer. But it symbolized more generally, especially in the new philanthropic currents, the specific carrier of the alienist's influence over the madman — a carrier which bore different messages and induced different responses according to the temper and state of his disorder. The physician's regard was not constantly severe or stern; on the contrary,

'A much greater effect is produced by looking the patient out of countenance with a mild and steady eye, and varying its aspect from the highest degree of sternness, down to the mildest degree of benignity; for there are keys in the eye, if I may be allowed the expression, which should be suited to the state of the patient's mind, with the same exactness that musical tones should be suited to the depression of spirits in hypochondriasis.' (Rush 1830: 173–74)

The rationale for such treatment, and for the modulations of the governor's countenance, was an exhortation to the madman to restrain *himself*; thus the system of moral management under the direction of the governor achieved an economy of mechanical restraints. In the older 'terrific' system of management inmates were 'kept in subjection and apparently orderly habits by the strong excitement of the principle of fear', which as the folklore of the institutions and later actual revelations demonstrated was often supported by liberal beatings and frequent resort to chains. The reformers regarded such practices as degrading and excessive; the terrorized inmates, as Samuel Tuke wrote,

'may be made to obey their keepers, with the greatest promptitude, to rise, to sit, to stand, to walk, or run at their pleasure; though only expressed by a look. Such an obedience, and even the appearance of affection, we not infrequently see in the poor animals who are exhibited to gratify our curiosity in natural history; but, who can avoid reflecting, in observing such spectacles, that the readiness with which the savage tiger obeys his master, is the result of treatment at which humanity would shudder.' (Tuke, S. 1813: 147–48)

To philanthropists of his own and succeeding generations Tuke's criticisms evoked unmistakeably the rhetoric of enlightenment, and obviously recalled the numerous descriptions of Bedlam as a variety of London 'attraction', a 'menagerie' for the curious to visit of a Sunday.

However powerful and thorough the repression possible by terror,

Tuke claimed, 'yet the *desire of esteem* is considered at the Retreat, as oper-
ating in general, still more powerfully' as an instrument of management;
and moreover it operates on the basis of 'rational and honourable' induce-
ments. 'When properly cultivated, it [the desire of esteem] leads many to
struggle to conceal and overcome their morbid propensities; and at least,
materially assists them in confining their deviations within such bounds,
as do not make them obnoxious to the family' (Tuke, S. 1813: 157).

In the 'family' at the Retreat, Tuke devised special occasions, like the
famous 'tea-parties', where patients could display exemplary self-restraint
and submit themselves to the appropriate social forms; the 'guests' would

'dress in their best clothes, and vie with each other in politeness and
propriety. The best fare is provided, and the visitors are treated with all
the attention of strangers. The evening generally passes with the
greatest harmony and enjoyment. It rarely happens that any unpleasant
circumstances occurs; the patients control, to a wonderful degree, their
different propensities; and the scene is at once curious and affectingly
gratifying.'   (Tuke, S. 1813: 178)

'Moral treatment' was not always associated so directly with the virtues
and atmosphere of the family, since it was fitted also to establishments far
larger than the 'household'. But the principles of psychological restraint
on which moral treatment was based invariably endowed the physician or
governor with the noble and philanthropic qualities of a paternal figure.
The governor so conspicuously lacking in Hogarth's Bedlam ward
became, in the reformers' representations of the model asylum, the watch-
ful and intelligent centre of the whole. The 'ideal governor', as the
American physician Benjamin Rush described him, would live constantly
with his inmates, 'and have the exclusive direction of their minds';

'his business should be to divert them from conversing upon all the
subjects upon which they had been deranged, to tell them pleasant
stories, to read them select passages from entertaining books, and to
oblige them to read to him; to superintend their labours of body and
mind; to preside at the table at which they take their meals, to protect
them from rudeness and insults from their keepers, to walk and ride
with them, to partake with them in their amusements, and to regulate
the nature and measure of their punishments.'   (Rush 1830: 239–40)

Over time, such a figure would invariably become, even for the insane, an
object of 'respect and affection' as familiar as a parent or spouse, and an

exemplary model for the inmates to imitate. Thus, as Rush succinctly expressed the ideals of moral treatment,

> 'by keeping the eyes and ears of mad people under the constant impressions of the countenance, gestures, and conversation of a man of a sound understanding, and correct conduct, we should create a pressure nearly as mechancial upon their minds [as the pressure of a splint on a broken limb], that could not fail of having a powerful influence, in conjunction with other remedies, in bringing their shattered and crooked thoughts into their original and natural order.'
>
> (Rush 1830: 240)

Such moral pressures, exerted with a force close to the intensity of a parent's bond to a child, were the fundamental motor of the new plan of 'management' in asylums, and its most telling symptom. They were the key to achieving the ideal of 'what asylums ought to be'.

The improvements in more prosaic aspects of management which the lunacy reforms accomplished, to provide better sanitation and ventilation, more adequate diet, and more organized activities, were far from inconsiderable; but these served themselves as marks of the new enlightened regime. What the new model asylum represented was not simply a summary of the several discrete improvements in conditions effected more or less widely in institutions; what was essential was the new 'atmosphere' of confinement evoked by images resonant with the rhetoric of enlightenment and of the new 'science of man'. Against the image of Bedlam, which served the reformers as an emblem for the many generations of neglect and cruelty under which the insane had languished, the new model asylum represented a salutary demonstration of the 'powers of kindness' and humane sympathy. 'Moral treatment' itself became in turn an emblem of the power of mind over mind, symbolized with especial force in the moral management of the insane. Treating the insane 'morally' was indeed a striking demonstration: by his psychological techniques the physician mastered and calmed animal furies which previous generations in their ignorance had held as objects of superstition, fear, loathing, and despair.

· 3 ·

THE ARCHITECTURE OF
CONFINEMENT

'An insane asylum is a therapeutic instrument in the hands of an able physician, and our most powerful weapon against mental diseases.'
(Esquirol)

The 'power of mind over mind' which moral treatment represented to the lunacy reformers, was exercised through the commanding presence of a physician newly endowed with this philanthropic work. But its exercise depended equally on the skills of architects; it was their task to prepare the physical spaces of confinement, where in turn physicians could create the proper therapeutic atmosphere.

The lunacy reformers accorded the physical dimensions of confinement a strikingly positive value, far beyond their functional purpose of securing the insane, and segregating them behind walls from the community at large. Within the walls of confinement the physical environment of inmates was, on the familiar premises of a pervasive associational psychology, an invaluable resource. If properly designed and exploited, the interior space of the asylum could be a therapeutic tool; properly manipulated it could yield the alienist an ever greater control over the inmate, and over all the 'impressions' which reached his mind. It was this therapeutic potential of confinement which initiated a close collaboration between architecture and psychological medicine. In the event a great fund of energy was devoted to ingenious and ambitious architectural schemes. The universal end was, by one or other 'simple idea in architecture', to enable a special atmosphere in the model asylum; to enhance through the design itself the individual inmate's relation to the physician; to render the physician's surveillance over the inmate more general and constant. The architectural schemes, of which among a profusion of plans Bentham's Panopticon was the most extreme and best known, thus served as means of enabling or facilitating the *moral* management of the insane, and of relaxing mechanical restraints.

Figure 1 Plan of an intended London asylum for the care and cure of the insane, by James Bevans

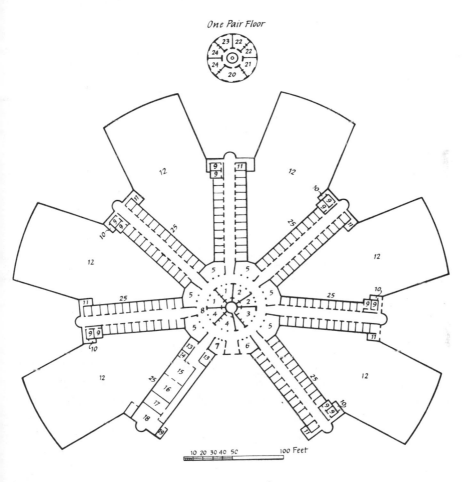

One Pair Floor

1 Stewards Apartments	14 Pantry
2 Matrons Apartments	15 Kitchen
3 Surgery	16 Wash-house
4 Apothecarys Apartments	17 Drying Room
5 Day Rooms	18 Straw Room
6 Porters Room	19 Servants Water Closet
7 Visitors Room	*One Pair Floor*
8 Inspection Gallery	20 Committee Room
9 Rooms for Noisy Patients	21 Women Servants Bed Rooms
10 Patients Water Closets	22 Matrons Bed Room
11 Warm Baths	23 Stewards Bed Room
12 Airing Grounds	24 Men Servants Bed Rooms
13 Store Room	25 Covered Walks

When John Conolly, who had been so moved by Tuke's *Description of the Retreat* (1813), took over the daunting task of managing the nearly 1000 patients in the Hanwell Asylum, he promptly abolished all mechanical restraints. He made the gesture dramatically, but it was only possible, he carefully explained, in the context of a specially prepared building and with the support of many attendants to represent (and multiply) his authority and presence. 'It must not really be supposed', Conolly later wrote,

'that though, in the shape of waist-coats, hobbles, &c., mechanical aid has in great measure disappeared, it has under other forms and combinations been altogether dispensed with, and that the unsound intellect submits itself to be set to rights by the simple and unassisted antagonism of the sound one. No such great mental triumph has ever been achieved. In truth, the functions of the carpenter, the smith, and the mason are as much in request as heretofore in surrounding the inmate of the lunatic-asylum with a complete atmosphere of *restraint.*'

(Conolly 1850: 92–3)

The inventive ingenuity of the architect created a 'semblance of liberty' amid a 'real and bona fide detention and security'; this allowed the governor or physician complete mastery over the inmates, but by predominantly moral means. Otherwise put, architecture itself could be a moral force.

The design of asylums, which became so important during the lunacy reforms, was a relatively novel concern. There were before the end of the eighteenth century relatively few mental institutions of any scale. From the 1780s the pace of developments quickened. A number of new provincial asylums were built; St Luke's was greatly expanded and the rebuilding of Bethlem first mooted. Questions of design became more pertinent and indeed central in the planning of asylums, as likewise for the planning of workhouses, prisons, and general and specialist hospitals, which were also spreading rapidly on a wave of new building. From the point of view of design these institutions had much in common, in part because architectural traditions served the various requirements of the new establishments rather poorly: they all stood in need of innovations.

In England, by contrast to the continent, few medieval monastic buildings survived in use as hospitals, pest-houses, or almshouses beyond the sixteenth or seventeenth century. There were in a few cases survivals of the monastic tradition in hospital architecture, with older buildings arranged in cloisters around a central church. But, in general, hospitals, almshouses, and the new houses of correction were, in the critical description of later centuries, 'conglomerates', or buildings without formal and geometrical design which often collected together parts of pre-existing buildings with new blocks of open wards, as need required. Few hospital buildings were purpose-built to any elaborated design until the eighteenth century; most were agglomerations of two- or three-storey structures huddling around a central court. In some places the city walls themselves still accommodated the hospital, almshouse, or lunatic cells, in rooms originally intended as keeps, barracks, or powder magazines.

Such lunatic asylums and madhouses as existed were in general indistinguishable, except by reputation, from ordinary domestic architecture, although the lunatic 'huts' were undoubtedly extremely mean and rude. Bethlem and St Luke's, by reason of their scale and their central situation in London, were exceptional in the formality of their design; but their plans, far from offering an instructive or influential example for later designs, were widely faulted by lunacy reformers. The new Bethlem Hospital raised in Moorfields in 1675–76 was conceived by Robert Hooke on a grand plan whose façade resembled the Tuileries. Two symmetrical wings of wards flanked a central pavilion, which served as the administrative offices; the whole building, with a frontage over 500 feet, was surrounded by a high stone wall. Inside, a broad gallery ran the length of the building; during the day it served as an open ward for the inmates who were allowed 'the liberty of the gallery', and among whom the visitors to Bethlem mingled. Off the gallery, cells were ranged, each sealed by a stout door and provided with a small, high, barred window for ventilation. Some inmates were apparently kept chained singly or in small groups in their cells, with the door bolted. John Howard visited the place in 1788 and found its wards 'quite clean and not offensive', although the single 'vault' (privy) which served upwards of 300 inmates was 'very offensive' (Howard 1789: 139). Since the whole interior of the building was open, however, Howard criticized the consequent failure to classify and segregate the inmates: 'The patients communicate with one another from the top to the bottom of the house, so that there is no separation of the calm and quiet from the noisy and turbulent, except those who are chained in their cells' (Howard 1789: 139). The pandemonium which resulted, and which was a characteristic feature in the representation of Bethlem, was in the lunacy reformers' view a flaw of faulty design (see especially Official Publications 1815–16: First Report).

St Luke's, which was founded in 1751, transferred in 1786 to a large and imposing new building designed by George Dance, the architect of

Newgate. Its façade was ungracefully neoclassical, and like Bethlem, it was built on the formal pattern of two wings (one for male inmates, the opposite female) flanking a central administration block, with two terminal pavilions. The lofty interior galleries, which stretched the length of the wings, were fifteen feet wide, and served as an open ward, with several common sitting-rooms. The galleries were flanked on both sides by rows of large cells (10' 4" × 8' × 13' 3" high), which had both windows and grilles over the doors to aid ventilation. The open plan of the wards, as in the case of Bethlem, prevented classification of inmates on either floor, and the wards were shut off from the central block only by upright bars and iron gates, which gave the whole a cavernous aspect.[1]

The designs of Bethlem and St Luke's reproduced with only minor modifications the contemporary fashions in building great residential institutions. Their plans were roundly criticized by the lunacy reformers as inadequate and faulty, as indeed the contemporaneous design of Newgate by George Dance was severely attacked by John Howard and later prison reformers for its open-ward plan and failure to separate prisoners. By contrast, the reformers produced in their collaboration with architects new *cellular* plans which eventually supplanted entirely the older type of 'conglomerate' and open-ward system, as likewise cellular prisons and penitentiaries eventually supplanted the out-moded designs like Dance's Newgate.

The growing interest in design derived in part from the technical problems in institutions of confinement which traditional plans whether formal or conglomerate failed to resolve, and which overcrowding compounded. Howard's great survey of the prisons, undertaken in the aftermath of the suspension of convict transportation to the American colonies, presented a compendium of errors of design and management, to which he attributed the foulness, insalubrity, and infamous low morality of the places. Few prisons were built with any but the most casual provisions for ventilation and cleanliness, and many were only rarely whitewashed. Their situation was often unhealthy, and dampness was a universal problem not simply in dungeons. In these respects prisons and common gaols suffered particularly, since they were often housed in ill-adapted buildings and were frequently crowded and close. But the problems were general in residential establishments, especially those of any scale. Howard made the same complaints against the hospitals and lazarettos he inspected. The problems of maintaining such places in reasonable salubrity and cleanliness under the prevailing unfavourable conditions were probably beyond the technical means available; thus the vogue for new 'ideas in architecture'.

Howard himself believed that a new design for prisons was the prerequisite for effective reforms; 'in order to redress these various evils', as he wrote, 'the first thing to be taken into consideration is the *prison itself*' (Howard 1792: 20). He suggested accordingly in his plan for a model County Gaol, raising the wards and cells to the first floor of the building, over open arcades at the ground level, which would allow freer circulation of air, light, and warmth and could materially aid hygienic measures. Such simple suggestions were a modest beginning to the practical redesigning of English prisons; half a century later the proposals would culminate with Sir Joshua Jebb's elaborate civil-engineering solutions which made possible huge penitentiaries on the Pentonville model.

Despite a flurry of proposals the practical and especially health-related problems in institutions were slow to abate. Hygienic conditions in many institutions remained deplorable until late in the nineteenth century; it was this fact which led men like the statistician William Farr to their life-long opposition to 'residential establishments'.

But the concerns of design were in any event not limited to hygienic problems. Howard demonstrated effectively how architectural plans could embody and enhance, or frustrate, the greater purposes of the prison as regards security of custody, the warders' exercise of control, and, as he added with emphasis, the separation and reform of the different classes of prisoners. Dungeons afforded the maximum in secure confinement, but the reformers sharply criticized them, not only on grounds of health, but as wrongly conceived. The changing conception of imprisonment itself in the reform period stimulated the search for new designs of the prison more appropriate to its reformed and enlarged purposes. As the purposes and rationales of imprisonment became more elaborated, the design of prisons required more or other than the familiar apparatus of restricted spaces and fetters.

The architecture of prisons, and of other varieties of confinement, accordingly grew specialized and distinctive, and more 'appropriate' to the character of the inmates. 'Fitting the building to its purposes' involved, in the case of prisons, a variety of structural innovations, stylistic refinements and new ways of organizing the space of confinement (by the so-called 'ideas in architecture'); together these changes would better support the reformed notions of prison management, and better embody the reformed *idea* of the prison by evoking its proper psychological atmosphere.

The vogue for new ideas in architecture revitalized a current in the aesthetic traditions which was concerned with the 'moods' buildings could embody. On a common view buildings evoke a range of impressions in the mind of an observer – by their dimensions, the play of light and shadow in their spaces, and their stylistic details. These impressions should ideally be appropriate to the purposes the buildings serve. Thus the essential character of the building would be self-evidently visible and sensible through the 'moods' and psychological impressions it embodied and evoked. In aesthetics the French architect Boullée advanced this principle most explicitly in a programmatic statement, although its significance and import were far broader. Burke's essay on the 'sublime', published in 1757, which commented on the impressions evoked by scale and awesome dimensions, and on the psychological effects of darkness, was for instance particularly suited to reflections on the design of prisons which would inspire terror. The notions Burke deployed seemed to later generations of critics to comment indirectly on Piranesi's 'Carceri d'Invenzione' – those imaginary sketches which nonetheless had a notable influence on the idea of the prison and its representation. The magnificent ruins Piranesi depicted, whose colossal spaces were littered with machines of torture, dwarfed and overwhelmed the few tiny, faceless human figures in their shadows.[2] These imaginary *'carceri'* which fascinated Coleridge and de Quincy as representations of great metaphysical prisons of the subject, also influenced architects like Dance, who self-consciously conceived the prison under its 'terrible' aspect (see Taylor 1973).

The reformed 'idea' of the prison was a world away from Piranesi; it evoked a more carefully modulated terror. The minutely sub-divided and organized space of the new prison was no longer awe-inspiring simply by reason of its vastness and dark recesses where no light penetrated. It did not evoke the same 'terrific' impressions. But the aspirations to embody 'moods' and to compose through the idioms of style an *architecture parlante* which expressed the building's purpose in its form, no less markedly influenced the design and representation of penitentiaries and model prisons. The 'separate system' and the 'silent system' had their own distinctive architectural 'moods'; these struck contemporary observers as forcibly, for different reasons, as the dungeon-like exercise yard designed by Dance for Newgate which, after a century, so fascinated Doré.

The designs of model asylums similarly ideally embodied a 'mood' and made an *architecture parlante* to express the proper forms for their purpose. Through the attentions of philanthropists the insane emerged in the

54

reform period as distinctive objects of a particular charity and sentimental concern, which, the reformers hoped, the setting, design, and 'impressions' of their confinement would properly represent. The design of the model-asylum building, and indeed its plan as a whole, to a large degree reflected this philanthropy, and supported a new conception of the social relations in confinement for which any allusion to the apparatus of the prison or to Bedlam was inapt. 'Moral management' required a distinctive architectural plan which not only materially supported and enabled the new social relations, but evoked their proper 'atmosphere'.

In the older asylums the aspect of terror and security had been obvious. Visitors to the places typically reported in fascinated detail the elaborate apparatus of terror: the hidden vats of cold water into which maniacs were suddenly and without warning precipitated for a 'surprise bath'; the steep stairs and artificial 'precipices' which were used to induce vertigo in the inmates; the tomb-like underground chambers in which maniacs and the refractory could be sealed; the chains, whips, restraint chairs, mechanical swings. The security of the places was often no less evident, in their high stone walls, barred windows, iron gates, their general fortress-like aspect and so on (see Conolly 1847: 7ff.).

The model asylum plans on the contrary organized a more prosaic 'terror' and security, befitting the reformed moral management of inmates. The reformers in fact avoided referring to 'terror' as an important principle of control, describing instead merely the 'salutary demonstrations' of various sorts which could, in the manner of terror but by calmer means, forcibly and suddenly impress the mind of the madman (in the epoch various 'shock' treatments remained commonplace). The architecture was accordingly not geared up to become itself a machine of terror.

Constant and general supervision and surveillance of inmates were instead the gentler means of producing an 'atmosphere' of restraint. The new model asylum afforded secure confinement, but not under the aspect of the prison fortress or dungeon. The apparatus of security was hidden, and cleansed of its prior associations with prisons. Thus, at the Retreat even the stone wall bounding the inmates' exercise yard was sited at the bottom of a slope which largely concealed it, so that it did not interrupt the view from the building itself over a verdant and apparently vast expanse. This was similarly the rationale for the explicit borrowing of details from domestic architecture in Tuke's plan for the Retreat, for instance in the telling matter of the windows without bars; or for the range of associations to the country manor which Dr Browne evoked in describing his model asylum colony. These were not incidental or peripheral details incorporated in a plan only as finishing decorative touches; they were central to the reformers' concern with design, and an essential means of establishing the proper 'tone' in model asylums to reflect the change in the status of the insane which the reformers had worked. The 'happy scenes' which Dr Browne described and displayed before an imaginary visitor were not rhetorical flourishes on the basic programme of moral treatment; they were its proper vindication, and a powerful demonstration of the philanthropists' efficacy and greater humanity in managing the mad.

It was, however, the structural innovations in the design of asylums, hospitals, and prisons which were in the event more enduring and influential. The ingenious attempts to signify or evoke appropriate 'moods' for the insane reveal much about the reformers' notions; but the structural innovations survived in stone, and helped to establish the bases for new principles of institutional planning and construction which survived into the twentieth century. In this respect the plans of asylums, hospitals, and prisons despite the divergent purposes of the places bore remarkable similarities. In each case the innovations served not only as the technical means of improving ventilation and hygiene in crowded establishments of scale, but also as the material basis enabling and supporting the new conceptions of social relations in confinement which the roughly simultaneous reforms in asylum and prison management, and the 'birth of the clinic', advanced (see Ackerknecht 1967, and Foucault 1973).

The plans were in each case based on a small, discrete unit – a cell or bed – which was multiplied and combined in geometrical patterns to form a composite whole. The hospital bed was the basic unit in the reorganized structure of the 'clinic', as were cells in the penitentiary and asylum. This separate 'cellular' unit allowed for the segregation, classification, and indeed insulation of inmates; and allowed also an individual approach in the matters of the inmate's management. These were the new resources in the architecture of confinement which grounded or helped to enable the reforms in management. Thus, in the model asylum, it was cellular insulation, and the schemes for 'opening up' individual inmates to improved and extended 'inspection' and surveillance, which were the architectural means of psychological restraint, and the essential key to 'moral treatment'.

The structural innovations in design – the new 'ideas in architecture' – were borrowed from diverse sources and recombined often ingeniously to suit the new purposes of the model asylums. They fell grossly into two large classes, although particular designs and actual buildings sometimes combined elements of both. The *carré isolé* was more characteristic of asylum planning in France, though the pavilion styles which derived from it were diffused everywhere; the Panopticon, and associated radial plans, were more common at the outset in Britain, and likewise were diffused (see Thompson and Goldin 1975: 53–77).

The origin of the *carré isolé* system is obscure, although the architect Tenon suggested plausibly that the pavilion plan derived from it imitated the siting of tents in an army encampment (Tenon 1788: 140; see also Blomfield 1921: 198–99). More fancifully others acknowledged the example of Louis XIV's palace at Marly, which featured a central royal residence (the 'sun') surrounded by twelve separate satellite pavilions (the 'planets'). The principle in either case was clear: the units of the design were separated, surrounded by open spaces between the buildings and amenable to specific uses (for instance, classification and segregation of the diseased and disordered). In the late eighteenth century despite architects' growing enthusiasm for pavilions and the break-up of large conglomerates into smaller, separate buildings, the Royal Naval Hospital at Stonehouse near Plymouth was the only perfectly realized pavilion hospital of its day. It was visited several times by the French hospital commissioners in the course of inquiries on redesigning the Hôtel-Dieu in Paris. The commissioners admired particularly the arrangements for ventilating the individual pavilions, the spaciousness of the plan as a whole – it arranged the pavilions in rows (placed in echelon) around an immense central court – and the virtually complete isolation of the separate buildings which were linked only by long, open, connecting corridors (see Tenon 1788, and Lavosier 1865: 603–704). The Plymouth pavilion design was ultimately not directly suitable for a new Hôtel-Dieu (which was being planned to accommodate several times as many patients) but the French visits and subsequent discussions further stimulated pavilion-type plans in France.

In 1786 Louis XVI's court architect François Viel began to rebuild the lunatics' rooms at the Salpêtrière, the huge female hospice in Paris which held large numbers of the insane. The original buildings, which dated from the late seventeenth century, had been built near the Seine on marshy ground which often flooded. Viel planned to build 600 'loges' (small cells communicating to the outside) arranged back-to-back in single storeys (which allowed ventilation through the ceilings), with eight or ten pairs of cells composing a separate building. The buildings themselves straddled narrow courts (onto which the loges opened), which were in some cases fenced or walled off to aid with the separation of the inmates. The plan lacked the spaciousness of the Plymouth Hospital, and crowded many more buildings into spaces which single rows of long pavilions occupied at Plymouth. But it marked a notable and symptomatic advance in hospital planning (Thompson and Goldin 1975: 54–8; see also Henry 1922: 28, and Vallery-Radot 1947: 206–07).

After some modifications in the Salpêtrière design a cluster of new loges for inmates was completed at Bicêtre, another enormous Paris hospice, in 1822. This marked the real beginning of the *carré isolé* system. The loges at Bicêtre were not placed back-to-back, which was an arrangement tending to aggravate dampness, but in single rows side-by-side, opening out to an arcade and courtyard beyond. The corridor which linked the cells on the higher storey of the loges was broken by numerous large windows and served, like the arcade below, to allow air and light into the cells. The rows of loges arranged at right angles enclosed a small court, and this unit formed the *carré*; it was a basic module which could be duplicated and repeated in series to form the design of larger hospitals, as it was later in the great Maison Nationale de Charenton outside Paris, which was begun in 1838 and eventually assembled sixteen separate *carrés isolés*. Apart from its important advantages for the salubrity of institutions, the basic plan – which could be multiplied and extended indefinitely – had the merit of building in sub-divisions within the space of confinement. The plan would be built up through progressively scaled units: from the individual cell or loge; to the cluster of cells at the corner of a *carré*, which would share a sitting-room; to the row of cells opening onto a common corridor, which could serve as a ward or day-room; to the rows of cells at right-angles, which enclosed a common court or a walled garden; and so forth (see Richard 1889, and Bru 1890: 158–60).

The physical resources of such a building, or series of buildings, allowed with easy flexibility complete classification and even perfect isolation of inmates, or likewise progressively greater degrees of association in the spaces available. From the 1820s the *carré isolé* system was widely used in France and elsewhere, and indeed survived well into the twentieth century as an important principle of hospital design.

The Panopticon plan offered similar advantages, although on the basis of a strikingly different 'idea in architecture'. Jeremy Bentham is still generally credited with responsibility for the original idea of the Panopticon; the name was his, and he presented an elaborated sketch of the design heavily marked by his own idiosyncrasies. But the various elements of the plan, and even their ingenious combination, were broadly anticipated in earlier designs and by several existing buildings. The larger purposes of the plan, however extremely Bentham himself presented them, were well-known and common to most of the reformers. Though none of the reformers wholeheartedly embraced Bentham's Panopticon plan in all its specifics, they nonetheless recognized what it was about, and happily endorsed other plans 'on the panopticon principle'.

The Panopticon was in Bentham's sketch, an 'inspection house' conceived in a general form which could be adapted to the specific purposes of prisons, workhouses, factories, madhouses, schools, and the like. The linking of these various institutions, which Bentham argued all depended on the 'inspection principle' for their management, was not so peculiar as historians have sometimes suggested in retrospect. Architecturally, the buildings of prisons, workhouses, factories, etc., did share certain common technical problems; and more pertinently, the problems of discipline in the various places were (to a degree) similar. There was at the time no well-elaborated 'science of management'; but there were nonetheless numerous discourses on how to manage. It is striking at first glance how much the proposals for reforming social relations in prisons and asylums repeated the same terms, as if the discipline of various categories of inmates depended on a few simple and general principles. This is perhaps less striking if one recalls that Bentham, who publicized his scheme as an ideal national penitentiary, had borrowed it in essentials from his brother's plan for a manufactory; the brother had come upon the idea in designing an arsenal in southwest Russia – a plan which had to be put forward in the face of a shortage of foremen and skilled workers, in order to facilitate the supervision and coordination of common labourers.

Structurally the 'inspection house' is a great cylinder of several storeys (as many as six storeys high in Bentham's later version). The cells are arranged along the outside walls, separated from each other by partitions radiating from the centre. An inspection tower fills the hub of the structure, and by virtue of its situation enjoys an open view into all the cells around the circumference. To ensure that the building would be genuinely a panopticon – or a place where everything is seen – Bentham had even taken the care to calculate the sight-lines between individual cells and the inspection tower, with as much attention to the matter as a director in the theatre. He had contrived further to shelter the inspection tower from the view of the cells; the essence of the plan, as he explained, consists in 'the *centrality* of the inspector's situation, combined with the well-known and most effectual contrivances for [his] *seeing without being seen*', which is the major principle of 'panoptism'. Since, on the premiss of the 'inspection principle', 'the more constantly the persons to be inspected are under the eyes of the persons who should inspect them, the more perfectly will the purposes of the establishment have been attained', the ideal is total and constant surveillance; barring this as humanly unfeasible, Bentham's plan tries nonetheless to effect 'the *apparent omnipresence* of the inspector', so that 'the persons to be inspected should always feel themselves as if under inspection' – 'in that predicament, during every instant of time' (Bentham 1843: IV, 40, 44). Through the insulation of 'the persons to be inspected' in separate cells and through their apparently constant surveillance, the Panopticon plan ingeniously accomplished, according to Bentham, a revolution in management; the enormous merits he intoned thus:

'Morals reformed – health preserved – industry invigorated – instruction diffused – public burthen lightened – economy seated as it were upon a rock – the Gordian knot of the Poor Laws not cut but untied – all by a simple idea in Architecture!' (Bentham 1843: IV, 39)

The 'simple idea' owed parts to many diverse sources, and not simply to the ingenious solution to a more specific problem that Bentham's brother had worked out. In essentials the Panopticon was a radial design; and indeed it was arguably the most important of all radial designs, since the publicity surrounding Bentham's attempts to have it built as the proposed national penitentiary was at least helpful in establishing radial plans as the model for asylums and prisons in Britain. The Panopticon carried forward more systematically and broadly the basic principles of Blackburn's earlier radial plans (Howard 1789: 155, 170–71; see also Markus 1954: 251–56).

On the continent such plans had a greater hold earlier, or at least figured more prominently in discussions of design. The famous Maison de Force at Ghent was the most important of the early radial prisons, and may actually have influenced Bentham in his conceptions of the Panopticon. It was begun in 1773 and projected as an octagon with eight radial wings, although it was never completed in this form. The long, narrow blocks which were actually put up, radiated from a common centre, and were conducted by other blocks at the outer circumference. This gave the whole from the exterior a circular aspect. The administrative buildings flanked the central court. The rationale for the plan, which the architect Count Vilain XIV expounded (Vilain 1775), was to increase the light and air in the cells, and to enhance the 'inspection' of inmates, largely for reasons of control and security.

In hospital design, radial plans dominated the important competition in projects for a new Hôtel-Dieu in Paris. In 1774 Antoine Petit proposed a circular building containing six radial blocks of three or four storeys around a central church. The open ward plans within the radii were designed to encourage ventilation, and act as conduits for the poison gases which would be swept on a wind toward the central church and evacuated through a huge conical dome (which was to act as an exhaust siphon). Poyet produced an equally ingenious (and unrealized) plan in 1785 for a huge wheel-shaped hospital with 5200 beds. The blocks of wards occupied the sixteen spokes of the wheel, with smaller blocks running round the outer circumference. The wards were separated by triangular courts, and there was a court planned for the central area around the church. There were many other such plans, each recommended by its special virtues and its superiority over the traditional 'conglomerate' or Greek-cross plans; each had virtues in the important matters of ventilation and drainage, and increasingly, separation and classification of inmates.

The circularity of the designs was in some cases apparently functional, since it eliminated corners (which were likely damp) and used space more efficiently than grid-like designs; but on the other hand circular buildings obviously could not be oriented to take full advantage of the sun and prevailing winds. The most famous of the circular plans was the Narrenturm (the Fool's Tower) at the Allgemeines Krankenhaus in Vienna, which dated from 1784. The Narrenturm was a forbidding five-storeyed cylindrical fortress, which stood as a striking anomaly against the rectilinear regularity of the greater hospital, laid out in its neat quadrangles. The rationale for the round tower is obscure, but perhaps echoed the familiar round towers in the walls of many central European towns which traditionally became lunatics' towers. The Narrenturm was not a panopticon; although the cells occupied the circumference of the building, they were closed off from the central court by a high wall, and thus could be inspected only as keepers actually walked the circular corridors and peered in. The cells were ventilated only by small windows opening to the exterior; as a consequence, Howard complained, 'the form of the building causing the air to stagnate in its centre, as in a deep well' (Howard 1789: 68).

The 'cellular' lay-out of the Panopticon acknowledged a long-standing ideal in prison design among the reformers – the idea reaches back at least as far as the earliest proposals for separate confinement in the early eighteenth century. Doubtless it was also an echo of monastery designs. There were, however, very few existing prisons (or hospitals, or asylums) which were actually cellular, and none which enforced so great a measure of insulation on the inmates in their respective cells. Bentham advanced the familiar rationale for separating the inmates: where the cells are 'divided from one another, and the prisoners by that means secluded from all communication with each other', 'in a spot so constructed, and under a course of discipline so insured, how should infection ever arise? or how should it continue?' (Bentham 1843: IV, 45–6). The design was thus meant to be effective in preventing communicable disease, and more germanely, in interdicting 'moral infections', the malign contagious influences of the inmates on each other.

The *focus* of the Panopticon plan, the central inspection tower, was the design's most original and ultimately important feature, on which the whole rationale rested. The lay-outs of hospitals, and of prisons, were of course traditionally oriented around a central church or chapel, which provided a focal point of the whole and the axis of its symmetry in the large geometrical plans. In smaller establishments the altar of the chapel served as a similar focus, which made visibility of the altar from the different areas and sections of the building an architectural ideal and often an organizing principle of design. The Greek-cross plan of wards was in part so common for this reason, since it allowed as many inmates as possible a direct view of a central altar placed at the cross-point itself.

In the design of the first large cellular prison in Europe, the so-called 'Silentium' for male prisoners in the Papal prison of San Michele built in 1704, the arrangement of altar *vis-à-vis* cells was similarly a central problem and the crux of the design for the architect. Since the prisoners remained constantly in their cells and could not associate even in a procession to go to the chapel to hear Mass, the design required that each prisoner enjoy a direct view of the altar, from his cell. The novel solution in the event arranged three tiers of individual cells on either side of a broad interior gallery, where the altar was placed at one end. The inmates could thus hear Mass from within their individual cells, without the risks of their associating in a common chapel.

In Bentham's design the problem of visibility was, as it were, directly inverted. The focus of the design, the central inspection tower, was not the point to be made visible, but the vantage itself. The design tried to build in complete visibility for an inspector at the centre of the banks of cells and the inmates within; for the inmates in their respective cells the visibility of the centre was contrariwise blocked, to preserve the principle of the inspector's 'seeing without being seen'. The central inspection tower thus displaced the altar or chapel in the design, and occupied its traditional site, while the central visual reference point became itself the source of a continuous (and mysterious) 'supervision' radiating out like the all-seeing eye of God.

In one version of the proposal Bentham introduced the Panopticon with a remarkable quotation from the Psalms:

> 'Thou art about my path, and about my bed: and spiest out all
>   my ways.
> If I say, peradventure the darkness shall cover me, then shall my
>   night be turned into day.
> Even there also shall thy hand lead me; and thy right hand shall
>   hold me.'   (Bentham 1843: XI, 96)

This was an unusual and striking citation from an unreligious man; and it is ironic considering the Benthamites' caustic criticisms of those more religiously-minded prison reformers who recommended solitude, darkness, and the 'separate system' as means of producing 'conversion experiences' in the inmates. The citation was, however, apt indeed since the 'apparent omnipresence' of the inspector in the scheme, his 'invisible eye' and constant providence, were characteristics hardly removed from the divine attributes. 'Inspection' easily found itself a place in the contemporary religious vocabulary, and in the language of moral preachers; but its secular meaning was equally important since it reflected the new notions of 'management' which asylum and prison reform broadly advanced. In significant ways the two senses advanced in parallel. The explicit rationales of Bentham's Panopticon and the 'inspection principle' were markedly different from the ostensibly religious rationales for other conceptions of prison management; but the practical measures which each recommended were remarkably similar. Benthamites to a great extent met with Quakers, Methodists and Evangelicals, and other philanthropists, in sharing a common interest in architectural schemes which could insulate inmates, and render more general and constant their supervision. The Panopticon, with its ingenious arrangements for inspection, was to this extent symptomatic of (and broadly influential in) a common programme; and this is the significant fact, whatever particular criticisms in detail Bentham's plan suffered (see Jetter 1962a and b, and Bumm 1903).

The influence of the Panopticon (or of the approach it represented) on the planning and construction of asylums was evident soon after Bentham first circulated the plan in 1787. In one of his first sketches of the plan Bentham elaborated its advantages for the specific purposes of the lunatic asylum:

> '[since] the powers of the insane, as well as those of the wicked, are
> capable of being directed either against their fellow-creatures or against

themselves, separate cells [for the insane], exposed, as in the case of prisons, to inspection, would render the use of chains and other modes of corporal sufference as unnecessary in this case as in any.'

(Bentham 1843: IV, 60)

The predicament of constant inspection would be itself restraining, even on the insane; and if necessary, from strict supervision regular and certain punishment for disobedience could follow. The system of moral restraints (backed up if necessary with threats of punishment) was, whether in prisons or asylums, the most lenient regime in Bentham's view. It would allow the governor to dispense finally with chains: for inmates 'confined in one of these cells, every motion of the limbs, and every muscle of the face exposed to view, what pretence could there be for exposing to [the hardship of chains] the most boisterous malefactor?' (Bentham 1843: IV, 47). The situation of the inmates within the Panopticon would make them, on the contrary, sensible of, and sensitive to, moral pressures. Since the design built in cellular insulation and general supervision, and ingeniously 'exposed' the inmates, it left them with only their channel of communication to the centre – with the sane man in the system – and thus enhanced the hold of this commanding presence over all those in parallel and exclusive relationships to him. The plan offered the physician, as Bentham argued,

'a method of becoming master of everything which might happen to a certain number of men by which to dispose of everything around so as to produce in them the desired impression, to make certain of their actions, of their connections, and of the circumstances of their lives, so that nothing could escape, nor oppose the desired effect.'

(See Halévy 1955: 82–3)

The Panopticon would thus realize the full positive potential and promise of confinement, conferring on the physician an unparalleled 'power of mind over mind' which he could wield in the interests of resocializing the inmates. Every inmate, alone in his cell, would earn his due on the utilitarian calculus, and feel the constant impressions from that sane mind in the centre who, like the commanding presence the asylum reformers described in their 'ideal governor', would be 'master of everything'.

The advantages of the Panopticon as Bentham noted them for a model asylum were of course very close to the lunacy reformers' own aims in reconceiving the asylum and its social relations. No asylum was in the event put up on Bentham's exact specifications, but the elements of the plan were very broadly imitated or copied. A large number of the new asylums were built 'on the panopticon principle', which generally meant that their plans adopted the notion of 'inspection' and at least certain of its architectural elements. Other new asylums often incorporated different specific features (all provided for some manner of classification), even where their plans failed to allow generalized inspection. In form, only a few of the plans were, however, genuinely panoptica in all essentials – notably the Glasgow Lunatic Asylum, which became a model of sorts throughout Europe, and the plan of James Bevans (see *Figure 1*, p. 49) for a new London Asylum solicited and endorsed by the 1815–16 Commons Select Committee investigating madhouses.

The Glasgow Lunatic Asylum, which was roughly contemporaneous with the Millbank Penitentiary and other modified panopticon prisons, was designed by the architect William Stark and put up in 1810–14. The building was in the form of a star, with four wings radiating from the centre. As Stark explained in his *Remarks on the Construction of Public Hospitals for the Cure of Mental Derangement*, this form conveniently separated the building and surrounding grounds 'into two equal parts; one of which is for males, the other for females';

'each of these is [further] divided into two subordinate parts; one for a higher, the other for a lower, class of patients. These last are sub-divided, each into four parts, for different cases, or degrees of insanity: 1st, Frantic patients. 2d, Incurables. 3d, Ordinary patients. 4th, Convalescent.' (Stark 1807: 15)

The principles of the sub-division achieved in the plan, by sex, 'rank in life', particular disorder and degree of insanity, demeanour and so forth, were commonly accepted and widely instituted. Stark took the matter of separation particularly seriously, however, and contrived 'separate passages, or stair-cases' to connect the wards of the 'several classes of patients' with their own 'distinct inclosures' in the carefully sub-divided exercise grounds; thus, 'by these means, the patients of each [class] will have, at all times, the most direct and immediate access to that inclosure which is assigned them for air and recreation. . . . In this way, each class may be formed into a society inaccessible to all the others' (Stark 1807: 15). The wards themselves were divided into individual cells, with some common spaces. Stark was, however, opposed to solitude for lunatics, even for 'patients in a convalescent state', and although the plan offered the possibility of complete isolation, it also encouraged and facilitated 'properly

65

regulated intercourse of the patients' which unlike their 'indiscriminate assemblage' could, under certain circumstances, be therapeutic.

Like so many others associated with the lunacy reforms, Stark argued that a 'fitting receptacle' was a prerequisite of improvement. He criticized 'those cheerless dismal dwellings – in the contrivance of which, nothing seems to have been considered, but how to inclose the victim of insanity in a cell, and to cover his misery from the light of day'; and argued that 'however desirable a good system of management may be, no such system can be prosecuted with effect in an ill-contrived building. The defects of arrangement must unavoidably affect the patient, and operate both against his comfort and his cure' (Stark 1807: 15).

The problem of security Stark thought easy to solve, but sensitive, since the plan ought to provide secure custody without needlessly upsetting the inmates. 'An insane person is capable of feeling acutely, and of recollecting distinctly, the treatment which he meets with, even in the accessions of frenzy' (Stark 1807: 5); and thus, the supposed 'animal insensibility' of the mad, to, for instance, extremes of cold or the degradations of chains, could not excuse their historic neglect and cruel treatment. Stark tried to design, on the contrary, for a system of management fitting to their condition; his plan provided 'a superintendence unusually active and efficient, which follows and watches every motion of the patient, while it assures to him a more than ordinary degree of individual liberty, of exemption from restraint and bondage, of personal security, of ease, comfort, and enjoyment'. Such a 'superintendence' was built into the plan itself, so that

> 'by a peculiar distribution of the day-rooms, galleries, and grounds, the patients, during the whole day, will be constantly in view of their keepers. . . . An advantage peculiarly resulting from this arrangement will be, that those patients who are quiet and submissive, are relieved of the irksome and disagreeable sensations occasioned by their having a keeper always present, and observing their motions. Those, again, who are inclined to disorder will be aware that an unseen eye is constantly following them, and watching their conduct.' (Stark 1807: 1, 16)

The mild and yet vigilant system of management based upon the 'unseen eye' and the architectural resources of a 'panopticon' was fully in accord with the ideals of the model asylum, and indeed represented an influential solution to the characteristic problems of asylum design. It fostered, most germanely, a new atmosphere appropriate to the lunatic as a moral subject sensible of ordinary human influences; and it helped to create in the asylum 'a new order of things' before the lunatic's eyes in order to break suddenly and violently his disordered train of ideas and associations.

Bevans's design (*Figure 1*) for a model London Asylum was in its essentials an imitation of the Glasgow building, adapted, however, to accommodate a larger number of inmates without sacrificing the advantages of Stark's plan. It provided for seven radii from the central inspection tower, of which six were wings with individual cells ranged across central galleries. The plan was widely praised and endorsed during the Parliamentary investigations, and although it was never realized as the new London Asylum it nonetheless survived through its influence elsewhere.

In general, the designs for model asylums which appeared in profusion across the early nineteenth century are probably more instructive as 'schemes' or ideas than as actual blueprints. Some did become blueprints for buildings actually put up; but the designs considered together (whether realized or not) well represent in a schematic fashion the principles of the reform programme. To this end the designs provide abundant evidence of the reformers' thinking on 'management' and their conception of the proper social relations in the asylum. The designs thus suggest unmistakably certain ideological grounds of the reform projects, which owed not to a simple humanitarian reflex but to more elaborated notions of contemporary social relations.

· 4 ·
THE INSANE

'Les fous, le folklore les aime plutôt un peu vifs, le bruit et la fureur, les cris de bête, la violence animale, l'agitation forcenée. . . . Convention tout cela: pour un vociférant vingt muets; pour un agité cent statues.'

(Gentis 1971)

The principal forms of insanity, according to the 1844 Report of the Metropolitan Commissioners in Lunacy, were:

1 mania
2 dementia
3 melancholia
4 monomania
5 moral insanity
6 congenital idiocy
7 congenital imbecility
8 general paralysis of the insane
9 epilepsy

and finally, as a subsidiary addition, delirium tremens (Official Publications 1844a: 102ff.). 'Insanity' was not a precise category, nor a uniform condition. Contemporary medical and legal theories established the limits of the category variously, but broadly enough to embrace at once clearly delineated organic conditions, a range of 'functional' mental disorders, and as well novel notions like 'moral insanity', which as Shaftesbury remarked was 'scarcely distinguishable' from ordinary crime. Medical psychology recognized not merely gross insanities, but 'finer shades' of disorder, and the medicine of insanity accordingly took into its purview a broad collection of symptoms including, *inter alia*: hallucinations and delusions, motor disturbances, speech disorders, minor behavioural disorders, sexual aberrations, defects in motor or intellectual development and adaptation, excessive irritability and excitability, violent and passionate outbursts, lethargy, dejection, immoderate changes in character, habits or morals.

The contemporary forms of insanity not only spread broadly, but were in themselves indefinite and often unfixed. The 'forms' which Shaftesbury enumerated were not in the main disease entities, but simply descriptive terms; nor did they constitute separate and distinct populations among the insane. In cases of insanity the 'forms' which alienists laid out analytically in tables of classification were very often combined with each other, to complicate diagnosis. Many insanities were thus hybrids of the different 'species' of disorders.

Among asylum inmates, as the Commissioners' Report noted, the most commonly diagnosed forms of insanity were mania and dementia, which were also significantly the broadest categories, comparable in their scope to the early categories under English law distinguishing insanity into madness and idiocy. 'Mania' referred to insanities of wild excitement and fury, characterized by extravagant delusions or hallucinations, and often great violent outbursts. It applied broadly to conditions of mental excitement and elevation, whatever their causes, and represented within medical discourse what in contemporary folklore and common speech were still the most characteristic feature of madness generally. The 'furiously mad' were, for practical reasons, among the first classes of the insane defined specifically under English law. The Vagrancy Act of 1744 applied in particular as a protection against those 'by lunacy furiously mad, or so far disordered in their senses that they may be dangerous to be permitted to go abroad'. In the thirteenth century Bracton's compilation of English law referred to the madman principally as *furiosus* or *frenetico passione detentus*, which were terms probably close in their sense to the early English expressions 'raving mad' and 'frenzied', with their common suggestion of violent, excited, and unpredictable behaviour (Bracton 1915).[1] The madman's *furor* was likewise the basis for the famous 'wild beast' test, which was widely in use as a judicial criterion of genuine insanity.

The causes of 'raving madness' were of course evidently various, including even intoxication by drink which led to a temporary insanity. 'Mania' was similarly a broadly descriptive term, and not a disease classification. The varieties of mania, including the common 'religious mania', differed in the content of their delusions and in their exciting causes; and the varieties isolated merely the special mental characteristics of particular cases, not different pathologies.

The Commissioners' Report in 1844 itself distinguished, on a pragmatic basis, several types of mania: acute conditions of 'raving madness'; 'ordinary' mania, or 'chronic madness'; and periodical or remittant madness with lucid intervals. Practically, these types of mania required different degrees of restraint and management, although mania of any sort required constant vigilance against the sudden outbreaks. The insanity of the 'furiously mad' was thus especially salient for its social consequences and the dangers it posed. The threat of mad outbreaks and their actual flaring-up were indeed the essential features of 'mania', and made the category particularly germane for the judicious management and control of insanity.

'Dementia' referred to the results of progressive decay, weakening, or obliteration of the intellectual powers and faculties, for whatever reason. It was logically linked with the category 'idiocy' (which was often termed 'amentia'), whose sense it limited to the congenital condition of those born idiots or imbeciles. 'Idiot' was an ancient legal term, which signified originally 'a private person', without civil office, but later by extension referred to someone without civil capacity. In the late thirteenth century the Statute on the King's Prerogative defined the condition of 'natural fools', who were by nature (i.e., by birth) deficient in intelligence, and thus incapable in civil society. The law recognized such idiocy as a permanent condition, distinguishable from madness which lucid periods often interpolated. Thus the Statute allowed permanent wardship for the *fatuus naturalis* and control over his estates, but only temporary trusteeship in the case of a madman of property while he was *non compos mentis* (Walker 1968: 25, 32). The law later developed or adopted various artificial criteria to establish 'idiocy', in the form of tests of an alleged idiot's capacity or failure to count twenty pence, tell his age, identify his parents, or name the days of the week. Because of the different legal consequences of madness and idiocy, such tests were often important in the distinctive procedures for obtaining a writ *de idiota inquirendo*, which pertained principally to idiots of property. The determination of idiocy was *ad hoc* and practical, and did not in any event follow from the application of a rigorous definition.

The broader condition, 'feeblemindedness', was not necessarily 'natural' or congenital, but often the effect of such pathologies or trauma as progressively weakened or destroyed the intellects and will. 'Dementia' was as broad a term as the individual cases of feeblemindedness were various. There were many different causes and no uniform onset of the condition, and it ran many particular courses, although 'dementia' was usually a prognosis as well implying further decay and atrophy of the faculties. The character of the condition was again notably social, since the 'demented' were progressively incapable and dependent, but in many cases were not victims of a fatal disease, and so lingered on.

70

Mania and dementia were the grossest varieties of insanity, according to the contemporary notions, and perhaps the most visible and problematic socially. By comparison, 'melancholia', 'moral insanity', and 'monomania' were 'partial' insanities or finer shades of disorder, whose diagnosis reflected advances in the medicine and jurisprudence of insanity.

Within legal practice the law traditionally disposed in matters of insanity by rough and rude canons of *non compos mentis*, close in their character to popular notions of insanity. *Non compos mentis* was itself not strictly limited in content to the varieties of insanity; it stretched indeed well beyond such insanities as resulted from disease. Apart from the general class of idiots who were incapable *a navitate*, as Blackstone formulated its definition:

'under the general name of *non compos mentis* (which sir Edward Coke says is the most legal name) are comprized not only lunatics, but persons under frenzies; or who lose their intellects by disease; those that *grow* deaf, dumb, and blind, not being *born* so; or such, in short, as are by any means rendered incapable of conducting their own affairs.'

(Blackstone 1765–69: Book IV, ch. 2)

The loose formula was further complicated since, as Blackstone acknowledged, such 'incapacity' could be merely temporary (considering, for example, that 'a lunatic is indeed one that hath lucid intervals; sometimes enjoying his senses, and sometimes not, and that frequently depending upon the change of the moon') or 'artificial' (as in the case of 'artificial, voluntarily contracted madness, by drunkenness or intoxication, which, depriving men of their reason, puts them in a temporary phrenzy'). *Non compos mentis* was thus a way of registering the *effects* of different conditions, including varieties of insanity; it was not simply the legal expression for insanity.

Between the time of Blackstone's *Commentaries* (1765) and the M'Naghten Rules (1843), the legal practices for defining insanity sharpened considerably against the earlier rough use of popular notions. A number of important trials in the interim involving the insanity defense left new precedents, notably because the trials raised general questions about the character of insanity and were fought with novel 'expert' assistance from prison doctors or independent physicians and alienists. As a result the 'right-wrong' test and the 'wild beast' test, which often previously represented simply a belief in the genuine madman's 'wildness' and *furor*, were more precisely and explicitly defined.

The consequent refining of notions of *non compos mentis* brought legal practices more closely in touch, and in potential conflict, with contemporary theories in medical psychology. The legal criteria and definitions of insanity became less rude, although medical notions influenced rather than replaced the older conceptions of the law courts, and the medico-legal definition of the criminally insane and their responsibility remained a contentious and problematic site in the criminal law.

In the most famous and consequential of nineteenth-century insanity trials, both sides in the case of M'Naghten in 1843 quoted lengthy passages from treatises of medical psychology. The legal arguments indeed concerned less the mental state of Daniel M'Naghten at the time of his crime, than the greater medical and legal questions of criminal responsibility and 'partial' insanity. M'Naghten's counsel argued in the course of a famous insanity defense that insanity was a more diverse condition than the law apparently acknowledged; the legal procedures for establishing criminal insanity were, he claimed, outmoded, overly restrictive and inappropriate, since they dated from a period when

> 'insanity was a much less frequent disease than it is now, and the popular notions concerning it were derived from the observation of those wretched inmates of the madhouses whom chains, and stripes, cold and filth, had reduced to the stupidity of the idiot, or exasperated to the fury of a demon. Those nice shades of the disease in which the mind, without being wholly driven from its propriety, pertinaciously clings to some absurd delusion, were either regarded as something very different from real madness, or were too far removed from the common gaze, and too soon converted by bad management into the more active forms of the disease, to enter much into the general idea entertained of madness.' (Cockburn cited in Walker 1968: 93)[2]

M'Naghten was of course acquitted by reason of his 'partial' insanity, and removed to Bethlem Hospital.

At the mid-century Bethlem and other asylums contained many inmates suffering one or other 'nice shades of the disease'. Alienists indeed commonly claimed that enlightened management in asylums had reduced the incidence of violent outbursts, and of extravagant and bizarre behaviour among the insane, and that the 'active' forms of insanity were thus becoming less typical.

Of the partial insanities which the Commissioners' Report enumerated, 'monomania' referred to derangement on one subject only, or an insanity with one particular delusion and obsessive preoccupation.[3] 'Moral insanity' signified most commonly a disorder of the affects or moral sensibilities; as Prichard originally defined the term, it was a form of madness

> 'consisting in a morbid perversion of the natural feelings, affections, inclinations, temper, habits, moral dispositions, and natural impulses, without any remarkable disorder or defect of the interest or knowing and reasoning faculties, and particularly without any insane illusion or hallucinations.' (Prichard 1835: 12–13)

'Melancholia' was an ancient category, and served for centuries as the logical couple to 'mania', since it referred broadly to mental conditions of depression, dejection, and 'low spirits'. By then prevailing notions of faculty psychology, however, melancholia implied a less than total loss of reason since often it left its victims with their intellectual powers fully intact, and undiseased. A diagnosis of melancholia was nonetheless prudent foresight, as the Commissioners' Report suggested, since

> 'a great number of persons . . . who betray no particular error of judgement or hallucination, are confined in Lunatic Asylums as a precaution against suicide, to which they are prone, in many instances, from a disgust of life.' (Official Publications 1844a: 106)

The organic conditions were the only clearly defined disease entities among the forms of insanity which tables of classification enumerated. By the mid-century several organic conditions associated with insanity, notably the general paralysis which Bayle defined in 1822, were widely established as disease entities, with specific causes and morbid agents, courses, and outcomes. Such organic conditions accounted for, or complicated, the cases of a fair proportion of asylum inmates late in the century, especially among the chronic or hopeless cases.

This then was the array of 'species' of insanity, as commonly set out for purposes of comprehensive classification in treatises. Despite advances in medical psychology and in its nosology, the so-called species or varieties of insanity were not in general different classes of disorder defined and understood by their pathology or aetiology. The list of 'forms' rather was loosely based on descriptions of mental and motor symptoms, which sometimes clustered together but were largely unanchored in the physiology of the body and were without consistent relation and connection to lesions of the brain or nervous system. The 'forms' of insanity without clear organic basis were accordingly labile, and susceptible to various and shifting definitions of their content, although the continuous use of ancient terms borrowed from Greek physicians and Roman jurists to represent the states of insanity has obscured historical changes in their character.

The table which the Commissioners' Report published was a representative example of the state of contemporary medical and legal theorizing of insanity. In contrast to modern psychiatric classifications, the different 'forms' were somewhat rudimentary and sketchily drawn; although clearly in the lineage of modern classifications, they are difficult to assimilate into modern diagnostic categories (which are elaborated into different systems), even in such cases as 'moral insanity' which directly anticipated the modern term 'psychopathy'.

In contrast to earlier tables of the species of insanity, the scope of mid-nineteenth century classifications was notably broader, especially since the recently defined 'partial insanities' could themselves be widely construed. 'Insanity' appeared grossly in some cases or finely shaded in others, and broke out in acute episodes or developed slowly with insidious progress into chronic conditions. Those who filled lunatic asylums at the time, and the insane in workhouses and elsewhere, suffered a great range of disorders in varying severity and with different outcomes and social consequences. The medicine of insanity embraced a broad range of the conditions, as later the classical systems of psychiatry defined seemingly diverse objects (including different disease entities and 'functional disorders') as falling within their purview.

In the contemporary institutional policies and in the day-to-day running of the asylums the niceties of medical classification were, however, less important than other practical classifications of the insane according to their demeanour or the social salience of their conditions. Similarly the path of a madman to the asylum was often determined more by social than by technically medical judgements. The confinement of lunatics and idiots to asylums served broadly social purposes; and hence the asylum populations who constituted the subject-matter of medical psychology and later of the classical psychiatric systems were often committed under non-medical auspices because of the social consequences of their disorders.

From the earliest times of English law, certain varieties of madmen have been isolated and defined, loosely and practically, by the behavioural criteria of laymen. The popular, legal, and medical representations of such madmen — and the practical designations of their condition — became in the forms which were carried over across several centuries part of the raw material out of which the novel and comprehensive discipline of medical psychology emerged. The insane populations in institutions likewise provided 'raw materials', but the relation between the range of conditions medical psychology described, and the ways the insane actually suffered, was complex and not a one-to-one correspondence. Between the theories of medical psychology, which were necessarily abstract, and the practical designations of the insane, which were important for their daily management; and between the practical uses of asylums for relief and secure detention, and the reformers' programme for moral treatment (which was never conceived to be an economic means of relief), the relations were multiple and shifting. No one order of information suffices to characterize the insane or the conditions of their confinement. The 'insane' were perceived, detained, isolated, classified, and studied at once according to popular norms, legal procedures, administrative practices, and more properly medical notions. From one to another of these vantages the 'insane' were a different group.

The insane in asylums were probably predominantly those suffering the grosser, more bizarre, and threatening varieties of insanity, and in particular those whose condition made them dangerous to be at large. Asylums were the more fitting receptacles for the dangerously insane, the suicidal, and in general the potentially curable, whatever their particular disorder; whereas workhouses could with some cause and appropriateness confine harmless and quiet lunatics or idiots, hopeless cases, the chronic, and aged insane.

Such practical designations of the insane (dangerous, suicidal, curable, harmless, quiet, etc.), which were so pertinent in their daily management, fit only loosely and approximately with medical classifications. As the medical categories developed and were grouped into systems, the practical uses of asylums, whether for relief or in the interests of public security, still determined the actual asylum populations in greater measure than the more narrowly medical rationales and recommendations for asylum confinement. The particular decisions leading to committal orders (which in cases of the pauper insane required no medical opinions or judgements of sanity until after 1828) were often largely pragmatic, and non-medical. The 'forms' of insanity described and enumerated in the interests of completeness within medical treatises were accordingly not representative of the actual inmates in asylums; their fate was often determined by other factors than the 'form' of their disorder, although the character and composition of asylum populations themselves doubtless affected in obvious and subtle ways the progress of theorizing 'insanity'.

Such 'interesting' cases among the asylum populations as fascinated and preoccupied alienists were often unique or far removed from the ordinary; and common classes of disorder which alienists struggled to theorize, such as 'mania', were themselves rather practical terms which acknowledged the important social aspects of insanity. Thus, although the asylum populations formed a critical part of the raw materials on which the theorizing of insanity worked, and were in a general sense the subject-matter of early psychiatry, the theories of insanity and their classifications were never a simple and direct representation of the 'insane' in their varieties. The scope of classifications and the emphases in medical treatises were indeed notably different from the actual bulk and weight of the different varieties of insanity in the total burden which these presented practically, as administrative or public health problems.

Although the 'insane' suffered many disorders and disabling conditions, it is difficult to know what particular varieties of the insane, and in what proportions, actually filled asylums. It is further difficult to form an impression of the greater social characteristics of the 'insane' or asylum populations. There is finally little evidence from which to infer the social factors which may have affected the occurrence, prevalence, and distribution of insanity or nervous disorders.

In some few cases, where for example police records have survived, the whole train of events leading to a particular lunatic or idiot's committal to asylum is clear but rarely is there any full record of the circumstances (or presenting symptoms) which led to the discovery or identification of lunatics and idiots, or of the decisions which typically led to their commitment, and passage to asylums. Nor are the asylum records of inmates particularly illuminating about the contemporary character of the insane and the disorders they suffered. Of most inmates there is no more record than the entries in an asylum case-book. Before 1845 even such entries were often scantily made; they frequently recorded an inmate's diagnosis and medications, but without any appreciable case-history. The general nursing comments on an inmate's demeanour occasionally mentioned whether he or she were suicidal, dangerous, 'subject to fits', or harmless. But asylum case-book entries rarely provided any systematic demographic information about inmates beyond listing their age and sex. The identity and character of asylum inmates, especially before 1845, and of the insane in workhouses and elsewhere long after, are thus often unclear and problematic to infer.

Contemporaries were not uninterested in these questions, but were not notably able to provide soundly based answers. The statistics of insanity were severely limited, and the subject never quite elicited in England the mixture of scientific interest and morbid fascination with which the 'moral statisticians' in France, Belgium, and parts of Germany approached it, as a telling index to the health of their civilizations (see Chevalier 1973; Quetelet 1827 and 1830). English writers across several generations of course drew moral lessons from the statistics of insanity, often in grand terms, as Cheyne had considered more impressionistically in the mid-eighteenth century whether insanity was indeed the characteristic 'English malady'. But the statisticians, and those numerate alienists who concerned themselves, focused generally on several more limited aspects of the 'insanity question': whether insanity were truly on the increase; and how the insane fared within confinement (for instance what their prospects of survival or recovery were; and how different medical treatments and regimens influenced the vital statistics of the institutions).

The pressure of numbers

'Madness strides like a Colossus in the country.' (Reid, J. 1808: 166)

The statistics of insanity took several forms, of which the earliest comprised very rough estimations of the statistical tendency to insanity in the kingdom. The prevalence of insanity in the population, and its putative increase, were a long-standing concern, and indeed a talking-point of moralists which periodically burst into 'fears' of an epidemic outbreak of insanity. From the times of the Spital Sermons and the 'hospital fevers' in the eighteenth century, such fears persisted; they revived in force at the turn of the eighteenth century when lunacy reformers were drafting their original institutional programme, then again in the mid-century with the rise of 'moral statistics', and finally through waves of eugenics propaganda nearly until the present.

Fears of an increase in insanity were associated particularly with the apparent concentration of the insane in confinement. The insane were conspicuous under many circumstances, even as solitary lunatics or idiots; in any numbers, they were doubtless recognized as such, and as peculiar, wherever they were confined. Their mad antics were long part of the folklore of Bethlem, and likewise of the bridewells and workhouses in the days of the great undifferentiated receptacles which mixed the insane with the infirm, the orphaned, idle beggars, and rogues; in the 'model manufactories' the insane were sometimes particular nuisances, since few of them could apparently work to any purpose.

The fears of insanity, however, concerned the threat of the insane as a malign influence, present in *numbers*, not as curiosities or minor nuisances. The malignity of the insane in confinement had in part a realistic basis since what contemporaries knew as 'gaol' or 'hospital' fever did occasionally spread abroad beyond the confines, and was popularly associated with the origin of epidemics. Such occurrences naturally strengthened the already lurid and frightening reputation of the insane.

The impression of numbers was equally important, although its basis was perhaps less clear. Before the mid-nineteenth century the dimensions of confinement of the insane were somewhat shadowy, though undoubtedly far greater than the available statistics suggested. To contemporaries even these partial accountings were often extremely alarming; the numbers which in retrospect seem small were at the time imposing, and represented a remarkable accumulation and concentration of the insane in confinement. The impression of numbers at the turn of the century was based less on a statistical reckoning than on the recent and dramatic growth of confinement, which to a degree concentrated the insane and rendered them more conspicuous, and put their receptacles on the reform agenda of philanthropists.

Defective as the statistics of insanity admittedly were, several alienists and early statisticians tried to amass them in order to calculate the incidence of insanity, across nations and in different historical periods, as a way of evaluating the then commonplace opinions about the increase in insanity; their efforts are still an important source of evidence, such as it is, about the extent of insanity and its contemporary estimation.

From the Bills of Mortality statisticians could derive one index of incidence, which allowed a base-line of sorts, although the categories of the Bills were ambiguous and shifting. Suicides, for instance, were in some places and some periods apparently listed as lunatics because of the manner of their deaths. As early as 1662 John Graunt had worked up some figures from the London Bills of Mortality, and had thereby estimated a Londoner's probability of dying in Bethlem. 'The Lunaticks', he concluded, were few,

'viz. 158 in 229, 250, though I fear many more than are set down in our Bills, few being entred for such, but those who die at Bedlam; and there all seem to die of their Lunacie, who died Lunaticks.

I dare ensure any man this present, well in his Wits, for one in the thousand, that he shall not die a Lunatick in Bedlam, within these seven years, because I finde not above one in about one thousand five hundred have done so.' (Graunt 1662: 22)

Such estimates were properly in the early nineteenth century no more than historical curiosities, but contemporaries made similar calculations and tried to establish likewise the prevalence of insanity by means of a rough census of inmates 'on the books' of asylums or madhouses at a given date, which of course yielded a very conservative estimate indeed of prevalence.

In 1813, Dr Richard Powell published his 'Observations on the Comparative Prevalence of Insanity at Different Periods', which were based on such procedures. Powell was Secretary to the Commissioners of the College of Physicians, the body of inspectors who were charged with visiting and licensing private madhouses in the London region; he thus had access to the Town and Country Registers of private licensed madhouses, which provided periodic returns of inmates in many madhouses for the period after the 1774 Act for Regulating Madhouses.

Until 1807 when a Parliamentary Select Committee sought returns of the numbers of pauper and criminal lunatics, these Registers were the only comprehensive lunacy statistics of any sort. Individual lunatic hospitals and asylums published only occasional reports, generally associated with an appeal for funds and to demonstrate the extent and successful results of their charity; Powell did not try to compile these infrequent reports into comparable figures. His only source for studying the 'comparative prevalence of insanity' was thus the series of Registers, which listed only the insane who were then fee-paying, private inmates in licensed madhouses, and some who were boarded out privately by parishes. The only available statistical source thus severely and arbitrarily limited the dimensions of the phenomenon.

Powell's ostensible purpose was to judge the 'popular opinions respecting the increase of that most difficult, delicate and important disease'; and he tried incidentally to note any connection between the prevalence of insanity, as he found it, and variations in the seasons, the climate, or political circumstances – which were natural queries at the time, after decades of polite speculation among men of letters about the effects of English weather on English melancholy, and after the recent denunciations of revolutionary France as a breeding-ground of madness in alarming proportions.

The statistics which Powell produced demonstrated a small rise in the numbers of the insane, by a proportion of 129/100 across the years from 1775 to 1809. The five-year aggregates of raw figures were 1783 inmates (in 1775–79), compared with 2271 (in 1805–09), which he regarded as smaller than expected, both in absolute terms and in the rate of increase, considering, as he put it, the 'supposed predisposition to', and predilection for, insanity in 'this commercial country' (Powell 1813: 139).

The prevalence of insanity calculated by his procedure was actually so low (he found a rate of 1/7300 in England by the 1801 census), that the disorder, as he suggested, 'ought not to be considered as a complaint of very common occurrence' (Powell 1813: 139).

Powell's estimates were manifestly far too low, and he himself acknowledged that they were distorted by his excluding the pauper insane, and the insane in public hospitals, asylums, workhouses, and elsewhere, from his calculations. He tried to correct for these omissions, and for other insane in private madhouses 'neglected to be returned' (who were likely a considerable number, including many paupers), on the interesting and remarkable assumption that these omissions numbered probably only half again as many as the numbers actually returned, which was a ludicrously low estimate, and reflected the bias that insanity was predominantly a disorder of the well-to-do and the refined classes.

Although vitiated by such assumptions, and by a very narrowly restrictive definition of 'insanity', Powell's article was one of the first serious essays in the statistics of insanity. It was clearly polemical in intents, and compiled against the contemporary impression of the rising numbers of the insane, at a time when many physicians regarded insanities and the nervous disorders as among the commonest and gravest of medical complaints.

Marshalling the available statistics of insanity did not dispel the impression of numbers, or the important dimensions of the problem, least of all for those mad-doctors and philanthropists who thought medical psychology one of the most basic and essential branches of contemporary medicine. But the lack of any reasonable accounting of the prevalence of insanity did trouble the planning of asylums, which required some more concrete estimation of how large 'insanity' bulked as a phenomenon. The 1807 Select Committee did gather some very partial returns of lunatics, which listed for a given date some 483 pauper lunatics in private custody across the country, and 1915 in poorhouses, houses of industry, workhouses, gaols, and houses of correction. These figures afforded some measure of the numbers of insane paupers and criminals burdening various institutions whose transfer to the more appropriate separate confinement of asylums was of course among the rationales of lunacy reform. The programme for building separate asylums was not, however, proposed simply as a means of siphoning off the several thousand insane who might become burdensome in their confinement in workhouses or bridewells; reformers had conceived rather more ambitious designs for asylums but clearly without any real estimation of the actual extent of 'insanity' or of the numbers and varieties of the insane for whom asylum confinement was 'appropriate'. The 1807 returns represented the 'insane' only by the most restrictive definition (those actually held in certain institutions, and recorded as lunatics or idiots, on some particular day), and were in any case notoriously defective since many counties returned no accounts of lunatics at all, and in the different counties the procedures and criteria for identifying the 'insane' were so varied that the figures actually returned were hardly comparable.

When Dr Andrew Halliday, on behalf of the 1807 Select Committee, investigated several of the returns personally to verify them, he found in Norfolk, for example, 112 pauper lunatics as opposed to the 22 officially returned. The Select Committee acknowledged that generally the figures were 'so evidently deficient in several instances, that a very large addition must be made in any computation of the whole number' (Official Publications 1807).

These were nonetheless the only statistics available, together with the Town and Country Registers and certain returns solicited from public hospitals, for consideration by the Select Committee which recommended what became the County Asylums Act of 1808.

The Committee's estimate that sixteen asylums of up to 300 inmates could each serve districts or unions of roughly 500,000 inhabitants, was thus purely notional.[4] There was little basis for such planning calculations, and indeed no procedure even for securing accurate and comprehensive returns from local authorities. Two of the first counties to establish new asylums under the 1808 Act, Bedfordshire and Staffordshire, had in fact returned no pauper lunatics in 1807, although Bedford Asylum held over 50 paupers soon after, and the Stafford Asylum opened to receive 120 inmates in 1818. However the local conditions had been reported, when the new county asylums opened they were often swamped with applicants, far beyond what they could accommodate; within several years after the 1808 Act was passed, the law allowed local Justices discretionary powers to send paupers elsewhere, and thus relieved what would otherwise have been impossible pressures on the institutions.

As the new county asylums were opened after 1811 and began to publish annual reports, the statistics of insanity became increasingly focused on public asylums, rather than on madhouses and the insane in workhouses and elsewhere. The numbers of the insane held in confinement, which were accordingly at least by part better documented, seemed to rise dramatically with the spread and expansion of county asylums. Twenty years after investigating the 1807 returns for the Select Committee, Dr Halliday estimated that the number of the insane had more than trebled in the interim. No real comparison in absolute terms was of course possible, since the earlier figures at least were so questionable and suspect. Nonetheless the 1827 insanity returns totalled over 12,500 lunatics and idiots, which represented a marked increase over the previous official returns of 1807 and 1819; even this number Halliday thought could be inflated considerably, to account for parishes which had failed to make returns.

The figures were in any case striking evidence of a continuing rise in the recorded numbers of the insane in asylums, in private care, and otherwise confined; such accumulating evidence undercut and eventually silenced the sceptical alienists like Dr George Man Burrows who regarded the increase of insanity as purely illusory. Burrows argued with some justice that the recent coincidence of unusual and prominent events somehow connected with insanity, notably George III's periodic insanities (especially during the Regency crisis), the several attempts on his life by lunatics, and the assassination of Spencer Perceval by a lunatic in 1812, had heightened temporarily awareness and general curiosity about the insanity question (which would, he suggested, later subside to its more normal and proper proportions) (Burrows 1820). Although such events no doubt quickened public discussions, and echoed in legal and legislative chambers, the trend of rising committals to asylums was not limited to a panic or rising emergency; it was more substantially grounded, and indeed increasingly supported by public policies.

By 1844 when the great Commissioners' Report appeared with its massive statistical appendix, there could be no question about the rise in numbers in confinement. The more pertinent questions concerned its interpretation (and extrapolation), and the less grand matters of studying asylum populations through their vital statistics. The recorded numbers of the insane in confinement grew even more rapidly after 1845, in part as a result of the new Lunacy Acts, and continued to grow (probably slightly in advance of population) nearly without interruption until after the Second World War. Over the course of the nineteenth century the actual rise in numbers was no doubt less dramatic than the recorded rise appeared, if only because the statistics of the insane progressively became more comprehensive and accurate. Many of the lunatics and idiots newly admitted to asylums were in fact already established or even long-standing cases transferred from other varieties of confinement; such individuals figured in the insanity statistics often only after their transfer. Thus some proportion of the apparent rise in numbers owed simply to administrative artefact, as cases were shifted between institutions and variously classified.

In forty-odd years after the Acts of 1845, the total number of inmates in lunatic asylums, public and private, increased more than five-fold, as the state's capacity to confine grew accordingly. The number of inmates in private licensed madhouses actually declined over this period (from over 6000 in 1850 to 4500 in 1890), and by the end of the century far the greater number of the more than 100,000 lunatic population were accommodated by public institutions.

Before 1845 by contrast the public asylums were less significant statistically for the numbers they held. In 1827 the original county asylums held fewer than 1500 inmates, and other public asylums probably not more than 1000. In the total dimensions of confinement of the insane, the share which the public asylums then bore was relatively small, although it was better represented in the statistics of insanity than the greater part of confinement, which was before 1845 largely hidden in terms of official records. From the decades around 1750, and more dramatically after 1800, the practices of confining the mad were doubtless increasing, but this increase added only to the contemporary 'impression of numbers' before there were any but fanciful statistics; the growth in confinement was not well-documented (or regulated) until decades later, when sponsored and funded under state control.

This was the background to discussions of the insanity question around the turn of the century and after. The discussions in fact revealed little about the 'insane', and their social characteristics, apart from very crude estimates of their numbers. Nor did the discussions really concern the prevalence or incidence of 'insanity' in a proper statistical sense. What contemporaries wrote about the increase in insanity and the historical waxing and waning of the various disorders and conditions which 'madness' represented, however revealing of current preoccupations and of their implicit understandings of the causes of madness, was largely speculative. The state of medical psychology could hardly have supported serious studies of the comparative incidence of madness, or even more humble and limited essays in medical topography (which constituted a rudimentary epidemiology and the primary means then in general medicine of investigating the social factors influencing diseases).

The other major varieties of insanity statistics at the time reported the cure-rates for insane patients, which were widely published, and the vital statistics of inmates, which were computed from asylum case-books. Lunatic hospitals, asylums, and individual mad-doctors had published statistics on their rates of cure routinely from the eighteenth century onwards. These statistics were a notable form of publicity, and were a prominent part of charitable appeals. The Spital Sermons preached about the insane and lunatic hospitals often provided recent figures about the numbers treated, relieved, and cured in Bethlem, which emphasized the extent of charity and its often successful outcome. Thus in 1683, as a Spital Sermon reported, Bethlem brought in 75 'distracted persons', cured 41, and buried only 13, which left then 'remaining there under Cure, and provided with Physick, Dyet and other Relief, at the charge of the said Hospital 118'. In 1741, the hospital admitted 173, discharged 119 as cured, and buried 46, which left 223 remaining.[5] Such figures became a point of rivalry between institutions, as well as the basis for the reputations of many mad-doctors. The figures are difficult to interpret, since the meaning of 'cure' is elusive (and certain of the figures were simply fabricated); they are notable for what they reveal indirectly about the conditions of medical practice, and for the reported numbers of deaths, which suggest a surprisingly low rate of mortality. In their patchy form, the statistics reveal nothing about the average or extreme durations of confinement, the average number of inmates or their character, or the sorts of inmate who were more likely to recover.

The vital statistics of insanity, which statisticians and a number of alienists assiduously compiled from the 1820s, were similarly limited, and based only on actual asylum populations. Alienists and mad-doctors before them, had long speculated about which groups in the greater population were most susceptible to madness, at what points in life, and so forth. Since asylum registers, which for Bethlem were complete from the early eighteenth century, provided basic information about the age and sex of inmates, and the duration of their confinement (or the date of their death), compiling simple vital statistics, as opposed to studying the incidence and distribution of insanity in the population at large, was relatively straightforward. For particular asylum populations the statisticians could compute grossly the mortality rate of the institutions, and the respective probabilities that various categories of inmates would die in confinement, survive as chronic or long-term inmates, or leave as 'cured'.

Such figures were interesting for several reasons, most notably since they contributed to the greater series of studies in the vital statistics of institutions, which tried to calculate rates of mortality in the large 'residential establishments' (workhouses, gaols, penitentiaries, foundling hospitals, etc.). They were likewise of service in time to medical psychologists in their work defining the different 'natural histories' of the 'species' of insanity, the courses and outcomes of the disorders, and conditions of madness.

The first study of vital statistics in this sense, concerned with the inmates of an institution and their various fates, was compiled from the case-books of Bethlem, the oldest and, until the late eighteenth century, largest asylum.

In 1789 Dr Richard Warren, one of the physicians to George III, consulted the books of Bethlem in order to offer a prognosis in the case of the King. He had been asked by the Parliamentary Committee appointed 'to examine the physicians who have attended His Majesty, during his illness, touching the state of His Majesty's health': 'Does Dr Warren know, whether the Majority of those who, at His Majesty's Time of Life, have been afflicted with the Disorder His Majesty now labours under, have recovered?' A number of physicians were asked similarly for such a prognosis, including Dr Francis Willis, a clerical mad-doctor with a thriving private practice, who was famed for his rapid ability to 'type' lunatics according to the different species of insanity by a rough and ready empiricism.

Dr Warren sought simply to compare the King, as a relatively elderly male, with the sample of similar victims (regardless of their particular disorder) among Bethlem's recent admissions. He could thus report on the elderly King's likely prospects of recovery. Although crude, such comparisons held out to early medical psychologists the possibility of discovering the courses and outcomes of the different insanities; the greater possibilities for observation and comparison of particular insanities or classes of inmates which the scale of asylum confinement allowed, provided indeed one of the principal medical rationales for the concentration of the insane in asylums, and held out the promise of a better understanding of the different species of disorder, and hence of better classification and typing of inmates.

In 1810 William Black published *A Dissertation on Insanity; Illustrated with Tables, and Extracted from between Two and Three Thousand Cases in Bedlam*. The several thousand cases were drawn from Bethlem records compiled in 1772–87 by John Gonza, the hospital's apothecary. Black was a specialist in 'the numerical method', and had originally published his insanity tables in *A Comparative View of the Mortality of the Human Species, and of the Diseases and Casualties by which They are Destroyed or Annoyed* in 1788. Gonza's records of Bethlem inmates were unusually detailed for the time, and although they revealed little about the inmates themselves apart from their disorders, they were well-suited to the compilation of vital statistics. Black produced tables illustrating his 'general propositions' on:

'the respective proportion of Insane males and females; the ages; the mischievous and the harmless; and those who attempted suicide; the length of time they were insane before admission; the various remote causes; the cured, incurable, relapses, discharges and deaths; the general prognosticks and remedies.'   (Black 1810: 12–14)

Compiled in such a fashion, the statistics of insanity resembled those general statistics computed on the morbidity and mortality rates of hospitals, gaols, workhouses, foundling homes, and their respective populations, rather than the statistics assembled for a 'natural history' of the disorder itself. Black's 'general propositions' on insanity were actually a collective portrait of the Bethlem inmates over a fifteen-year period. The vital statistics were a way of describing the fate of those already confined, and thus were not representative for the insane in the population at large, although Black and later statisticians largely assumed the general validity and application of the figures.

The tables which Black published were generally unremarkable, and did not substantiate the wilder speculations about the character of the insane which were current. Females predominated, but only barely, and the greatest number of admissions (over 85 per cent) were aged between 20 and 50 years, with a small proportion of the elderly. Many of the admissions were thus probably heads of households. The 'mischievous' were roughly equal to those who were not. Almost 20 per cent had attempted suicide (and many more doubtless were suicide-prone). There were twice as many 'incurables' as the number released 'cured'. Less than 10 per cent of admissions died while in confinement, which was creditable by contemporary standards, since formerly 'the Mortality in Bedlam was swelled by Small Pox and Scurvy'.

The most interesting of the tables presented Black's ranking in importance of the different causes of insanity, both physical and 'moral'. 'Misfortunes, troubles, disappointments, grief' formed the leading class of causes, followed in their frequency by 'family and hereditary' causes (which were both physical and moral), 'religion and Methodism', 'love', 'drink and intoxication', among others. Later statisticians returned to this listing of causes with interest; even in the 1830s the range of acknowledged causes of insanity was hardly different. The brief case-histories recorded in asylum registers still typically cited one or other of such leading causes, with the regularity of formulae, and thus illustrated through particular cases what medical psychology established as the general patterns of insanity in its onset and exciting causes.

However revealing of current understandings of insanity, the listing of apparent causes to which mad outbreaks or declining conditions were attributed, was in fact the least sound of the approaches to vital statistics. The causes of insanity were open to highly individual and indeed idiosyncratic interpretations (which left the resulting ranking of 'causes' barely comparable from one alienist to the next), and this was so even later when the more advanced theories of medical psychology were better diffused and after 1845 when the law had fixed protocols for collecting standardized vital statistics.

From the mid-century the practices of standard record-taking spread, generally after the model of John Thurnam, one of the early presidents of the Medico-Psychological Association who provided a detailed protocol for taking patients' medical histories and recording their personal circumstances. The vital statistics of various institutions accordingly became more genuinely comparable, although diagnoses were never even within the terms of a highly formalized system of classification fully standardized.

The dominant statistical approach remained nonetheless the study of the vital statistics of a particular institution, often by comparison with other institutions. When Thurnam published his *Observations and Essays on the Statistics of Insanity* in 1845, he presented the statistics primarily as an index to the 'results of treatment' under different particular regimes. Thus the proportion of inmates who recovered, and the number who died, were taken as a guide to evaluating the medical practices and general standards of administration (the adequacy of the diet, cleanliness, ventilation, and so on) in the institution.

For different discrete asylum populations (in particular with reference to the Retreat, where he was medical superintendent from 1838 to 1849), Thurnam tried to calculate 'circumstances in the character of the cases admitted, influencing the results of treatment' (i.e., the influence on prognosis of age, sex, station in life, and previous habits, the duration and exciting causes of the disorder, etc.). By isolating these various 'influences' he tried to control for them, and thus to distinguish the general character of the asylum population from the specific influences of the 'several particulars of treatment' on their fate in confinement. He tried further to weigh the different influences on inmates' prospects of recovery of the general hygienic conditions, on the one hand, and of the medical treatment proper (physical, pharmaceutic, and especially moral treatment), on the other. The statistical procedures for weighting these various factors, which involved Thurnam in the useful exercise of explaining something about statistics to a largely innumerate medical audience, were naturally not very exacting.

Thurnam's use of statistics in fact buttressed rather unremarkable conclusions which need hardly have been derived from the figures. With regard to the circumstances influencing patients' recovery, he concluded for instance that the poor were in general less likely to recover; indeed 'it is highly probable that many of the causes of insanity, which to a great degree consist in deviations from sound hygiene rules, exert a decided influence upon the probable termination of the attack' (Thurnam 1845: II, 37).

The most important contribution to the statistics of insanity was undoubtedly the work of Willian Farr. In a series of articles after 1835 he surveyed the whole range of then existing statistics of insanity to draw, in most cases judiciously, the limited conclusions about certain of the social characteristics of the insane which the figures warranted. Farr's greater concern was the morbidity of public institutions, and he studied accordingly the available statistics of the fever hospitals (notably the London Small-pox Hospital), foundling hospitals, workhouses, prisons, and general hospitals, as well as asylums, in order to compare their salubrity. It was the appalling, and apparently excessive and unnecessary, mortality of the large establishments, especially those which received numbers of the 'sickly and depressed classes', which led to Farr's despairing comments on the current state institutional policies. Confinement seemed to erode further the health of those already weak or diseased, and risked creating epidemic conditions (Farr 1841: 17–33).

From the available statistics of insanity Farr estimated for the mid-1830s a total of roughly 20,000 lunatics and idiots in England, Wales, and Scotland. The prevalence of insanity appeared on the basis of the figures available, greater in Scotland (1/574 of the population) than in England (1/1000), and greater in agricultural than in manufacturing districts. The returns from twelve 'agricultural' counties represented a rate of 1/820 compared with 1/1200 in twelve predominantly 'manufacturing or mining' counties.

Farr was, however, sceptical of such computations, which represented simply the number of reported and officially recorded cases of insanity (usually those confined as lunatics or idiots) per thousand of the population. As he argued these figures did not provide a measure of the relative *tendency* to insanity in particular populations but were simply based upon an accounting (usually quite defective, as he demonstrated) of reported cases. The number of cases was never a true measure of real incidence, since, for instance, more congenital idiots survived infancy and more lived longer in the countryside, although there were not necessarily more born there. At any one time there were thus likely to be more idiots living in the countryside. As Farr argued:

'In Wales, and remote villages, the idiot lodges in a cottage, and, supported by the parish, is the qualified butt, and of course the favourite, of the neighbourhood: in towns, he would have more difficulty to survive the nursing in a workhouse.' (Farr 1837b: 588)

Since, further, rural idiots had greater opportunities to produce idiot children compared with idiots confined in workhouses and asylums who could not breed and often died young in confinement, Farr concluded with respect to the incidence of insanity:

'If we exclude the congenital idiots, and only calculate the proportions insane, it is likely that the tendency to madness would be found greater in towns than in the country, – in England than in Wales and Scotland. If lunatics in this and other countries be now better treated than formerly, – and this is incontestibly the case, – their life is necessarily prolonged; and the proportion to the population is increased although the tendency to insanity may be diminished.' (Farr 1837b: 588)

On the basis of such inferences Farr suggested that the incidence of insanity was doubtless greater in the towns and other industrial areas than in the countryside, although he did not try to explain this difference nor establish what other social factors might affect the incidence and prevalence of insanity.

From other figures Farr was able to establish that lunatics and idiots made up at least 10 per cent of the pauper population (and more, including the dependents of pauper lunatics and idiots); insanity seemed, further, to be among the significant causes of pauperism. In London asylums, madhouses, and workhouses, seven out of ten lunatics were paupers, and since many of these were apparently heads of households, their insanity as Farr inferred reduced whole families to destitution. As the 1844 Commissioners' Report later suggested, insanity most frequently attacked those aged 25–40, the group with largest family responsibilities (Farr 1841: 18).

Such findings of course lent weight to recommendations that the pauper insane be sent to asylum for treatment as soon as possible after their first outbreak of madness, and not only as and when they latterly became nuisances in the workhouse, and were perhaps already 'incurably insane'. Farr acknowledged that confinement in workhouses seemed far more economic (since workhouses could keep lunatics and idiots for roughly 2s 10d – 3s 6d per week; whereas in Bethlem weekly costs per inmate often exceeded 15s); but he tried to establish that this was in the long term false economy. Among the inmates of the Middlesex Asylum at Hanwell he calculated the average term of confinement lasted four and a half years (for the decade 1831–40). As others had previously suggested, Farr thought this length of term owed partly to the increased difficulty of cure in those cases where lunatics were transferred from workhouses and other institutions which denied them proper treatment. Of over 800 inmates at Hanwell at the end of 1839, about 650 had indeed previously been confined 'for considerable periods' in workhouses or other asylums (Farr 1841: 23ff.). For matters of policy such calculations were obviously highly relevant; Farr's efforts to demonstrate the real economy of proper treatment of lunatics, and his observations on the statistics of insanity more generally, were largely dictated by the immediate 'institutional question' and pressing problems of policy as they appeared. About the character of insanity itself, and its social distribution, however, Farr ventured little into speculation. Though he established the remarkable prevalence of insanity among paupers, he wrote about pauperism primarily as a factor influencing, clearly to the worse, the survival and recovery prospects of inmates already in institutions. Those inmates who were paupers more often died, or became chronic and incurable. Similarly, although Farr also acknowledged the remarkable proportion of the insane who were paupers, he did not use such findings as the starting point for any epidemiological investigation into how various social factors might influence the patterns of incidence of insanity. There were in any case no medical topographies of insanity of the sort that became so useful in understanding contemporary infectious diseases.

Within medical psychology such 'social influences' were a talking-point and curiosity, although the arguments about influences often rested again on deducing 'causes' from a specific inmate population, or even less systematically were frankly speculative. The apparently greater prevalence (four-fold) of insanity in America (gathered from figures which were not comparable with the English or British figures, and reflected primarily rather different confinement practices) was the source of considerable speculation, much of which is interesting in its own terms. The comparison was not of course a proper statistical exercise; but it opened a revealing line of speculations which exposed certain contemporary pre-occupations about insanity, and the vague outlines of certain notions about its causes which were only obliquely reflected in the theories of medical psychology.

The contemporary vital statistics concerned as they were with institutional questions are in fact in general not especially revealing about who the insane actually were. Nor are there other sources of systematic information, until after 1845, which give even simple details about the lives of inmates before their confinement.

The medical case-books of asylums generally contained little systematic information of a social kind about inmates. For many institutions, and almost all workhouses containing lunatics, no 'medical registers' were kept until after 1845; in many cases there are no records of admissions, deaths, or discharges, or at most lists of inmates' names, ages, and parishes of origin.

Long runs of case-books have survived from several institutions, notably Bethlem, but these contain in fact little beyond the medical short-hand comments on the frequency of bleeding or the particular drugs or other powders administered. There are few developed case-histories, or details about the circumstances leading to someone's confinement, or even administrative details of how anyone was ordered, committed, and conveyed to the asylum, whether by police, family, parish officials, or at the King's pleasure. A few 'interesting' and sensational cases are better documented, both by more substantial physicians' comments and by other official records. These, however telling and interesting in their own terms, are at best only incidentally revealing about more general conditions. 'Typical' inmates were almost by definition uninteresting for such anecdotal purposes and very rarely sat for their case-book portrait or caught the physician's curious eye when he set about to describe someone's 'extravagant antics'.

Among published works there are several first-person records of a confinement and recovery, which again are interesting documents, but unenlightening where not deliberately misleading about general conditions. Such narratives describe with varying detail a number of private madhouses, often from the aggrieved and jaundiced memory of one nursing old wounds. Extended case-histories prepared for publication by physicians were rare, except where they were merely illustrative in a medical or management treatise. Many of the separate case-histories published concerned troublesome inmates, whose detention had caused wide publicity or whose family had protested widely, and thus cast a shadow on the physician's reputation. At the extreme, such histories were simple vindications of the physician's judgements, and thus paraded the lunatic's delusion perhaps enhanced with poetic license so as best to display his outrageous and self-evident lunacy.

Other published case-histories were primarily literary in their intended effects, and ranged from the pathetic, in the sometimes affecting descriptions of 'Ophelias' wronged in love and maddened, to the baldly moralistic, the sensational, the lowly humorous. Popular collections like the anonymous *Sketches in Bedlam*, published in 1823 'by a Constant Observer', are in general deliberately 'colourful' or extravagant, in the tradition of Swiftian or more popular *grotesquerie*. The 'sketches' are almost exclusively drawn from well-known criminal lunatics housed in Bethlem, in its separate criminal wing, who were of course in no way representative. The fascination of the portraits and images of madness in such documents, however, hardly enhances their value or usefulness in forming an impression of the actual character of the insane.

This is of course a general problem with literary evidence; the distinct texts all depend upon, refer to, and comment about a common stock of images in the cultural code concerning 'madness', and a common vocabulary of terms. Yet to establish their singularity the texts draw only selectively from this code, and indeed characteristically strain away from it; and thus not only do the individual texts fail to represent the general code in its entirety or representatively, they often make ironic comments on it. However rich and suggestive, such texts are difficult to square with the varieties of sociological description and more systematic representation and enumeration.

Beyond the simplest details the insane as a class are largely unknown, at least until after the mid-nineteenth century. There are the familiar breakdowns of asylum inmates by sex and age, which indeed corrected certain ideologically-induced confusions of the time. The gross proportions of paupers among the confined are clear, but little else about them; as regards what sorts of paupers these were, in what degrees of distress, whether aged, idiotic, paralytic, stunted, or retarded by diet deficiencies, suffering organic complications, etc., there is very little reliable information. Nor, beyond plausible guesswork, is it possible to make many secure inferences about the probable incidence of mental disorders under conditions which have long ago disappeared. The conditions of existence of mental disorders at present are themselves poorly understood. But it is clear in addition that across broad periods the character of 'insanity' itself has shifted considerably, in part because certain of the conditions associated at different times with madness have newly emerged or disappeared, worsened and spread, or waned. The conditions, physical, emotional, and intellectual, which 'insanity' has represented have themselves shifted, decomposed, and been restructured, in part as a consequence of the advances in medical psychology and later of psychiatry in extending their powers of description and in reconceptualizing mental disorders.

Certain of the organic conditions associated with peculiar mental states (although not invariably or necessarily diagnosed or recognized as 'insanity' or the like, in individual cases) have also suffered notable fluctuations in the past. The variety and degree of diet deficiencies were traditionally far greater and far more damaging in their consequences, which doubtless included many states verging on 'madness'. Fevers with delirium were probably under certain recurrent circumstances more common and note-worthy formerly. Toxic conditions were probably more varied and some-times more dangerous; mercury and lead poisoning (each closely associated with forms of mental disorder) were over long periods commonplace risks, and were endemic in certain artisan occupations (*vide* the 'mad hatters'); adulteration and spoilage of food were more common. Conversely, the 'general paralysis of the insane' so common until the early twentieth century in the last stages of syphilis, must have been very rare in Europe before the mid-sixteenth century, as similarly the mental disorders associated with advanced alcoholism and alcoholic poisoning were relatively rare before the advent of cheap distilled spirits.

Changes in the structure of the population have also doubtless affected the prevalence of certain insanities. Increased longevity and the secular decline in the adult death-rate have, for instance, doubtless extended the risks and occurrence of 'senility' and other forms of cerebral deterioration which affect individuals sometime after 'middle-age'.

The policies over the last century or more of confining idiots in mental institutions have obviously reduced their fertility, and have (perhaps) reduced the incidence and tendency to congenital idiocy in the general population. On the other hand, surgical techniques have allowed the survival of many more severely or partially brain-damaged accident victims.

The list of such changes and fluctuations in organic and environmental conditions could easily be extended and refined. But their import for understanding the character of the insane population is actually rather limited, since charting the fluctuations allows only a more or less plausible comparison of the prevalence of a particular organic condition at different moments; there is no way to reconstruct the likely *incidence* of, for instance, advanced syphilis at some point in the early nineteenth century (and in any case, in the vicissitudes of diagnosis, many genuine cases of general paralysis of the insane were not classified among the 'insane'). Thus even in the case of clearly defined organic conditions associated with 'madness', it is impossible to reconstruct the absolute extent of the conditions at any time in the past until very recently; it is difficult even to relate the apparently fluctuating prevalence of the different organic conditions to the phenomena of 'madness' more broadly, which are much more complexly determined. In the case of 'functional' disorders (which have been most likely always the predominant forms of madness) the problems even of charting the fluctuations in different diagnoses are intractable. The 'forms' of madness are in general so closely bound up with contemporary social practices and the state of the medical arts, that genuine comparisons across time are effectively impossible; it is difficult even to locate or select a unit of comparison.

In the early nineteenth century the efforts of alienists and statisticians to chart the history of mental disorders, to draw up medical topographies, or to describe the various social factors influencing the incidence of the disorders, were necessarily rudimentary (and often frankly speculative). William Farr was probably correct to emphasize the especially bleak survival prospects of idiots in manufacturing towns, as compared with the prospects of village idiots, which were hardly rosy. There were in rural areas, and more generally before the Industrial Revolution, more marginal economic niches in which a harmless lunatic or idiot might find a means to subsistence; there were few viable marginal places in Coketown. Similarly there were probably more 'domestic' arrangements for relieving the insane in the countryside, whereas households in growing and crowded towns could not easily absorb numbers of dependants and burdensome lunatics and idiots. In such reasonings contemporaries like Farr were probably correct enough, but the results cannot carry the analysis very far.

The numbers of the insane, and their condition, were undoubtedly profoundly affected by the dramatic social changes around the turn of the century, and through the early years of the nineteenth century, as were the character of illness generally, of pauperism, and of crime. The consequences of industrialization and the development of towns on the numbers of the insane, and on their fate and standards of care, are however difficult to specify. The consequences as regards the conditions which produced madness are a matter for speculation. The increase in population, and the dramatic changes in its age structure, doubtless swelled the numbers of the insane, as other social changes were probably killing them off more quickly.

The growth of the towns, as many contemporaries realized, made 'domestic' care of the insane far more problematic, and increased the likelihood of their institutional confinement. The demoralizing effects of the towns, and of rural dislocations, doubtless themselves generated discontents bordering upon madness, and were probably connected with the rapid diffusion of the concept 'moral insanity'.

The insane were an increasingly visible and troublesome 'social problem' by most accounts, particularly in the towns. But beyond such impressions their pressure of numbers is remarkably difficult to demonstrate or to quantify. The actual social character of the insane in general remains unclear, and can indeed only be inferred, at several removes, from the different contemporary representations of the insane, although these are limited and often markedly skewed.

To specify the character and numbers of the 'insane' in retrospect thus remains in large measure an intractable historical problem. In contrast, for instance, either to pauperism or to a range of infectious diseases, 'madness' and the extent of its former incidence are effectively impossible to reconstruct in any representative fashion. Documentary evidence on the 'insane' before 1845 is too patchy, unsystematic, and difficult to interpret; the early statistics of insanity provide at best partial and faulty accountings of the insane recorded in asylums and madhouses alone, at a time when a greater number of lunatics and idiots were still confined elsewhere (and thus did not appear in the official figures), and when many languished in neglect. The causes and conditions of the existence of 'madness' are further too little understood to permit any but rather banal inferences about the historic dimensions of the various disorders which 'madness' and like categories have (probably) represented.

Who actually filled the new county asylums as they opened is generally unclear. Some were chronic lunatics or idiots; others had recently suffered acute attacks; some were dangerous, others harmless. A large but indeterminate number were old or established cases transferred from other places of confinement; many were new cases detected by a more vigilant and energetic system of 'medical police', which employed rather wider social criteria of 'madness' and authoritatively extended the rationales for confinement in parallel with the state's growing capacity to house the insane in its own receptacles.

The apparent increase in the numbers of the insane owed clearly to their increasing visibility as a class in separate confinement; statistically, it owed by parts and in various proportions to the transfer of established cases into asylums when further accommodation became available (which by administrative artefact often resulted in such old cases being officially classified and recorded as 'insane' for the first time); to an increasing vigilance which extended the boundaries of 'madness' as an 'actionable' category, and resulted in a greater estimation of a previously 'submerged' problem; and obviously to the increase in population across the decades around the turn of the century, which was likely at least to be matched by an increase in the numbers of the insane, in a similar ratio. Many would indeed doubtless be inclined to suggest that the turbulence and social dislocations of these decades may well have increased the relative tendency to madness and its incidence in the population, as well as the absolute numbers of lunatics and idiots. But about whether insanity was 'on the increase' (i.e., whether the conditions which predispose individuals to madness were increasing over these years, or whether mental suffering and strains erupted more frequently into madness), an historian can only speculate.

The population rise alone of these several factors would probably have been sufficient to strain severely the established (and largely expedient) procedures for confining the dangerously insane and those idiots and lunatics who were put away on practical grounds for purposes of relief. The instituional capacities for confinement were limited and often already filled to their limits; residential institutions of all sorts were already infamous in the mid-eighteenth century, on account of the appalling conditions which overcrowding, poor provisions, and the contract system bred and fostered.

Despite the undoubted pressure of numbers, however, what initiated and directed the emerging programme for separate confinement of the insane, remains an outstanding problem still to be adequately resolved. Social policies toward the 'insane' changed radically and dramatically, especially in the years from the turn of the eighteenth century to the 1850s; in whatever measure this owed to the pressure of numbers, it marked nonetheless a decisive and qualitative shift, which altered the fate of the 'insane', the methods of their treatment, the criteria and categories for recognizing and designating them as a class, and to a large degree the significance of 'madness' as a form of human experience.

To chart the history of these new practices obviously requires an estimation (as far as is possible) of 'insanity' in its contemporary forms, since the numbers of the insane were clearly a pressure on the provisions for confinement and relief as a whole. Separate confinement of the insane emerged against the background of these unprecedented pressures on confinement, contemporaneously with the reorganization of the criminal law and penal system (toward dramatically greater reliance on the punishment of imprisonment), and changes in the provision of poor relief.

But the rationales for separate confinement of the insane, and its associated programme for moral treatment, were developed not simply pragmatically or humanely in response to the 'needs' of the insane themselves or to demands for the public safety. The rationales and the new treatments developed within an ideologically charged climate of philanthropy, and under the sway of a new autonomous medical discipline which arose to inherit the burden of studying, and interpreting authoritatively, the forms of madness.

Although the structural pressures on the system of confinement are in retrospect unmistakeable, as they were to some contemporaries, the reorganization of confinement and its new designs depended upon a series of elaborated ideological programmes, which offered their distinctive evaluation of the problems, the proper functions, and the promise of confinement, and thereby palpably influenced the plans actually realized. Penitentiaries, the newly constructed or reformed workhouses, and asylums, spread when and where they did in response to structural factors; there was in this sense clearly an independent dynamic increasing the spaces of confinement. But the views which informed the reorganization and design of confinement, and the ideological practices installed within the different varieties of institution, were the real and lingering basis of the 'reforms' and marked their achievement.

Separate confinement of the insane developed under the guidance and through the agencies of philanthropy, and provided the institutional site for the practices of medical psychology. The conjunction of these developments in the rise of new and reformed 'moral-treatment' asylums in the first half of the nineteenth century, established the first distinctively modern 'mental institutions' and the context in which psychiatry developed. The character of the 'insane', their legal and social status, and their very likelihood of survival, changed dramatically as a result; and thus it is appropriate to reconstruct the medical and psychological discourse and the rather more diffuse environing 'perceptions' of madness, which informed and directed the programme for moral-treatment asylums – and which made those asylums 'fitting receptacles'. The ideological basis of the separate asylums is indeed especially interesting since there is so little reliable, systematic, or representative information available on the contemporary character of the 'insane'.

PART II
MEDICAL PSYCHOLOGY AND ALLIED DISCOURSES

INTRODUCTION

'Mental illness was constituted by all that was said in all the statements that named it, divided it up, described it, explained it, traced its developments, indicated its various correlations, judged it, and possibly gave it speech by articulating, in its name, discourses that were to be taken as its own. . . . This group of statements is far from referring to a single object, formed once and for all, and to preserving it indefinitely as its horizon of inexhaustible ideality; the object presented as their correlative by medical statements of the seventeenth or eighteenth century is not identical with the object that emerges in legal sentences or police action; similarly, all the objects of psychopathological discourses were modified from Pinel or Esquirol to Bleuler: it is not the same illnesses that are at issue in each of these cases; we are not dealing with the same madmen.'   (Foucault 1972: 32)

'All the statements that named' madness or 'divided it up' constitute in Foucault's use of the term, a 'discourse' on madness. At any historical moment such statements are not necessarily consistent, one with the next; they do not indeed make up a system or express a uniform whole whose parts are assembled internally with scientific rigour. On the contrary they are, as Foucault has argued explicitly in the case of psychopathology, 'dispersed', not mutually consistent, and pegged at different levels of generality and abstraction. The statements deployed about madness in Romantic novels, for instance, compose a particular cultural code which is not unrelated to the contemporary statements deployed in clinical case-studies (nor unrelated to their manner of presentation), but is clearly not their accurate reflection, and moreover serves different, literary purposes. On Foucault's argument it is the ensemble of, and the interaction among, such different orders of statements and the social practices to which they are related, which has constituted and circumscribed 'madness' at different historical moments; and thus by implication a history of 'madness' properly charts not the vicissitudes of the referent 'madness' itself, but rather changing 'statements' about madness, their interrelations, their inscription and establishment in social practices and policies, the authority and prestige they command, etc.

From such a vantage, the establishment of medical psychology in the early part of the nineteenth century marked a decisive 'break' in discourses about madness. This is not to suggest that around a certain arbitrarily selected date anterior and posterior 'statements' divided sharply or neatly; the 'break' in so far as it is demonstrable was not a 'mutation' but a process, which depended on the gradual elaboration of new concepts and psychological techniques, and on the spread of the new institutional spaces in which a discipline of medical psychology became authoritative. There were, across this 'break', aspects of continuity. Many discrete 'statements' on madness persisted unchanged; those derived, for instance, from reflections on the ethics of the Stoics were uttered continuously with at most variations in emphasis, from Pope and Dr Johnson to the alienists of the late nineteenth century. Much of the received wisdom about madness in the early nineteenth century has similarly a 'timeless' air, since it was heavily coloured in its articulation by texts of the moralists of classical antiquity. But more importantly, the greater set of statements on madness was radically different, and assembled on a different basis, under the aegis of a newly emerging medical discipline.

Before the development of medical psychology, the medicine of insanity formed only a subsidiary chapter in general medicine. Many symptoms and indeed syndromes associated with insanity were fixed, and in some cases exhaustively described and catalogued. But their pathologies were poorly defined, if at all; and since 'disease', however florid or varied in the symptoms through which it appeared, was conceived as a single morbid condition (owing to the imbalance of the humours or to disturbances in the 'tensions' of bodily tissues), madness was judged susceptible of the same remedies as other manifestations of disease, with only minor distinguishing differences. Even after the division of 'disease' into a plurality of specific disease entities from the late seventeenth century, the insanities were often assembled into a puzzling, residual category placed under 'diseases of the head' or 'neuroses', to which only speculative pathologies could generally be assigned; the therapeutics of madness, after Sydenham, remained general. The subject of madness despite its inherent interest and social import commanded more significant attention from philosophers, priests, and moralists than from medical practitioners.

The early medicine of insanity was thus an ill-defined pursuit at the periphery or margins of general medicine. It inspired little confidence. Although the symptoms of madness were often striking and alarming, and undoubtedly formed part of many medical practices, the medicine of insanity remained rudimentary.[1] It was guided by the speculative principles of humoural or solidist theory, and by the empiricism of those conscientious mad-doctors who left their valuable 'practical hints' on the 'management' of the insane. The theoretical contributions of such practitioners and of non-specialists were understandably few, and perhaps more importantly the physicians' contact with the mad and disordered was severely limited. The practice of medicine was private (asylum medicine was not organized until the early nineteenth century, as the number of superintendent posts multiplied), and only in special circumstances did the insane receive medical attentions of any sort. Most of the insane who were confined were held under non-medical auspices; if they received any medical care, it was likely for physical complaints alone. Thus to a degree contemporaries' pessimism about the prospects of cure and recovery from the insanities reflected and endorsed the prevailing conditions of medical practice. Within the range of 'statements' on madness, the medicine of insanity offered little that was authoritative, and it was further limited in the scope of its application in practice.

By contrast, the rise of medical psychology ensured the ascendancy and authority of a medical discourse on madness. The new discipline, which developed in large measure independently from the body of general medicine, was installed in the mental institutions which increasingly became the treatment of choice for the insane, and thus decisively altered their fate. The spread of separate confinement of the insane provided the institutional sites in which the specific practices of medical psychology developed; medical psychology itself supplied in turn one of the principal ideological rationales for the new asylums, which alone allowed the new science its unprecedented opportunity for observing systematically and simultaneously the course of insanities in many inmates, under what appeared to be carefully controlled conditions.

In conjunction, the spread of separate confinement and the elaboration of new treatment procedures within the asylum marked the beginnings of the era of mental institutions. At the level of discourse these beginnings were associated with a new and radically altered grouping of 'statements' on madness, which provide the first clear antecedent analogue of a recognizably modern knowledge of mental disorders.

The changes which allowed the new discipline to emerge were first widely visible from the last decades of the eighteenth century. By 1803 the German physician Reil announced pointedly that he regarded medical psychology as one of the three principal branches of the *ars et scientia medica*, equal in importance to internal medicine and surgery. Contemporaneously in France, the *idéologues'* programme for a 'moral medicine', which bore so directly on the disorders of madness, was well-advanced and gaining ground in the Paris school (see Ackerknecht 1967, and Foucault 1973). In Britain the task of advancing the domestic variant of 'moral medicine' fell primarily to philanthropists, both lay and medical. The lineaments of medical psychology were clearly evident in the early asylum-reform programme and in a number of theoretical and practical treatises from the 1790s. Nonetheless the new discipline was slow to achieve a full professional status, according to the common criteria, and its advance depended on the general philanthropic and 'reforming' climate which environed the articulation of specific 'statements' on madness. There were indeed indispensable broader cultural currents, not ostensibly medical or peculiarly relevant for medical psychology, which prepared the change and allowed the gradual codification of a discipline some years before it became established formally as a recognized medical speciality.

Medical psychology was not widely acknowledged as a fully-fledged speciality until the 1830s or 1840s. It did not emerge with its full complement of professional societies, journals, formalized instruction and certification procedures, until even later. The medical superintendents in the early state-run county asylums communicated to a degree among their number, and circulated their respective asylums' annual reports. These provide evidence of the gradual standardization of asylum administration, but it was not until 1841 that the inaugural meeting of an Association of Medical Officers of Asylums and Hospitals for the Insane was held, and the group began publishing its *Asylum Journal of Mental Science* only in 1853. The other major professional journal, *The Journal of Psychological Medicine and Mental Pathology*, had been started by Forbes Winslow several years before, in 1848.

As late as 1834 John Abercrombie was proselytizing the British Association for the Advancement of Science 'On the interest and importance to the medical profession of the study of mental philosophy', and proposing a 'philosophy of mind', based in large measure on the study of the mentally disordered, as a valid and important branch of physiology.[2]

In the same decades medical psychology made only minor inroads into the programme and courses of lectures and clinical instruction in medical faculties; much of the instruction in the speciality remained informal and personal.[3] Until the appearance in 1858 of Sir John Bucknill and Daniel Hack Tuke's *A Manual of Psychological Medicine* (1858), there was no widely used textbook of medical psychology for clinical training which was truly comprehensive.[4]

Although on such criteria of 'maturity', a discipline of medical psychology did not fully emerge until the mid-century, the changes over the preceding decades which prepared the ground are in some ways a more important and interesting herald of the discourse on madness. By their very nature these changes were not narrowly medical, but were attuned to broader philanthropic and social currents. A study of the conditions in which the nascent discipline of medical psychology emerged thus requires more and other than a description of the shift in the medical discourse. The impetus for change came largely from outside the medical system itself, and thus a more adequate account requires some greater catalogue of the contemporary perceptions of madness, irrationality, and the human personality, which environed the change, but were themselves too diffuse to constitute immediately a discipline or to ground new social policies and practices. These contemporary perceptions can be conveniently, if somewhat arbitrarily, listed thematically under several heads, including: the problem of the irrational; the psychology of the classes; universal reason and individual differences; techniques of moral influence. The various themes are each clearly related to the subject-matter of the more formalized systems in medical psychology, and can thus serve to introduce a discussion of the signal changes in discourse which constituted medical psychology as a break from the older subsidiary medicine of insanity.

THE PROBLEM OF THE IRRATIONAL

'If through defects that may happen out of the ordinary course of Nature, any one comes not to such a degree of Reason, wherein he might be supposed capable of knowing the Law, and so living within the Rules of it, he is *never capable of being a Free Man*.' The famous sixtieth section of Locke's *Second Treatise* draws toward its conclusion the discussion of the Law of Reason, on whose observance the whole order of Civil Society rests. The fate of those 'immature' individuals who are not sufficiently rational is the subject of a brief digression: if someone, by natural or unnatural defect, is deprived of reason or of its proper exercise, then, as Locke argued,

> 'he is never let loose to the disposure of his own Will (because he knows no bounds to it, has not Understanding, its proper Guide) but is continued under the Tuition and Government of others, all the time his own Understanding is incapable of that Charge. And so *Lunaticks* and *Ideots* are never set free from the Government of their Parents; *Children, who are not yet come unto those years whereat they may have; and Innocents which are excluded by a natural defect from ever having*; Thirdly, *Madmen*, which for the present cannot possibly have the use of right Reason to guide themselves, have for their Guide, the Reason that guideth other Men which are Tutors over them, to seek and procure their good for them.'   (Locke 1698: §60).

To link like this madmen, lunatics and idiots, and children, as categories of irrational and therefore incapable and immature individuals, was of course not original to Locke, although in his formulation it was particularly influential. The different categories required in common some guardian to act over them, in place of their own deficient or alienated reason; and thus the link of the categories served to point up a common dependency or state of wardship which, in the case of madmen and idiots, English law had acknowledged and allowed from its earliest period.

The link of the categories served also, more pertinently, to mark off certain of the boundaries of Reason, in Locke's account and similarly in many other contemporary texts. The character of Reason, 'right reason' or 'reasonableness' was widely discussed in seventeenth-century England; opposing sides in the religious, philosophical, and political conflicts often each claimed the mantle and prestige of Reason for their respective positions (see Hill 1965). The Law of Reason which Locke expounded represented a particular stance within such debates, but more broadly it codified in its outlines what was progressively taken as the 'norm' of adult conduct and independence. In its advance this emerging norm of the free-standing masterless individual profoundly altered the contemporary character of irrationality and dependency. The norm in itself emphasized the independence of a free individual achieved through labour, as it high-lighted the values associated with bourgeois calculation; by contrast it also spawned or recomposed a whole complex of social categories which stood variously *outside* Reason, including idlers, indigents, vagrants and crimi-nals, children, brutes, savages, religious enthusiasts, and idiots and mad-men. The contemporary categories of irrationality and abnormality were indeed largely composed with reference to the norms of Reason and 'reasonableness'.

Among the exemplars of irrationality and unreason, the madman occupied a distinctive and central place. 'Madness' was of course an ancient category, around which over many centuries long cultural tra-ditions had accreted. By the seventeenth century the representation of the madman as a social figure was relatively stable, and indeed to a degree fixed in stereotypy. The same clusters of images and metaphors recurred commonly, characterizing this or that distinguishing feature of madness. In graphic representation the stereotype was equally old and established; a pictorial tradition captured madness by an economy of allusions to, for instance, the madman's straw crown, his near-naked condition, the drool or foam at his mouth, the staring or fascinated eyes – an array of stereo-typical allusions which has remained secure and widely grounded even to the present day. These were, by tradition, the distinguishing signs and symptoms of the genuine madman.

Despite this distinctive representation, the actual usages of 'madness' as a description were extraordinarily varied; the usages spread across virtually the whole range of figures who in one or other aspect exemplified the irrational. 'Madness' was thus not simply a particular example of 'ir-rationality', but in some respects approached its essence; beyond its specific outlines it suggested more broadly the general state of disorderly

107

unreason. 'Madness' was a plastic and labile term which apparently lent itself readily to many extended and metaphoric senses; it was, perhaps for this reason, a constant mainstay in the rhetoric of derogation. Because of its broad uses, 'madness' and its myriad referents were historically very significant in marking the contours of reason. Indeed how the bounds and contours of reason developed was well-reflected in the practices of marking off 'madness'.

This was the background against which the modern vocabulary of 'mental disorders' appeared. The background itself was very slow to fade. Even across the years when 'madness' was reconceived and assimilated authoritatively into discrete disease conditions susceptible of treatment in medical psychology, the referents of 'madness' were never primarily medical. 'Madness' continued to represent many diverse varieties and manifestations of the irrational; and in turn there was a continuing interplay of senses between 'madness' (specifically construed as one or other mental disorder) and the more encompassing notion of the 'irrational'. In the interplay something reflected back on the clinical notions of 'madness' themselves. Something survived, in other terms, of the older links between madness and the vague, suggestible perceptions of the 'irrational' – the threatening groundswell atop which reason perched uneasily. The insane energies of the madman thus continued to serve as an emblem, far beyond the confines of medical treatises, for the dangerous and overwhelming powers ranged against Reason.

It was such a threat which the many and wide metaphoric uses of 'madness' as a description doubtless evoked. In a single volume (1809) of The *Examiner* (a journal where one could otherwise read reports on the progress of lunacy reforms) within a score of pages one article reviewed an exhibition by 'an unfortunate lunatic' named William Blake, finding it 'a farrago of nonsense, unintelligibleness, and egregious vanity, the wild effusions of a distempered brain';[1] a second reprinted an account of Joanna Southcott and her prophecies, which complained in summary: 'Where such impious bedlamites are allowed to walk abroad, it is not to be wondered at that madness should become epidemic' (*Examiner* 1809: 622). Such examples could be multiplied many-fold, and often by cases which bear even less perceptible resemblance *strictu senso* to the clinical senses of 'madness', as they were then being elaborated in medical discourse.

Yet despite the great range of usages, and their frequent distance from the more properly clinical senses, there are no grounds *a priori* for regarding the non-medical uses of 'madness' and related terms as merely incidental, metaphoric, or figurative. On the contrary the range of

extended uses of 'madness' was itself an important influence on and reference point for the developing medical notions. The medical discourse
depended to a degree in its choice and description of its objects on more
general cultural perceptions of 'irrationality', although these were themselves often hardly amenable to rigorous or systematic statement. In many
contexts the use of 'madness' and related terms as descriptions was clearly
metaphoric, and clearly distinguishable from 'genuine' (i.e., clinical)
madness; nonetheless the whole range of uses stood as the background
against which 'madness' (clinically defined) appeared. The statements of
medical psychology on madness were thus less a product of an emerging
discipline itself than of the greater culture. The discipline would doubtless
strive toward medical precision, the general culture, however, was
fascinated by diffuse perceptions of unruliness and irrationality, and fixed
with the force of obsession by its 'reveries' on madness – in the greater
sense.

The problem of the irrational, to which the descriptions of 'madness'
and their wide scope in large measure testify, accordingly persisted; it lay
as one of the historically and logically prior sedimentary levels atop which
the more distinctively medical notions were overlaid.

Among philosophers the problem of the irrational was presented, until the
Romantics, largely in intellectualist terms; it was a matter of disturbed or
false reasoning.[2] Locke for instance distinguished the mad from 'naturals'
(congenital idiots). 'Naturals' were those 'deprived of reason' and hence
of the mature uses of any of their mental faculties, whereas the mad had
disturbed but still active faculties. A famous passage of the *Essay concerning
Human Understanding* elaborates the distinction; madmen, as compared
with idiots,

> 'seem to suffer by the other extreme. For they do not appear to me to
> have lost the faculty of reasoning, but having joined together some ideas
> very wrongly, they mistake them for truths; and they err as men do that
> argue right from wrong principles.' (Locke 1690: II, xi, 13)

This was a widely cited and influential definition, which later graced a
whole array of treatises on madness. It was not in the event, however,
ultimately appropriate for medical psychology. As Tuke argued, for
instance, in the *Manual of Psychological Medicine* (1858), the definition
seemed to conceive madness merely as a 'lesion of the intellectual
faculties'; this was pertinent for describing hallucinations, delusions, and

other disorders of perception, or *folie raisonante*, monomania, and melancholia, but was hardly a formula to encompass the broad range of conditions, perceptual, affective, organic, etc., which clustered among the insanities (Bucknill and Tuke 1858: 87).

From the vantage of Locke's own psychology, however, the definition was intentionally drawn broadly and meant to capture the essential *error* which characterized madnesses. It extended the notion of madness indeed even to embrace an individual's personal 'hobbyhorse' or his occasional idiosyncratic and unwarranted opinion, of which Locke wrote:

> 'I shall be pardoned for calling it by so harsh a name as *madness*, when it is considered, that opposition to reason deserves that name, and is really madness; and there is scarce a man so free from it, but that if he should always, on all occasions, argue or do as in some cases he constantly does, would not be thought fitter for Bedlam than civil conversation.'
>
> (Locke 1690: II, xxxiii, 4)

'Opposition to reason' was an exceptionally wide criterion for construing madness or its essence, and a criterion which did not underscore the wild bizarreness of the mad, or their 'otherness'. On the premises of Locke's psychology and epistemology, madmen were 'mistaken', and their errors were by way of an exaggeration of the errors into which all men occasionally fall.

Discovering the sources of error, and its perpetuation, thus provided the key to Locke's understanding of the problem of the irrational. Since, barring defects 'out of the ordinary course of Nature', all men are endowed by birthright with the mental faculties, the great empirical variations among them must owe to their experience, to their particular, accidental circumstances, and to the distinctive influences (including education) which shape them from outside, and effect how the exterior world will strike their minds. Madness constitutes an 'opposition to reason' in so far as it is a false impression or perception of the exterior world; it is the product of errors or deceits of the senses, conveying wrong information about the external world to the mind, and of errors in the (proper and fitting) connection or combination of ideas. Although all men are prone to error (Locke's conception of the limitations of right reason was indeed somewhat gloomy), in the madman error becomes habitual and eventually imperious, so that the madman's mind grows progressively less and less faithful in apprehending or reflecting the external world. Where truth and reason depend upon veracity to nature, errors (whether false sensations or false reflections) can prove eventually the undoing of the mind, and the original madness.

In the form in which it was bequeathed to mad-doctors and to the early medical psychologists, via David Hartley's interpretation and reformulation, Locke's epistemology was widely influential. It was doubtless vulgarized and merged into greater amalgams which were in effect philosophically hybrid, and more in the nature of suggestive and plastic images than elaborated concepts; but it was perhaps for this reason the more suggestive for conceiving and treating madness. Locke's description of the mind as a *camera obscura*, connected to the world by the apertures of the senses, stood in easy affinity with the image of the prism refracting light, derived originally from Newton's *Optiks*, which contemporaries commonly deployed to represent the white light of reason. Reason, the 'white light', perceives the world unrefracted, whereas 'coloured', distorted images of the world are filtered by imagination and the passions. 'The *understanding* is not so much unlike a closet wholly shut from light', Locke wrote,

'with only some little opening left, to let in external visible resemblances, or *ideas* of things without: would the pictures coming into such a dark room but stay there, and lie so orderly as to be found upon occasion, it would very much resemble the understanding of a man, in reference to all objects of sight, and the *ideas* of them.'

(Locke 1690: II, xi, 7)

Combined with the image of the prism, this description of the mind allowed a ready distinction between Reason and, on the other hand, Fancy, Imagination, Madness; Reason always sees clearly (light enters the opening unrefracted), whereas if across the 'little opening' the passions spread their influence, the resulting 'imperfect', 'faint', 'confused', or 'deluded' sight suffers the characteristic distorting effects of Fancy, the Imagination, or, at the extreme, Madness.

The new optical theories provided similarly a corpuscular physics which Hartley exploited in his 'associationist' psychology. The notions Hartley developed depend on an extended comparison between the combination of ideas into chains of 'association', and the physical communication of sensations via their respective 'vibrations'. The doctrine of vibrations seemed to provide, at least by analogy, a physical basis for the association of ideas, and to suggest in a rough and ready way a theory of memory – of why certain chains of associations become habitual. 'The perpetual recurrency of particular ideas and terms makes the vibrations belonging there to become more than ordinarily vivid' (Hartley 1749: I, 397), and indeed in the end habitual.

111

For conceptions of madness this mechanism of mental habituation, explaining how 'tracks' of associations might be laid down, proved widely serviceable. The notion of vibrations and of their varying intensities suggested a mode of representing the overwhelming force of mad ideas; or a way of explaining how mad ideas might compete with and then supersede the 'natural' rhythms and associations of reflection and perception.

The disorders of the mind were accordingly conceived as forms of 'delirium' − or literally going 'off the track' or 'out of the furrow'; the pervasive manner of representing the mind in its 'tracks' allowed, by a metaphoric leap, a direct comparison between the supposed physical state and structure of the mind and the qualities or patterns of its 'ideas'. Thus, as theorists argued, in the condition of mania it is the velocity of over-heated ideas in the mind which causes their indiscriminate (and false) association; once combined and laid down in new 'tracks' or neurological networks in the brain, such perverse associations then become an obstacle to the orderly and 'natural' succession of ideas in their train. Similarly, in the condition of melancholia the heavy fixity of thoughts hardens the mind into a new track, derived not from nature, but from an absurd, fanciful, or deluded connection of ideas, by a morbid habit.

Dr Thomas Arnold described the mind of a maniac 'carried along with the stream of that activity of the brain, and those violent vibrations which it can no longer control, or resist'; from the effects of 'vibrations arising with little order, and succeeding each other by the slightest, and most accidental connections, the most unnatural, and fantastical associations, will acquire the force, and possess the authority, of the most powerful and just' (Arnold 1782–86: II, 300). Such is the madness of a mind crowded with thoughts, which jostle and combine promiscuously, against the nature of things. Other descriptions drew on more elaborate metaphors, including the action of a shout moving through a crowd, growing in intensity and violence until all take it up in a general cry; this too was a popular way to represent the accidental connections and unnatural associations which, unchecked, can grow in intensity and authority over the mind.

At the other extreme of madness, at the depth of 'low spirits', the same terms were adduced to describe the fixity and gloomy, unrelieved weight on the mind of morbid trains of thought. In a memorable passage in *Rasselas*, Dr Johnson recorded the course of such a madness, to which those of saturnine temperament were most susceptible:

'some particular train of ideas fixes the attention; . . . the mind, in weariness or leisure, recurs constantly to the favourite conception, and feasts on the luscious falsehood whenever she is offended with the bitterness of truth. By degrees the reign of fancy is confirmed; she grows first imperious, and in time despotic. Then fictions begin to operate as realities, false opinions fasten upon the mind, and life passes in dreams of rapture or of anguish.'

(Johnson 1887: 140–41)

The description is not in its particulars faithful to Locke's or to Hartley's theories, but is in their spirit, and well represents the psychology of mind which was widely diffused in these decades. It was such a wide-ranging and flexible associationism which gave new substance and content to the older conceptions of madness as 'delirium', and enhanced the manner of describing the errors at the centre of madness.

As regards treatment procedures, the terms (if not the logical principles) of associationism were readily advanced as rationales, although it is unclear how far treatments were actually deduced from Locke's or Hartley's theories. The corpuscular physics suggested by the doctrine of vibrations was doubtless part of the basis for the varied 'shock' therapies. The 'fastening' or grip on the mind of malign and false associations of ideas, and the 'weight' of disordered, habitual trains of thought, were accorded a reified concreteness, as if understood almost in a gross physical sense. The continental physician Jerome Gaub recommended a therapeutics of powerful drugs, to 'tear loose a mind fast bound to some particular subject, which will force her to rest by effacing thought and temporarily inducing oblivion' (quoted in Rather 1965). Tearing the mind loose thus allowed the physician to 'expel overfixed ideas and substitute others in their place' (see Rather 1965: 185), for which end there were also available a remarkable array of machines to shock or momentarily terrorize a madman.

Shock, and the therapeutic terror which so many mad-doctors recommended at appropriate points in treatment, had the intended effect of throwing the body and mind of the madman into a new disorder; terror would raise extreme emotion (and often great physical discomfort), stronger in intensity and violence than the madness itself. Such practices went under the general name therapies of 'distraction', or alternatively of 'awakening'.

The error of madness had long been assimilated to the irrationalities of dreams, those nocturnal errors which individuals suffer while asleep. 'Delirium' broadly represented the dream of waking persons, that state of quasi-sleep or quasi-unconsciousness for which wakefulness and the full return of correcting evidence from the senses, were the proper remedies.

'Invasion by wakefulness is one of the most constant forms among the therapeutics of madness', as Foucault has observed (Foucault 1965: 185); and
through the early part of the nineteenth century there were many available
means described in the medical treatises for 'awakening' the madman, or, in
Conolly's phrase, for forcing 'the extravagant and erring senses, when
caught out of bounds, to hie back to their confine' (Conolly 1850: 96).
'Gathering up the senses' was intended to right the mind by restoring sound
sensory contact with the external world, and thus banishing the free reign of
the imagination. The mind could err or wander, mad-doctors argued in
terms roughly and reasonably faithful to Locke's epistemology, because of
some defect in the senses or block on the 'path' by which sense impressions of
external objects reach the mind. The external world is thus not properly
being impressed on the mind; lacking the correction of the senses, the mind
confuses fancies ('ideal pictures') with realities.

Dr Thomas Arnold, in common with many of his contemporaries, attributed the chaos which disturbed sound sensory experience to the 'terrible
imagination'; he described the 'high degree of delirium, in which the
patient's imagination has so lively an ideal picture for ever in view, as over-
comes, and confounds, the impressions made by external objects' (Arnold
1782–86: I, 76). His distrust of the imagination was characteristic and
general; he asked of the poet's 'ideal picture': 'what indeed can be a nearer
approach to Madness, than that of a man of genius, in the act of poetical
invention?' (Arnold 1782–86: I, 109), and by way of evidence he adduced
the familiar passage on the imagination from *A Midsummer Night's Dream*:

> 'Lovers and madmen have such seething brains
> Such shaping fantasies, that apprehend
> More than cool reason ever comprehends.
> The lunatic, the lover and the poet
> Are of imagination all compact:
> One sees more devils than the vast hell can hold,
> That is, the madman: the lover, all as frantic,
> Sees Helen's beauty in a brow of Egypt:
> The poet's eye, in fine frenzy rolling,
> Doth glance from heaven to earth, from earth to heaven;
> And as imagination bodies forth
> The forms of things unknown, the poet's pen
> Turns them to shapes, and gives to airy nothings
> A local habitation and a name.
> Such tricks hath strong imagination.'   (V, i, 4–18)

The mind's eye of the poet, in 'fine frenzy rolling', shaping 'airy nothings', was from Arnold's view the exact evil in delirium.

The imagination figured in such views at the margins of 'reasonableness' as a variety of trickster, locked in a protracted contest with right perception. In moments of insanity, the imagination tyrannized, and in the conventional imagery of the period, 'raised an army of false ideas'. Such a view had deep roots in the widely diffused distrust of the imagination and of enthusiasm in the classical period; and similarly to Locke's general account of the error of madness, distrust of the imagination allowed scope for explaining a range of intellectual disorders and superstitions.

The theologian John Trenchard conceived hallucinations, in typical fashion, as errors allowed by want of proper *experience*: the madman (and Trenchard was writing with reference to a particular religious enthusiast) hallucinates 'when the Organs of Sense (which are the Avenues and Doors to let in external objects) are shut and locked up'. Thus images generated from 'within', idle fancies, 'reign without Rival', constantly 'striking strongly upon, and affecting the Brain, Spirits, or Organ where the imaginative faculty resides' (Trenchard 1709: 9). Tissot explained Pascal's hallucination similarly:

'The brain of the celebrated Monsieur Pascal, was so much injured, by the severe labours of study, reflection, and imagination, . . . that certain of its fibres were agitated with a perpetual vibration, which excited incessantly the same sensation in the soul, as would have been produced by a *ball of fire* fixed in his side; and reason, overcome by the influence of the nerves, could scarcely ever lay aside the idea of the actual presence of such a ball.'

(Tissot 1781, quoted in Arnold: 1782–86, I, 167)

The 'idea of the actual presence' described a physical event, which by constant exercise (treading its path) would grow stronger (wearing the path smooth). The wearing of such a path, outside the right furrow, leads in this conception to an entrenchment of the madness.

The contrast of imagination and sense perception ended ultimately with an equation of delirium and dreaming – that state where no sense experience (apparently) is available, since the senses are shut up. Hence nothing corrects that fabric of errors, illusions, and flights of fancy, which the dream is taken to be. Dreaming is a transient madness from which we (usually) awaken. Benjamin Rush even identified the physical events occurring during dream sleep as the essential physical basis of madness itself; the dream, he imagined, 'is always induced by morbid or irregular action in the blood-vessels of the brain, and hence it is accompanied with the same erroneous *train*, or the same incoherence of thought, which takes place in delirium' (Rush 1830: 194). Madness and the dream were thus taken as of the same substance.

The equation inspired some limited hope in the 'awakening' cures, or in the sudden remission and disappearance of symptoms as the metaphoric sleep gave way to wakefulness. Arnold suggested that 'just as the dreams of children often continue for a while after they are apparently awake, their senses being with difficulty roused, and drawing off the attention by slow degrees from the *ideal picture* presented during sleep, to the *real representation* of surrounding objects' (Arnold 1782–86: I, 71–2), so could arousing the madman's senses disperse the ideas of his dream-like insanity. Thomas Bakewell used the same terms in presenting an actual cure or recovery, as if the madman had been suffering nightmares without being able to wake:

'I know a gentleman, who suddenly recovered from insanity, in consequence of a violent shock, the effect of a heavy fall. He seemed to awake, as if he had been walking in his sleep, and said, that it appeared as if he had been in a long and troublesome dream; but had no idea that it had continued longer than one night, and expressed the greatest astonishment, when told, that, time had stolen a march of three years upon him.'   (Bakewell 1809: 84)

The violent shock in this example was accidental, but shock was purposeful and a typical feature in many 'awakening' cures. In the physician's hands shock was one weapon among others for fighting illusions. Pinel stressed the 'importance of frequently and variously repeated attempts to counteract' hallucinations, and he relied on Montaigne's naturalistic verdict that 'visions and enchantments' were generally instances of the power of the imagination 'over the unenlightened minds of the vulgar'. Pinel carried over the remark directly to apply to the insane:

'this judicious remark, will more especially apply to the fantastic illusions, the gloomy suspicions and groundless fears of melancholics. Impressions of this kind, rooted in the temperament and matured by habit, are exceedingly difficult of removal. How are we to combat the prejudices of a contracted mind, that takes for reality every chimera of its own creation?'   (Pinel 1806: 177)

Against such 'superstitions', the therapy was yet again shock:

> 'Strong impressions on the senses may in these cases counteract the tendency of these morbid feelings. We can here oppose sensation to sensation; clear and distinct sensation to that which is obscure: the latter of course yields to the former, and without the train of imaginary evils.' (Cox 1806: 72)

The Cartesian phrase 'clear and distinct' sensation meant vivid sensory experience, which could be made stronger and given a more powerful hold on the mind than the fancies (obscure sensations) of a madness. The various cures depending on terror were of this form; they inflicted enough physical pain or anxiety to interrupt the insanity, and so give thoughts a new course or track to run.

There were also more mild therapies, or 'salutary demonstrations', which relied on theatrical tricks to divert or ridicule the madman from his particular insanity; this is a sampling:

1 The American physician Benjamin Rush suggested: 'Cures of patients, who suppose themselves to be glass, may be easily performed by pulling a chair, upon which they are about to sit, from under them, and afterwards showing them a collection of pieces of glass as their bodies' (Rush 1830: 108).
2 'If our patient imagine he has a living animal in his body, and he cannot be reasoned out of a belief of it, medicines must be given to destroy it; and if an animal, such as he supposes to be in his body, should be secretly conveyed into his close stool, the deception would be a justifiable one. . . .' (Rush 1830: 107).
3 A man who thought himself a plant was cured in this way: one of his companions humoured the delusion, and persuaded him he could not thrive without being watered. While the inmate believed, for some moments, his companion was watering him from a tea-pot, the companion was actually urinating on his head. 'The remedy in this case was resentment and mortification' (Rush 1830: 108).
4 'It is certainly allowable to try the effect of certain deceptions, contrived to make strong impressions on the senses, by means of unexpected, unusual, striking, or apparently supernatural agents; such as after waking the party from sleep, either suddenly or by a gradual process, by imitated thunder or soft music, according to the peculiarity of the case, combating the erroneous deranged notions

117

either by some pointed sentence, or signs executed in phosphorous upon the wall of the bed chamber, or by some tale, assertion, or reasoning; by one in the character of an angel, prophet, or devil: but the actor in this drama must possess much skill, and be very perfect in his part.' (Cox 1806: 47)

In each of these 'awakenings' the end is plainly to restore a mind to sound sensory activity — as against the wrong impressions of madness.

The pervasive Lockean epistemology provided a basis for explaining intellectual differences among individuals, as the products of their respective experiences; and it offered likewise a mode of identifying the sources of error whereby individuals deviate from the Law of Reason. From a different foundation, in Scottish conjectural history and in Enlightenment philosophies of history, another approach to the problem of the irrational which Charles Frankel has aptly styled the 'sociology of error' developed across roughly the same years (see Frankel 1948). This second approach was concerned with social sources of 'error', or more broadly non-rational behaviours; and specifically with explaining the persistence of 'irrational' practices and beliefs which seemed to constitute deviations from the progress of the human species, or obstacles to the advance of its rationality. For theories of progress which depended upon a concept of human rationality and its ever-increasing powers, the persistence of such 'irrational' practices and beliefs naturally posed important conceptual problems. The advance of rationality as a programme indeed depended upon an adequate understanding of the obstacles to 'rationality', which a series of empirical and conjectural histories, and sketches of the stages in the development of the human mind (toward rationality), attempted to provide. Although these histories and sketches related most centrally to the understanding of 'savages' and of enduring barbarisms, superstitions, and mystifications in 'civilized' societies, their approach was also pertinent to the contemporary perceptions of madness, albeit less directly or immediately than in the case of Lockean epistemology.

The method of this 'sociology of error', amply illustrated by Condorcet's *Outlines of an Historical View of the Progress of the Human Mind* (1795), was to demonstrate the limiting conditions imposed on reason and rationality by the accidents and contingencies of a particular time and place. Montesquieu's essays provided a model of sorts, since they described the alien manners, habits, morals, and modes of thought as these were conditioned by accidents of history and geography. The 'sociology of error' as a method wielded its critical tools somewhat more systematically. It passed judgement on the true and the false in a range of beliefs and practices, as for instance in the many critical accounts of religious mystification; and beyond passing judgement it attributed responsibility for the false, in this case to the deliberate perversion of truth by priestly castes in the service of their own vested interests. Rational criticism thus served itself as a method in the attack on 'unclear notions' which grounded and supported irrational behaviour and belief.

In its broad outlines this approach to the 'irrational' well survived among the philanthropists and ideologues of 'improvement' at the turn of the eighteenth century and after. The contemporary impressions of 'savagery' were a thorough pastiche, formed by parts from travellers' reports, early ethnographies, prejudice, and racialist stereotypes. The very looseness of such impressions, however, allowed the varieties of 'savagery' to be assimilated easily into a common category, opposed to an equally unitary notion of 'civilization'. The lability of the notion of the 'savage' allowed, further, a range of comparisons between genuine 'savagery' and the superstitions, folk ways and mores, or intellectual backwardness which survived in civilized societies. At the extreme it was not unusual to find the domestic labouring poor, or sections among them, described as 'savage', as if the lower orders stood in the same relation to civilization, 'rationality', and improvement as alien and barbarous peoples.

The Philanthropist, a humane and influential journal edited by the Quaker William Allen, well illustrates this amalgam which formed around the opposed notions of savagery and civilization. Across its publishing history, from 1811 onwards, the concerns of the journal were spread from penal reforms, education of the labouring classes, the condition of the insane, the Poor Law, to the abolition of the slave trade and missionary efforts to bring civilization or religion to alien peoples. The articles on domestic problems were naturally attuned to the terms of the on-going debates and their particular details; and hence the more general articles (for instance, 'On the Duty and Pleasure of Cultivating Benevolent Dispositions') often provide far more direct clues of the greater programme on which the whole range of concerns rested and was unified. Indeed it is striking how deeply articles entitled variously, 'On the Most Rational Means of Promoting Civilization in Barbarous States', 'On the Progress of Civilization in Africa', or 'Comparison of the Sixteenth Century with the Nineteenth, in Circumstances which Regard the Intellectual and Moral State of the Public Mind', evidence the same unified perspective which equally well provided the rationale for reforms in Britain.

Enlightenment theories of progress, albeit vulgarized, clearly underlay the journal's programme; in the interests of 'philanthropy' it also embodied a special emphasis on the 'benevolent dispositions' and 'cultivating the powers of humane sympathy'. Thus the remarkable article comparing 'the Sixteenth Century with the Nineteenth' criticizes by parts the cruelty and callousness of the earlier period as well as the 'intellectual weakness' and thraldom at the base of its barbarisms. 'We have added these anecdotes relative to the belief in witchcraft', as the anonymous reviewer wrote, 'not only as curious proofs of the weakness of the human mind, when it was still capable of being governed by such delusions; but as proofs of the horrid cruelty of the times, when men proceeded without remorse to burn their fellow-creatures, upon the allegation of imaginary crimes like these.' The 'barbarous sacrifices to the daemon of superstition' were evidence of collective delusion diffused through the culture, and one proof among many of 'the great mental inferiority of antecedent to present times' (*Philanthropist* 1814: IV, 363–64).

To account for such mental inferiority the reviewer adduced first 'pomp and circumstance' – the sway of authority and official prestige which would operate powerfully upon 'persons of weak and ignorant minds'; but this led to the reviewer to consider more generally the surprising if not incredible 'power of the imagination' in earlier centuries. He compared this power of the imagination, apparently so widely diffused in the culture at the time, with a similar weakness of mind 'which is abundantly exemplified in cases of partial madness; where a man will imagine almost anything, in some one particular direction, while the sanity of the mind, in other directions, continues unimpaired'. As regards 'madness', 'the truth is, that in many cases which are treated as madness, the mental disorder is nothing more than a very unhappy propensity to believe what the imagination shadows forth, in some particular direction in which it has been vehemently indulged' (*Philanthropist* 1814: II, 364). By implication witchcraft beliefs were thus a form of socially sanctioned collective madness, in which the power of the imagination was unchecked by reason.

The reference to 'madness' by way of explaining 'irrational' beliefs and practices was thoroughly fitting and conventional in this context. The single example from the *Philanthropist*, to which so many other cases could be added, can thus perhaps suffice to suggest the pertinence for perceptions of 'madness' of this approach to explaining savagery, barbarism, and superstition. The link established between the madman and the savage, or superstitious and vulgar mind, was to a degree common also to Lockean epistemology, since superstition and savage belief, equally with madness, were varieties of intellectual disorder. But the link of savage and madman allowed further a loose identification of madness with degeneracy, atavism, or lower forms of mental organization. This long antedated the theories of degeneracy produced in the wake of evolutionary biology and social Darwinism, and the modern concept of regression. The comparison of madman and savage was thus another way of forging connections between the apparently distinct categories established in common by reference to the advancing norms of 'reason'; it was a way of providing further sociological referents for 'madness' and of locating the category in the wider social landscape.

Although there was little apart from vague perceptions to ground the comparison of savage and madman (and as yet no well-conceived neurological account of a hierarchy of mental organization which could even plausibly be correlated with stages of 'civilization' or the development of the 'ego'), this was hardly inhibiting; the vagueness of the notions perhaps even enhanced their combination, and thus added to the halo of images and metaphors of the irrational which surrounded and environed the contemporary perceptions of madness.

The reviewer in the *Philanthropist* concluded his comparison of the 'public mind' in the sixteenth and nineteenth centuries, finally, with a plea for 'education', construed not simply as learning but as intellectual and moral training and formation in the broadest sense. 'It is the business of that strength of mind which education gives, to separate the cases in which that pliancy of mind to the beliefs of others is excessive and dangerous, from those in which it is reasonable and advantageous' (*Philanthropist* 1814: IV, 365); the strength and advance of civilization depended on such education, contributing to the moral and intellectual development of the 'public mind'. Thus under the influence of civilization, the mind, properly strengthened and supported, would be disposed, even 'in times of superstition', to resist the strong impressions which threaten to overwhelm weaker, more suggestible minds, and able to arbitrate dispassionately between the false and the true. In the 'treatment' and prevention, as in the diagnosis, of intellectual error, this prescription is again notably pertinent to conceptions of madness, since the programme for 'improvement', moral training, and character formation which it advanced, constituted the broader and more general plan in which the movement of 'moral medicine' and the moral treatment of the insane fit so tidily as distinctive specialities.

· 6 ·

THE PSYCHOLOGY OF SOCIAL CLASSES

As an exemplar of 'irrationality' the madman was one of a number of social figures who stood beyond the pale of adult rationality; his distance 'outside' was in addition marked off in a particular direction on the social scale. One 'fell' into insanity, or was 'reduced' to it, much as one would be reduced to bestiality or to helpless fatuity. Madness itself, and by its consequences, was a degradation, and there is no question of the contemporary social significance of falling to the level of the madman. It was thoroughly fitting that the outcast 'poor Tom, mad Tom' was emblematic for the condition of madmen; and likewise fitting that Tom Rakewell's Bedlam cell represented the lowest point in human declension and the pit of 'low life' in Hogarth's morality tale. Even gentlemen lunatics, however pitied on account of their loss of station, were reduced by the consequences of madness to brutish insensibility and incapacity; they thus required to be tended under the firm authority of keepers who were far their social inferiors. Madness was termed in some accounts a 'loss of the human station'. It was in practical terms a great leveller of social distinctions, in so far as it reduced all its victims, even a king, to the humiliations of being without reason. Despite their avowed sympathy for the insane, and their respect of them as 'moral beings', the philanthropists hardly shifted this long-standing sense of the madman's degradation, at the nadir of human society.

Beside this image of the madman as a general figure, with its base associations, there were however a series of more nuanced perceptions of different varieties of the mad, which recouped some measure of social status and respect for individuals among them. The descriptions of young female patients, for instance, were often affectingly drawn; these 'Ophelias' whose delicate and refined sensibilities had been wounded (perhaps) and maddened by a disappointment in love, evoked a dramatically different response and degree of sympathy from the naked figure of mad Tom. Although madness was a leveller, there were in fact often great distinctions made in the care and treatment of the mad according to their social background and degree of respectability. In medical theory, the different mental characteristics attributed to various social classes were likewise most influential in the delineation of clinical case-pictures; such characteristics were often directly associated with the (apparent) causes of insanity, physical and moral. To a significant degree the rich and poor suffered different insanities. The variations in mental capacities, inclinations, passions, etc. which apparently followed from the division of labour were highly relevant to conceptions of madness; and this was undoubtedly so, however much alienists claimed to approach and to observe the individual case, as a specimen of 'natural history'. The categories of medical psychology were shot-through with sociological allusions.

Contemporaries were, not surprisingly, quite interested in these matters. There was in particular a large body of speculation concerning the different susceptibilities to insanity, and to special forms of insanity, of the respective social classes. This literature was by and large frankly speculative and probably provides little other than a reflection of the prevailing ideological climate; but exactly for this reason it is extremely interesting as an index to the contemporary polite notions about the psychology or mental life of different social groups. There were it seemed varieties of madness, and exciting causes, to which the different classes appeared more or less susceptible. For broad purposes the varieties were subsumed under the general name madness, but nonetheless the contours of the category itself were drawn in considerable relief. The 'Ophelias' found a different spot or level than the 'poor Toms'. In turn the treatments prescribed for the myriad insanities were often deeply affected by such nuanced perceptions of social factors involved in the course of an insanity; and likewise they varied with the social character of its victim. In this respect as in so many others, madness was a social, and not a purely technical, category and as such was open to the sweeping influences of ideological currents. Pinel claimed to base his clinical work upon the 'natural history' of insanities; if 'naturalistic' by comparison to demonology, the practices of medical psychology were nonetheless thoroughly ideological. They were indeed hedged-in by moral judgements which reflected directly or indirectly the greater relations between the classes in the early nineteenth century.

'In proportion as man emerges from his primaeval State, do the Furies of disease advance upon him, and would seem to scourge him back into the paths of nature and simplicity.'

(*Quarterly Review* 1816: XV, 398)

The contemporary discussion about social factors affecting insanity occurred principally within a larger debate on madness and civilization. Whether insanity was 'on the increase' was the great statistical question; and this involved alienists and laymen in the largely fruitless task of trying to compare the prevalence of insanity in different times and places. The statistical inquiry invariably led to speculations about the causes of insanity and of its increase. In the English discussions the common theme was the 'advance of civilization', in which England was judged (perhaps not incidentally) the vanguard. Hence the greater likelihood of insanity there. The statistical question was thus referred to a greater discussion on whether, or in what measure, insanity was a distinctive disease of civilization. Since the statistical procedures were so very limited, and by their nature inconclusive, the frankly speculative discussions on the relation of madness to civilization are all the more important and revealing. What alienists and laymen tried to demonstrate with the statistics were in fact largely pre-formed opinions on the character of madness within their society. Similarly, in lieu of any systematic medical topographies, or genuine approaches to the epidemiology of contemporary mental disorders, the lists of the causes of insanity assembled by alienists – in which social factors bulk so largely – grow immensely in interest. Although these are difficult to distil down for any systematic information about the insane themselves, they are an invaluable clue to the contemporary state of opinion, and well reflect what alienists thought they knew about the social distribution of insanities in the population.

The theme 'madness and civilization' was elaborated along several different lines of inference, whose implications were at times mutually contradictory. One common line of argument derived from the description of madness as intellectual error, and its consequent assimilation to the class of superstition or savage thought. If madness represented, as some argued, an atavistic regression or throw-back from civilization, then the 'moral improvement' which the process of 'civilization' brought in its train could be conceived as its appropriate remedy. 'Civilization' in this sense would thus foster conditions which were inimical or unfavourable to such intellectual disorders as madness often represented. An older and more common view derived from a rather different sense of 'civilization'; here the advance of civilization seemed an unsettling force which inevitably disturbed individuals and disposed a portion of them to madness, as to other of the characteristic complaints of civilized life. In this fashion of expressing the 'madness and civilization' theme, insanity was not atavism but a disease of the highest civilization: those most cultured and refined indeed suffered its greatest incidence, since their minds were most taxed and most vulnerable to over-excitation, whereas savages were on the contrary too insensitive even to be capable of madness. There was finally a middle ground, of sorts, around the view that insanity was indeed a disease of civilization but one generally limited to those who experienced its anxieties without receiving its full benefits – notably proper education. If savages were happily immune, not so those 'marginal people' who suffered the strains and unnatural desires of modern life with few defences and thus were prone to madness as to ill health and debauchery generally. Schematically, in the most general terms of discussion, madness thus seemed variously a disorder characteristic of the savage and 'uncivilized', of the civilized and most refined, or of the imperfectly civilized. In fact the different views were not so disparate as a bald summary alone makes them seem; a summary better suggests the plasticity of terms in the discussion which for various purposes could be bent to measure.

The oldest of these views, placing madness among the risks attending civilized 'refinement', had roots at least as deep as the Renaissance. Burton's *The Anatomy of Melancholy* (1621), for instance, which offered a comprehensive summation of the varied expressions of the 'Elizabethan malady', was in general limited to disorders of the leisured and well-to-do, those for whom the term 'nervous complaints' had some possible bearing. Accordingly, it focused also on the particular susceptibilities to madness or melancholy which the well-to-do suffered, on account of their way of life and their mental characteristics. It was not at all a treatise on madness in the gross sense which Burton presented, and in this it faithfully reflected the prevailing conditions of medical practice. In Burton's day and for more than a century afterwards, the medicine of 'insanity' and related conditions was quite circumscribed in scope; it was generally limited to the well-to-do and to the treatment of their apparently characteristic nervous complaints. Under such circumstances it was natural for physicians servicing a rich clientele, to reflect principally and disproportionately on such nervous disorders as they actually treated. The early conditions under which the medicine of insanity was practiced thus provided one base for a tradition of thinking on the special 'madness' of the refined, the leisured, and the wealthy.

By 1733, when Cheyne published his study *The English Malady*, the link of madness with civilization was further developed, and elaborated in more general terms. Cheyne transformed, as if by ironic inversion, what foreigners intended as a libel against England into what he explained was an unfortunate fact and consequence of her greatness, but nonetheless a

125

mark of superior civilization. Apart from climatic influences, which he freely acknowledged, Cheyne attributed the characteristic 'English malady' to

> 'the Richness and Heaviness of our Food, the Wealth and Abundance of the Inhabitants (from their universal Trade), the Inactivity and sedentary Occupations of the better Sort (among whom this Evil mostly rages) and the Humour of living in great, populous and consequently unhealthy Towns, which have brought forth a Class and Set of Distempers, with atrocious and frightful Symptoms, scarce known to our Ancestors, and never rising to such fatal heights, nor afflicting such Numbers in any other known Nation. These nervous Disorders being computed to make almost one third of the Complaints of the People of Condition in England.' (Cheyne 1733: i–ii)

Among individuals, the 'liveliest' and 'quickest' spirits were most prone, whereas 'Fools, weak or stupid Persons, heavy and dull Souls, are seldom troubled with Vapours or Lowness of Spirits'. Because of her civilization, as Cheyne's argument implied, England numbered a greater proportion of such lively and quick spirits among her inhabitants than other nations.

The 'English malady' was not of course representative of the senses of 'madness' in contemporary usage, which were far broader. (Some seventeenth- and eighteenth-century physicians argued in fact that the 'nervous complaints' were not 'genuine madness' – or anything so gross – but stood only at its brink.) Nonetheless among nervous or mental conditions defined at the time, the apparently distinctive complaints ('hyps', 'spleen', 'vapours', 'nerves', lowness of spirits, melancholy, hysteria, etc.) of the leisured or prosperous were undoubtedly those most widely discussed in the medical literature; and most commonly treated, in private practices, at the spas and in the better madhouses. Thus to a degree the forms of 'madness' which most occupied professional attention were the prerogative of the upper ranks, since only they enjoyed the leisure to suffer them; and although other forms of madness were not ignored in medicine, it was obviously rather difficult in theory to assimilate gross madness immediately to the refined and often genteel complaints which 'nerves' generally represented.

From the end of the eighteenth century the medicine of insanity expanded in its scope dramatically, and its specialists, particularly in the public asylums, faced seemingly ever-increasing numbers of insane paupers. The change in the conditions of medical practice naturally affected at a remove the discussion in medical treatises of the 'madness and civilization' theme. For a time, despite the diversifying of medical practice, many treatises still continued to associate madness principally with the risks to which refined sensibilities were vulnerable. The alienists who lingered over the theme in this form were themselves primarily involved in private practices, away from the great towns; in the conditions of their work they probably actually observed something of the link they described. But there was an elaborated theoretical argument as well linking madness with refinement; and this was buttressed by a series of explanations (part novel, part traditional to the vocabulary of moralists) which linked specific features of 'civilized' life with the distinctive mental strains which were the undoing of the mind, and to which the 'refined' in particular were susceptible. Virtually all treatises in medical psychology contained references to the apparently low incidence of insanity among savages and among the ancients, by comparison with the rising numbers of the day which were attributed globally to the influences of 'civilization'. Thus 'civilization' in one or other sense figured widely in treatises as one way of marking out the distinctive character of contemporary madness.

Sir William Ellis expressed the conventional view succinctly in these terms:

'From the habits and mode of education of the upper ranks, particularly of the females, the brain and nervous system are kept in a state of constant over-excitement, whilst the frame is debilitated, from the muscles being rarely called into proper and regular exercise. Hence arises a high degree of susceptibility of disease, with little constitutional stamina, to resist the over-anxiety and other effects of the sudden changes in circumstances, peculiarly incident to the present times.' (Ellis 1838: v–vi)

Out of such causes, 'the fearful extent to which Insanity prevails'. Ellis's argument was of course widely familiar and virtually continuous with the view of Augustan moralists: madness was invariably brought on by such a weakening of the 'fibres', physical and moral, or alternatively, by other imprudent conduct supported by habits of 'extravagance', intemperance, or dissipation. With the familiar moral overtones so common among physicians of the period, Ellis reminded his readers that most owed their continuing sanity to the effects of their education and early formation; in 'unsettled times' only proper education, inculcating 'habits of self-government', 'thwarting inclinations, subduing passions', teaching the mind restraint and providing it with the capacity to 'abstract itself from consideration of painful events', could serve as a bulwark against insanity. The practical measures Dr Ellis counselled as precautions against madness were in fact hardly removed from what Augustan moralists, and notably Dr Johnson, had recommended (see Byrd 1974, and Fussell 1965). The famous work of John Barlow, *Man's Power over Himself to Prevent or Control Insanity* (1843), was likewise only the most egregious example of a lively and widely diffused tradition; this was a legacy from the past which left its marks scattered broadly in treatises of medical psychology.

The precise causes which excited madness in such 'unsettled times' were, however, the subject of more novel discussions, albeit rather inconclusively. Tuke, in summarizing several decades' argument for the *Manual of Psychological Medicine*, expressed the matter simply: 'There is an acuteness of sensibility, a susceptibility of the emotions, an intensive activity of the feelings, which seem to be peculiar to highly-civilized life' (Bucknill and Tuke 1858: 50). On the general principle that the susceptibility of an organ, physical or mental, to disease would increase in proportion to the amount of work required from it, insanity would naturally appear more frequently under civilized conditions. Civilization obviously required much greater work from the organs of the mental faculties; and within advanced nations insanity would naturally be concentrated among those who bore the greatest burdens of 'civilization'. The outstanding moral causes of insanity, which Tuke enumerated as 'fear, grief, reverses of fortune, speculation, domestic trouble, pride, ambition, great successes of any kind, religious fanaticism, etc.', were similarly more common among civilized than barbarous nations, more common among the refined than the vulgar; they took their toll accordingly (Bucknill and Tuke 1858: 50). Such arguments were very commonly advanced, doubtless in part because their very vagueness and generality allowed such a wide scope of explanation.

In one widely read account Dr Browne tried to explain the (reportedly) greater incidence of insanity in the United States, as compared with England, Wales, and Scotland. 'With luxury, indeed, insanity appears to keep equal pace'; this was Browne's starting point. The greater incidence of insanity in America 'probably depends on the rapid acquisition of wealth, and the luxurious social habits to which the good fortune of our transatlantic brethren has exposed them'. Thus far, the explanation appears consistent with Cheyne's description a century earlier of the debilitating effects of wealth in a prosperous nation. But Browne elaborated the argument with a long coda on the notion of 'civilization' which effectively blunts the force of the older explanation:

'the opinion has been hazarded, that as we recede, step by step, from the simple, that is, the savage manners of our ancestors, and advance in industry and knowledge and happiness, this malignant persecutor strides onward, signalizing every era in the social progress by an increase, a new hetacomb, of victims. Is insanity an inseparable adjunct to civilization? I spurn the supposition. The truth seems to be, that the barbarian escapes this scourge because he is exempt from many of the physical, and almost all the moral sources of mental excitement; and that the members of civilized communities are subjected to it, because the enjoyment and blessings of augmented power are abused; because the mind is roused to exertion without being disciplined, it is stimulated without being strengthened; because our selfish propensities are cultivated while our moral nature is left barren, our pleasures becoming poisonous; and because in the midst of a blaze of scientific light, and in the presence of a thousand temptations to multiply our immediate by a sacrifice of our ultimate gratifications, we remain in the darkest ignorance of our own mind, its true relations, its danger and its destiny. With civilization then come sudden and agitating changes and vicissitudes of fortune; vicious effeminacy of manners; complicated transactions; misdirected views of the objects of life; ambition and hopes, and fears, which man in his primitive state does not and cannot know. But these neither constitute, nor are they necessarily connected with, civilization. They are defects, obstacles which retard the advancement of that amelioration of condition towards which every discovery in art, or ethics, must ultimately tend. To these defects, and not to the amount of improvement, or refinement of a people is insanity to be traced.'

(Browne 1837: 52–3)

In certain of its echoes this could well be an evocation of Tocqueville. Dr Browne continued to believe himself that insanity was a risk to which the wealthier were particularly exposed, and to which they succumbed out of all proportion to their numbers in the population. 'The situation, education and habits of the wealthy classes are all more favourable to the development of the moral causes of insanity, than can be affirmed of the condition of the poor' (Browne 1837: 59), as he wrote, and he instances 'panics in the commercial classes', 'rapid influx and reflux of wealth' and 'ambitious projects', as moral causes especially fertile of insanities. The upper classes further were vastly more liable to hereditary madness, considering the wide extent of 'taint' in their stock. In 1837 when Dr Browne published his series of lectures on asylums, the statistics of insanity could still be used plausibly to support the contention that the rich fell insane far out of proportion to their numbers; among the inmates of asylums and private madhouses as officially recorded, a considerable proportion, concentrated in the private licensed madhouses, were 'wealthy' by some index, or at least not paupers. But the available figures massively over-represented the 'wealthy' insane, and in part simply reflected their far greater access to medical attentions; there was at the time little barring the commitment of as many private, fee-paying patients as presented themselves, whereas the public receptacles were overcrowded with insane paupers, and their over-spill into workhouses, for instance, was in no way reflected in the statistics of insanity.

In the event the greater and growing number of pauper lunatics was finally more telling. The theme of 'madness and civilization' was shifted further and further away from the old notion of 'refined' disorders of the leisured; the theme itself became diffuse and general, with only the broadest sociological referents. 'Civilization' came to suggest loosely the modern condition itself, which was commonplace – not the reserve of a special cultured or otherwise refined élite. The arguments about the effects of 'civilization' became accordingly more vague and unspecific, and doubtless weaker in their force. Dr Andrew Halliday, for instance, argued in 1828:

> 'The finer the organs of the mind have become by their greater development, or their better cultivation, if health is not made a part of the process, the more easily they are disordered. We seldom meet with insanity among the savage tribes of men; not one of our African travellers remark their having seen a single madman. Among the slaves in the West Indies it very rarely occurs; and, as we have elsewhere shown from actual returns, the contented peasantry of the Welsh mountains, the western Hebrides, and the wilds of Ireland, are almost free from this complaint. It is by the over-exertion of the mind, in overworking its instruments so as to weaken them, while the healthy functions of the body are, by a kind of reaction, interfered with, that insanity may be said to take place in a great number of instances.'
>
> (Halliday 1828: 79–80)

Such terms evoked a cluster of associations to 'nature', against which an 'artificial' society was counterposed along with its benefits and characteristic vices. The phrase 'over-exertion of the mind' recalls an old theme common in theories of the temperaments. It was prominent in Burton's *The Anatomy of Melancholy*, which associated any intense application of the mind with the risks of overstraining it, and thus treated madness almost in the nature of an occupational or constitutional hazard particular to those professions and temperaments which are too one-sidedly 'mental'. By comparison to Burton's, Halliday's arguments hardly convince in their crude generality.

Dr George Man Burrows suggested a still more diffuse link of madness with civilization:

> 'many of the causes inducing intellectual derangement, and which are called moral, have their origin not in individual passions or feelings, but in the state of society at large; and the more artificial, i.e., civilized, society is, the more do these causes multiply and extensively operate. The vices of civilization, of course, must conduce to their increase; but even the moral virtues, religion, politics, nay philosophy itself, and all the best feelings of our nature, if too enthusiastically incited, class among the causes producing intellectual disorders. The circumstances influencing their occurrence are to be sought in all the various relations of life, in constitutional propensities, and, above all, perhaps in education.' (Burrows 1828: 18)

The 'state of society at large' of course influenced the 'moral condition' of its citizenry in manifold ways, most dramatically during the

> 'great political or civil revolutions in states [which] are always productive of great enthusiasms in the people, and correspondent vicissitudes in their moral condition; and as all extremes in society are exciting causes [of insanity], it will occur, that in proportion as the feelings are acted upon, so will insanity be more or less frequent.'
>
> (Burrows 1828: 20)

Lesser perturbations and upsets produced accordingly fewer or more minor insanities. Carried to such lengths, the effort to link madness with advancing civilization lost any specific reference to the 'refined' as a social group and pertained rather to the 'moral condition' of the population as a whole. Toward the end of the century Henry Maudsley expressed the theme, as he and his generation received it, by a simple comparison of the savage and the civilized man, which anticipated in its overtones Freud's *Civilisation and its Discontents*:

> 'the savage has few and simple wants springing from his appetites, and them he gratifies; he is free from the manifold artificial passions and desires which go along with the multiplied industries, the eager competitions, the social ambitions of an active civilisation; he is free too from the conventional restraints upon his natural passions which

131

civilisation imposes, and suffers not from a conflict between urgent desire of gratification and the duty to suppress all manifestations thereof, a conflict which sometimes proves too great a strain upon the mind of a civilised person.'   (Maudsley 1879: 129–32)

(See also Rothman 1971: 113–19, and Altschule 1957: ch. 7.) This was in general the fate of the discussion on madness and civilization, and its redirection was evident from the early part of the century. As a result the 'lay sermons' which the spectacle of madness moved so many physicians to pronounce widened dramatically in their scope. Physicians had in the eighteenth century criticized the vestiges of an aristocratic ethos, in the manner of Fielding or Hogarth; from the beginning of the nineteenth century they would take in the whole sweep of manners and mores in the population in so far as these reflected the 'moral condition' of the nation.

Diagnosing 'madness' was hence an easy route to moralizing. It was typical to refer madness back to its exciting moral causes; and this allowed physicians from an early period to comment upon those aspects of the way of life, and those mental characteristics, of the victim which provided madness its seat. Since the fate of the madman was so widely believed to contain a cautionary moral tale, physicians hardly overstepped their position by drawing the appropriate lesson. Not surprisingly so many case-histories, from the seventeenth century onwards, read like senti-mental tales, or indeed minor morality plays; they provide not merely the customary advice on preventing and treating madness, but the appropriate moral evaluations of the excesses from which madness in so many if not most cases resulted. The 'nervous complaints' so common from the seven-teenth century, which furnished much of the clinical material for phys-icians and mad-doctors, prompted comment specifically on the 'refined' or decadent aspects of life among the wealthy which seemed broadly the basis of their characteristic disorders. Later, when the conditions of medical practice widened, and greater and greater numbers of the pauper insane began to receive medical attentions, the scope for moral comment widened accordingly. Although specific insanities of refinement continued to be described, increasingly the bulk of insanities were referred by their moral causes to the conditions of life, and the mental characteristics, of the labouring classes.

The 'physical and moral condition of the labouring classes' became an important topic of investigation for a variety of medical and philanthropic ends; and it was likewise notably pertinent for the understanding and description of madness. The general demoralization of the labouring poor, particularly in large towns, was easily associated in the rhetoric of moralists with such unruliness and disorder as 'madness' commonly and loosely suggested. Beyond vague and associative links in perceptions, a range of more specific sociological allusions was also important in the theorizing of medical psychology. The novel category 'moral insanity', for instance, well illustrates how far the understanding of 'madness' could come to depend upon sociological referents. Although in its incidence this 'moral insanity' was not of course an exclusive prerogative of the poor, it owed a great deal to the investigations of the 'moral and physical condition' sort. In its essentials the category was effectively constructed as a generalization (and exaggeration) of attributes which polite society recognized widely among sections of the labouring classes. In this and other ways the link of madness with specific aspects of the way of life and the supposed mental characteristics of the labouring poor was vigorously proposed – and in muddled and baldly prejudicial terms. In consequence, more dramatically even than in the earlier medicine of insanity, the perceptions of 'madness' (especially in its grosser forms) emerged in the early nineteenth century ideologically charged; what was 'madness' was refracted by moral evaluations which inhered in the relations between the classes.

There were, of course, still traces of an older moralism about the poor. The same Dr Browne who wrote acutely about the psychology of restless Americans suggested that madness was less likely among the poor. 'Poverty enjoins a compulsory temperance; it shuts out the longings of ambition; it acquaints with the realities of life, and excludes the effects of sentimentalism; it often trains the body to vigour, and in all these respects may be styled a prophylactic'. Thus, 'the agricultural population, which presents poverty in its more attractive forms and enjoys its best privileges, is to a great degree exempt from insanity'. Sources of this argument, with asides about the 'contented peasantry' and the limited mental horizons of the poor which disciplined severely their flights of fancy, are not difficult to locate. It was, however, increasingly exceptional within discussions on madness and civilization; ironically Browne expressed these opinions in roughly the same years when Dr James Cowles Prichard was developing out of his contact in practice with the pauper insane of Bristol the concept of 'moral insanity', which found such broad and ready assent.

Browne's was very much an old fashion. From the early decades of the nineteenth century alienists were characteristically preoccupied not with the 'vigours' which poverty bred, but with demoralization. The social factors which were held to influence insanity, and which were listed among its moral causes, were increasingly factors around and about the poor. There were most evidently the 'disorders', physical and moral, which seemed characteristic of the life in which the poor subsisted, and which came to represent in the general shape of the 'residuum' the principal defect and festering sore on the body of civilization. The image itself evoked an endless vocabulary for criticizing aspects of life among the poor which could pertinently be adduced as explanations of madness.

The simple, massive fact of pauper insanity took some time to be registered. It was not until the mid-century that improved statistics of insanity finally demonstrated beyond question what had doubtless been the case for generations: the overwhelming preponderance of paupers among the 'insane'. Hack Tuke pointed out simply that, based on returns of the numbers of officially registered 'insane' on 1 January 1877 (which were considerable underestimates), out of a total of some 66,000 lunatics more than 59,000 were recorded as paupers. 'The large majority of lunatics under legal restraint', he concluded 'undoubtedly belong to the pauper population' (Tuke, D. H. 1878: 89). Further, over the previous half-century and more, 'the apparent increase of insanity was mainly marked among those who became pauper patients' (Tuke, D. H. 1878: 91). The registering of such numbers was in the event several steps away from eugenics proposals.

From the mid-century onwards discussion of the pauper insane in Britain, and even more dramatically in France and Germany, drew heavily on the notion of 'degeneracy' (see for example the widely influential work of Morel 1857). It is less well known that earlier discourses on the moral causes of insanity (and likewise of criminality) in fact long antedated the rise of theories which flirted with genetic determinism; and indeed these provided the subsoil in which the vague and pseudo-scientific notions of 'degeneration' later rooted. The older views, however inchoately expressed, were in this respect perhaps the more significant and interesting.

At the height of the vogue for notions of degeneracy Tuke expressed in conventional terms the argument which had persisted over half a century: 'wherever there is most pauperism, there, as a general rule, will be the largest amount of insanity; not merely because insanity pauperises, but because malnutrition and the manifold miseries attendant upon want favour the development of mental disease' (Tuke, D. H. 1878: 95). These 'manifold miseries' were responsible for the 'mental stagnation', intellectual debility, irresponsibility, and irrationality of the poor; and behind the miseries the common 'moral causes' of insanity were prominent.

'Intemperance stands out in lurid relief, as the foremost cause of the disorder.' Since intemperance was a characteristic immorality of civilized society, this prompted Tuke to a further conventional allusion to the 'madness and civilization' theme:

'Mr Bright's "residuum" of a civilised people, and a tribe of North American Indians are alike uneducated, but, notwithstanding, present totally different conditions of life. [However mean or savage the Indians' existence] almost anything is better than that substratum of civilised society which is squalid, and drunken and sensual; cursed with whatever of evil the ingenuity of the civilised man has invented, but not blessed with the counteracting advantages of civilisation.'

(Tuke, D. H. 1878: 92–4)

Across the half-century before 1878 when Tuke's article (on 'Insanity chiefly in relation to the working classes') appeared, this line of argument had become commonplace. It enjoyed several different supports and expressions: notably in the lists compiled of the 'moral causes' of madness; in the language of derogation which the reformers of manners and the writers on 'police' bequeathed to lay and medical philanthropists of the early nineteenth century; in the diffusion of the concept of 'moral insanity' and its analogues; and in the revived importance within the linguistic texture of medical psychology of ancient metaphors which represented the mind as a hierarchically ordered system of parties or faculties in quasi-political relations.

To the so-called 'moral causes' of insanity the early practitioners of medical psychology devoted a disproportionate amount of their interest, which was of course fitting considering their common predilections for 'moral treatment'. Virtually all serious medical treatises on the insanities contained a discussion of their 'physical' causes, whether from brain lesions or cerebral deterioration, hereditary predispositions, or other 'constitutional' factors. But apart from the case of a few clearly defined organic complaints, there was little understanding of 'physical' causes which was not rudimentary or often fanciful. Post-mortem examinations of the brains of the insane yielded few consistent findings, and the advance to understanding madness through pathological anatomy was effectively blocked. Hereditary influences were subsumed under the vague notion of 'taint' or 'impure stock', since there were of course no means for studying the inheritance of specific traits. An understanding of 'physical' causes offered in any case few opportunities for treatment, whereas the referral of madness to a series of exciting and predisposing 'moral causes' opened large possibilities for treatment by moral influences, designed to undo and counteract the effects of earlier moral factors. In the contemporary ideological climate, so animated by talk of 'moral improvement', it was hardly remarkable that the primary approach to madness, wherever plausible, lay via positing some intellectual, 'moral', or emotional 'lesion' of which it was an effect.

The contemporary discussion of the moral causes, both predisposing and exciting, associated with such 'lesions' was thus highly significant – and also highly revealing of the greater themes to which alienists and likewise laymen referred the problem of madness. The early table 'of the causes of insanity' which Dr Black compiled from the records of Bethlem was a simple enumeration of often random factors associated with the circumstances of the inmates' admission; it was a rag-bag of causes which included prominently: 'misfortunes, troubles, disappointments, grief' (the most frequent cause), 'family and hereditary' factors, 'fevers', 'religion and Methodism', 'love', 'drink and intoxication', 'fright'. Later lists, particularly with the increasing vogue for moral treatment, were rather more specific and focused on particular moral influences. Beyond identifying some or other gross precipitating event which seemed an obvious prelude or catalyst to the outbreak of madness (in 1851, for example, 'overexcitement at the Great Exhibition' was one notable moral cause), alienists tried also to characterize the habits and general demeanour of the victim; such enduring characteristics were then implicated in the madness, for which some exciting event had supplied the igniting spark. Thus Thomas Bakewell listed 'all violent passions', 'indeed, all that train of painful feelings which arise from our sinful natures' as moral causes of insanity, and he cautioned accordingly: 'Let the proud man reflect, that the extreme indulgence of his arrogant notions, may bring him to be humbled in the dust, by wearing the chains of the maniac' (Bakewell 1809: 21). Faulty or 'injudicious' education was, on the grounds of such an argument, the principal predisposing cause of madness; it was actually conducive to madness, in so far as it imposed 'too lenient a government, allowing the passions to act uncontrolled and unsubdued, and never exercising that wholesome moral restraint which seems necessary to promote the happiness, as well as to conduce to the integrity of the health of the individual'. Although expressed in general and traditional terms, such criticism of faulty or immoral education was of course often focused in the event on the poor and on families of labourers who failed to instil proper norms of behaviour and self-discipline in their offspring. The moralism of alienists merged easily with moralisms from other quarters.

Among the moral causes which excited madness, 'pecuniary embarrass-ments', 'reverses of fortune', 'intense mental exertion', etc., were commonplace, but there were also and characteristically a range of con-ditions and events more distinctively pertinent to the culture of the urban poor. Many descriptions of the moral causes of insanity in fact echoed the language of derogation in which observers described the general 'physical and moral condition' of the poor, as if madness, like crime, suicide, and ill health, were a natural consequence and correlate of the disorder in which the poor lived. Intemperance, which was both a physical and moral cause, 'the hydra of modern days', appeared as Earle suggested, 'to be the most prolific [cause] of mental disease' of all; public drunkenness was especially to be criticized, since it fostered a whole subculture which proved the seed-bed of unruliness and 'extravagant passions' (Earle 1837: 117).

The 'want of finer moral feelings' among the poor, of which many signs were adduced, was similarly taken as a frequent source and correlate of madness; this was the suggestion among many that the emotional life of the poor was more primitive and less checked by civilized restraints. Because of the character of their labour the poor or the labouring masses generally developed more the 'animal' than the intellectual or moral nature of man, and thus fell prey more frequently to 'animal excesses'. The improvidence of the poor, their love of cruelty, their repugnance for continuous labour, and so on, were again involved at a remove among such cultural factors as could dispose people to certain varieties of mad-ness.

The novel concept 'moral insanity' served with its wide diffusion eventually to summarize a number of these notions. Although anticipated by Dr Arnold and by Pinel and Esquirol in France, the concept was spread in England principally through the work of Dr James Cowles Prichard, physician to St Peter's Hospital and the Infirmary at Bristol. By 'moral insanity' (which prefigured the modern notion 'psychopathy') Prichard referred to a madness without delusions or hallucination, characterized by 'a morbid perversion of the natural feelings, affections, inclinations, temper, habits, moral dispositions, and natural impulses' (Prichard 1835: 12–13). In the case-history examples of moral insanity which he published, he included an alcoholic squire, a middle-aged gentlewoman who suffered a strange restlessness, a gentleman who developed an ob-sessional tidiness, and so forth. In its general formulation, however, the category seemed evidently more suitable to describe serious and threaten-ing disorders than quirks and personal eccentricities; and its greater use was in fact to describe criminal activity and vicious, immoral, or anti-social behaviour. It spread across many varieties of anti-social conduct, some-what in the manner of the modern term 'psychopathy' but on a far greater scale and with even vaguer referents. The diagnosis was even in its own terms vague; since moral insanity arose as a 'lesion' of the moral faculties, it was evident only through its symptoms, i.e. through the 'perverted' and generally callous anti-social behaviour of an individual who was other-wise not deranged. The potential scope of the category was accordingly very wide; the actual uses of the category expanded greatly the boundaries of 'genuine madness' as a medical term; and indeed opened a long con-troversy with the legal profession as to the merits and precise definition of a concept of limited or diminished responsibility in the disposition of the law.

In its strictly formal sense 'moral insanity', like other categories of madness, was a neutral, psychological term which did not depend upon any sociological referents; it was strictly applicable only to individual case-histories which evidenced sudden or inexplicable changes in a person's 'moral sensibility', demeanour, and disposition. The norms from which it represented gross deviation, were themselves 'individual', given in the person's past 'normal' self, which the madness had perverted. Thus the case-histories of the morally insane commonly described their perversion of affections by contrast to, and often as a sudden and immoderate depar-ture from, their previous normal and sane conduct and feelings. As a medical category 'moral insanity' likewise implied in itself no social aetiology; although its predisposing and exciting causes were apparently far more often 'moral' (or 'environmental') than 'constitutional', alienists were loath, beyond the individual case, to suggest formally, explicitly, and in general terms any social causation or indeed consistent social correlates of the condition.

Nonetheless, through the uses to which they were actually put, 'moral insanity' and like terms acquired a halo of social connotations, and sug-gested a range of allusions to the conditions of life of different social groups. The morbid perversion of the affections and inclinations which moral insanity represented was thus referred, by a loose associative logic, not simply to events and upsets in an individual patient's case-history, but also and more significantly to cultural traits, ways of living, and mental characteristics which pertained to social groups at large. Alienists com-monly suggested that widely based cultural traits were in some measure pathogenic, although they rarely formalized such suggestions into explicit statements on the social aetiology of madness. The links between madness and cultural traits were not the weaker for being in part implicit; on the contrary, they were doubtless more pervasive and suggestive for not being rigorously examined.

How the different social groups variously fell insane was a question which clearly engaged alienists but to which, lacking any serious epidemiological investigations, they brought only largely impressionistic answers. The link of madness with cultural traits and ways of living was widely posited (implicitly, for example, in the case of 'moral insanity'), but it was principally supported by the evidence of moralists, who characterized the manners and mores of different groups loosely enough that these could plausibly be construed as 'moral causes' of insanity. From criticizing manners and mores, it was but a short leap to suggesting that the 'excesses' of blameworthy social practices and habits were the prelude to, or indeed the cause of, madness; many of the contemporary connections of madness with manners and mores were established across the conduits of this moral evaluation.

There was yet another level, finally, on which social categories invaded medical descriptions. The very naming of madness itself as a condition was commonly made in terms ripe with social allusions. Whatever groups were more or less prone to madness, the condition itself was often represented and conceived in figurative language which invariably recalled social life. It was the language of social order, hierarchy, the division of classes and factions, and political strife.

The contempory metaphors of mind were commonly 'political' – in a loose or extended sense. They represented the mind as a hierarchy of orders or parties. Madness accordingly was described as a variety of internal 'political conflict' – much in the manner of Freud's phrase describing the instinctual 'revolt from below'. Such metaphors of mind were of course common among the ancients; the *Republic*, most famously, is an extended comparison of the soul (and the proper relations, in harmony and health, between its parts) and the state, whose justice and order owe equally to a proper relation of parties.

Among the early medical psychologists, and earlier among the Augustan moralists, such metaphors were again commonplace, and doubtless not simply for incidental reasons. The famous passage in Cicero's *Tusculan Disputations* which describes the soul on the pattern of a hierarchical state, was one of the more popular citations used to embellish medical treatises on insanity. The part of the soul gifted with reason, 'the mistress and queen of the world', was in Cicero's comparison, destined to assume ascendancy over the elements of 'weakness, despondency, servility', much as the ruler stood in relation to the crowd, or 'even as the master over the slave, or the general over the soldier, or the parent over the son'. Extending the comparison, Cicero suggested further that if any soul succumbed to his weaker elements and wavered from the firm control of reason, he could 'be fettered and tightly bound by the guardianship of friends and relations'; such persons 'therefore we shall have almost to keep in chains and guard closely like slaves, whilst those who will be found more steadfast, though not of the highest strength, we shall have to warn to be mindful of honour, like good soldiers recalled to duty' (Cicero 1927: 201–03). Metaphors of this type are so pervasive in Western ethics that it is perhaps hardly noteworthy to point out how fundamentally the attributes of reason are borrowings from descriptions of government and authority. But given the importance of other, more particular allusions to social factors in the contemporary conceptions of madness, such pervasive metaphors are perhaps worthy of some attention.

When Pinel suggested that 'the doctrine in ethics of balancing the passions of men by others of equal or superior force, is not less applicable to the practice of medicine, than to the science of politics' (Pinel 1806: 228), this was not a decorative metaphor; it announced a cardinal principle of the 'moral medicine' which the *idéologues* promoted. There was a constant and explicit analogy drawn out of the 'resemblance between the art of governing mankind and that of healing their diseases'; the enlightened physician accordingly took the place of authority, representing the sovereignty and the royal function of reason, which were alienated and overthrown in the madman. To the madman in this political and social metaphor was left the part of the irrational, the vulgar and yet powerful energies which required the direction of reason vested in authority (Pinel 1806: 228).

From the other side, representing not the government of reason, but its overthrow, Dickens's famous description of the Gordon Riots in *Barnaby Rudge* well illustrates the forces of unreason and irrationality, of which the madman's wild energies could serve as broadly emblematic:

'If Bedlam gates had been flung open wide, there would not have issued forth such maniacs as the frenzy of that night had made. There were men there who danced and trampled on the beds of flowers as though they trod down human enemies, and wrenched them from their stalks, like savages who twisted human necks. There were men who cast their lighted torches in the air, and suffered them to fall upon their heads and faces, blistering the skin with deep unseemly burns. There were men who rushed up to the fire, and paddled in it with their hands as if in water; and others who were restrained by force from plunging in, to gratify their deadly longing. On the skull of one drunken lad – not twenty, by his looks – who lay upon the ground with a bottle to his mouth, the lead from the roof came streaming down in a shower of liquid fire, white hot, melting his head like wax. . . . But of all the howling throng not one learnt mercy from, or sickened at, these sights; nor was the fierce, besotted, senseless rage of one man glutted.'

(Dickens 1841: IV, 140)

The fury of the 'mob', sketched with such excited strokes, is perhaps finally the best reminder of the mass of images – of disorder, unreason, and irrationality – which clustered around 'madness'; and which, through the links of vague and diffuse perceptions, provided some measure of its content and of the language for its description.

· 7 ·

UNIVERSAL REASON
AND
INDIVIDUAL DIFFERENCES

In the history of psychology less than half a century separated Condillac's *Traité des sensations* (1754) from the writings on physiognomy of Lavater and Gall, and the physiological researches of Cabanis. The changes in the interim were momentous; the new styles of research emerging at the end of the eighteenth century reflect a turn in the development of psychology. Across the several intervening decades the confident enlightened belief in universal reason and the psychological unity of mankind was progressively displaced and increasingly supplanted by a newer 'science of man'. The newer science was not premissed on 'universal reason' but oriented rather toward the study and documentation of human variation and individual differences.

This broad change of direction in the history of psychology has long been associated with the Romantic movement, and in the history of social thought, with the vogue for 'organicism' and historicism as against the variants of Enlightenment rationalism.[1] For the study of the mind the change was also reflected prominently in, and partly explains, the growing interest at the end of the eighteenth century in mental disorders, and the increasing import for moral medicine and for psychology of their systematic study. The development of medical psychology through its early years indeed represented one of the more important branches of inquiry into 'individual differences', of which the peculiarities of the mad were an endlessly fertile and fascinating source.

The diversity of human types, genius and idiocy, the unique personality, the extremes of human experience, the pathological and abnormal: such themes were accorded a special status within the new psychological and physiological researches. The topics themselves were not absent from earlier mental philosophy, but their role and place were decidedly marginal. Madness and idiocy in particular were interesting principally as

142

boundary-markers of the limits of reason, and not as instances of diversity. 'Individual differences' broadly were of course explicable on the premises of Lockean psychology, as consequences of men's different education and particular experience; they represented, however, more often challenges to its epistemology than its characteristic objects of study. The dominant tenor of Lockean sensationalism stressed the basic psychological unity and equality of men, not their diversity. However varied, men themselves *qua* men were taken as equal or very closely similar in their natural faculties and in their capacities to receive sense impressions of the external world. Even great empirical variations among men were thus ultimately referred, with some plausibility or with straining ingenuity, to the different experiences which had impressed themselves on their minds. Helvétius wrote simply: 'Quintilien, Locke, et moi, disons: *L'inégalité des esprits est l'effet d'une cause connue, et cette cause est la différence de l'éducation*' (Helvétius 1818: II, 71). Apart from the boundary cases, like idiots, the blind, the deaf, and those grossly deformed, which were problematic for any contemporary epistemology, 'tous les hommes jouissant des facultés attachés à leur nature sont égaux', as the article on equality in Voltaire's *Dictionnaire philosophique* proclaimed (Voltaire 1835: VII, 472).

In the event Lockean sensationalism proved most vulnerable in the form in which it was represented by the French followers of Locke, notably Helvétius and Condillac, who asserted virtually an absolute equality and equivalence of men at birth. By the end of the eighteenth century the accumulating evidence of moral and physical variability, much of it assembled from the practices of the new clinical medicine and medical psychology, was brought to bear in an overwhelming challenge to sensationalism; the target was in particular Condillac. The *Traité des sensations* which Condillac published in 1754, was perhaps the most radical statement of sensationalism, since it treated sensations alone as the source of all ideas and mental powers, and as the sufficient unit of analysis for explaining all mental life.

The *Traité* introduced the famous explanatory fiction of the sentient statue. This was later highly vulnerable to the physiologists, but it well served Condillac as a paradigm to demonstrate how an individual organism might acquire faculties. The statue itself represents man's perfect organic structure; were it depicted, it would doubtless appear with the regular and harmonious proportions and the generalized physiognomy characteristic of neoclassical beauty. It signified in Condillac's exposition the universal organic substratum and sensorium, which was the endowment of all men and which provided the foundation and seat of all mental powers. As the exposition opens, the senses of the statue are described as 'asleep', and hence the 'soul' which later animates the statue is conceived as totally lacking in 'ideas'. It has by definition never been penetrated by any sense impression. In its course the text proceeds to awaken and unlock the sleeping senses one by one, beginning with smell as the sense which contributes least to human knowledge. Progessively step by step the text tries to demonstrate how from simple sense experiences alone (like the smell of a rose), the soul in the statue would acquire its full complement of desires and passions, and the faculties of memory, association, judgement, etc.

The only concession to diversity which the *Traité* allowed was an acknowledgement that some individuals, at times, experience their sense impressions more vividly than others. But this barely marred the generality and consistent universalism of the text, which was premissed on the notion that all individuals receive, with fundamentally identical sensory equipment, the same impressions from nature.

By contrast, the physiologists at the end of the eighteenth century documented a remarkable variability in human 'sensitivity' or receptivity to 'experience', and a wide variation in different organisms' capacities to adjust to their environments. When Cabanis in the Years IV and V presented a series of physiological papers to the Classes des sciences morales et politique of the Institut, he launched implicitly a sustained critique of the notion of psychological equality. Against Condillac, he suggested that the sentient statue was an unreal and tendentious abstraction; it was not a useful explanatory fiction, since it badly misrepresented the true, and immensely variable, character of discrete active organisms in their respective environments. The papers which Cabanis himself produced on physiology hence did not concern the sensations of a single (abstracted) subject, like the Condillac statue; they described a range of *typical* subjects whose mental lives varied considerably depending upon their age, temperament, sex, state of health, diet, environing climate, and so on. There was indeed no 'type commun à tout le genre humain', but many variations (Cabanis Year VI: 66). The papers published in the *Mémoires de l'Institut* accordingly describe a wide variability; what Cabanis began to study were the different interconnections between man's physical and moral states. How, for instance, did 'sensitivity' (*sensibilité*) vary, depending on an individual subject's age, sex, temperament, state of health, history of disease, passions, and dispositions. The consequences of such factors on men's 'capacity to feel' were evidently enormous; 'les hommes ne se resemblent point par la manière de sentir', as Cabanis wrote (Year VI 66). Thus in his research programme for a more adequate descriptive psychology and physiology, it was clearly more important to study variations among men, and not primarily their similarities or their abstract 'capacity to feel' in the manner of Condillac's statue.

Much of the evidence on which Cabanis relied and which he brought to bear derived from physicians, and from mad-doctors and early alienists. Physicians had of course long been concerned to describe variations in the 'strength' of organs or the general 'tension of the fibres' which were symptomatic of pathology. Under the conditions of the new clinical medicine in hospitals, such observation of differences became more comprehensive and systematic; the gradual diffusion of uniform procedures and standard methods of examination and record-taking also allowed in time the establishment of broadly-based 'norms'.[2] Against such norms individual differences could easily be registered, and indeed measured.

The medicine of insanity was likewise a fertile source of evidence. Mad-doctors had traditionally relied on one or other doctrine of human 'constitutions'. What they described was accordingly often an array of human types (representing the different constitutions), in which different sorts of madness could arise. Hence the link of melancholy with the 'Saturnine temperament', and the like. Across centuries a great welter of such notions grew up, though with little appreciable impact on the prevailing philosophical psychologies. From the late eighteenth century the opportunities of actually observing the mad multiplied dramatically. The prestige of treating (and studying) the mad likewise increased enormously; it became indeed an emblem of philanthropy and 'moral medicine'. It was perhaps the coincidence of these two facts which accounts for the sudden and remarkable prominence of madness as a topic – in medical, psychological, and philanthropic discussions. For whatever reasons the cataloguing of human differences which medical psychology signally advanced reflected back quickly on discussions of 'man' in philosophic discourse.

The observations on 'difference' from medicine and medical psychology accumulated in some respects helter-skelter, without at times the benefit of explicit or elaborated systems. It was the work of Cabanis and other physiological researchers which served to systematize and generalize, or at least to frame the diverse observations. The so-called 'physiological' researches actually stretched from studies on reflexes and descriptions of the higher mental processes to the laws of individual human development and prescriptions in ethics (conceived as a physiologically informed 'moral science'). For Cabanis and his associates, who were still faithful to Enlightenment philosophies of history, equality remained the *telos* of human society and advancing civilization. But its realization evidently required finer attention to particular human weaknesses, frailties, and inequalities than Helvétius or Condillac had understood. On this view the work of 'moral medicine' within the range of human inequalities still promised, beyond returning diseased individuals to their previously 'normal' state, the greater perfection of the human species.

However the *idéologues* formulated their notions, the new psychology and 'science of man' which drew upon and systematized evidence of physiological diversity and mental dissimilarities marked a sharp break with the notions of 'universal reason' or psychological equality; and thus the forms of madness, among other 'differences', acquired a new pertinence for psychology and for the greater conception of 'man'. The *idéologues'* work illustrates this connection strongly and directly; it was also, however, more generally based, even long after the *idéologues* had dropped from fashion.

In other contemporary branches of inquiry into 'individual differences', madness was likewise a central object. The observation of mental disorders provided important materials and impetus notably for physiognomy, 'craniology', and later phrenology. Lavater's influential essays and hodge-podge *Fragments* on physiognomy included numerous profiles of idiots, maniacs, melancholics, and so on.[3] For the physiognomist the case of the madman or the idiot was indeed particularly interesting. According to Lavater, 'physiognomy is the science or knowledge of the correspondence between the external and internal man, the visible superficies and the invisible contents' (see Lavater 1806). The general problem for this 'science' was to divine or discover what 'invisible contents' would correspond regularly with certain observable or 'visible superficies'. The point was not simply to describe or catalogue external (superficial) variations, but to learn how from such signs to 'read' what was within. The madman and the idiot were for these ends rare and valuable cases: their 'invisible contents' were in fact unusually if not uniquely familiar, and visible. Madmen and idiots were extreme types who were singled out to receive treatment precisely because their inner contents had become visible. Hence an actual collection of madmen in an asylum was a highly promising subject for physiognomists, who could attempt simply to assemble empirically some set of physical traits correlated with the different, self-evident mental characters of the mad. For a 'science' attentive to human variations, the extreme differences and pronounced abnormalities which madness and idiocy represented were naturally particularly revealing – or by their exaggeration they facilitated the physiognomists' task of 'reading' character.

Opponents of Pastor Lavater, notably Professor Lichtenberg and Sir Charles Bell, were equally interested if on different grounds in examining the insane. Lichtenberg and Bell styled their researches 'pathognomy', or the science of the varying expressions of the human face as these reflect different emotions. (Physiognomy more typically correlated character traits with fixed aspects of anatomy, including the structure of the skull; on pathognomy, see Lichtenberg 1966.) The search to describe the characteristic *expressions* of the mad and the idiotic was as persistent as efforts to discover their distinctive cranial anatomy or fixed facial features. Bell's great work on *The Anatomy and Philosophy of Expression* included a famous discussion on the proper pictorial representation of madness; this required of the artist, Bell suggested, a close understanding of its active passions and of the facial muscles these engaged. The representation of the madman was not just incidentally interesting. The greater purpose of Bell's work was 'to lay the foundation for studying the influence of the mind upon the body . . . [as] deduced from the structure of man, and the comparative anatomy of animals' (Bell, C. 1847, cited in Hunter and Macalpine 1963: 599); the madman was particularly interesting for this purpose since his condition represented a reversion of sorts to animal-like expressivity.[4] The madman accordingly revealed certain basic passions with unique vividness, stripped of their overlay of the higher emotions whose configuration of facial muscles was often so complicated. Hence the madman was close to brute, simple, uncivilized expressivity.

Bell sketched for his treatise 'the prevailing character and physiognomy of a madman', evidently a 'raving maniac', after making a visit to Bedlam in July 1805. He described his typical subject 'lying in his cell regardless of every thing, with a death-like settled gloom upon his countenance';

> 'If you watch him in his paroxysm you may see the blood working to his head; his face acquires a darker red, he becomes restless; then rising from his couch he paces his cell and tugs his chains; now his inflamed eye is fixed upon you, and his features lighten up into wildness and ferocity.' (Bell, C. 1847: 179)

This was the scene as Bell himself drew it. In his gloss on the sketch Bell wrote that it would be wrong 'to represent this expression by the swelling features of passion and the frowning eyebrow'; the mad were not simply victims of an overbearing passion, since there was also 'a vacancy in their laugh, and a want of meaning in their ferociousness'. Thus,

> 'The theory upon which we are to proceed in attempting to convey this peculiar look of ferocity amidst the utter wreck of the intellect, I conceive

147

to be, that the expression of mental energy should be avoided, and consequently the action of all those muscles which indicate senti-ment. . . . To learn the character of the countenance, when devoid of human expression, and reduced to the state of brutality, we must have recourse to the lower animals, and study their looks of timidity, of watchfulness, of excitement, and of ferocity. If these expressions are transferred to the human face, I should conceive that they will irresist-ibly convey the idea of madness, vacancy of mind, and mere animal passion.'   (Bell, C. 1847: 180–01)

Within a comprehensive 'science of expressions' the madman was again a critical and interesting case; his abnormality presented both problems for the order and scope of the science, and intriguing possibilities for its advance. Other students of the expressions disputed Bell's suggestions on the 'vacancy' of the mad, and their mere animal-like ferocity, but they would have understood immediately the reasons which led Bell to the asylum as an observer.

The anatomist Franz Josef Gall had similarly visited asylums to observe the insane; indeed he probably formulated the early stages of his 'crani-ology' during several months when he frequented the asylums and gaols of Vienna. Idiots and lunatics, like criminals, were interesting to a 'crani-ologist' as to a physiognomist, because of their marked propensities and deficiencies. Like the other subjects Gall examined, including children and the elderly, the deaf and dumb, gifted musicians, they seemed to offer evidence of the differential development of specific mental faculties. Since his general method was to read the 'inner man' from external signs, Gall was naturally interested in those whose propensities were self-evidently extreme or marked. Such extreme types offered the most promising material for a method of rough empiricism.

In assembling his range of evidence to establish the separate faculties of mind, Gall also drew heavily on the clinical observations of medical psychology. Many of the medical states and conditions which were of interest to medical psychologists – notably hallucination, the partial insanities and monomanias, dreaming and somnambulism – seemed to offer particularly clear evidence for the existence of independent mental faculties. Likewise the uneven effects on the mental faculties of brain defects and localized trauma, and certain phenomena of speech defects, suggested to the anatomically-inclined that the brain was indeed the 'organ of mind', and further that particular parts of the brain were the organs of specific mental faculties.

In their turn 'craniology' and the 'phrenology' which Gall's less scientific associate Spurzheim later popularized, were notably significant in the development of psychology and allied fields. 'Craniology' was of inestimable importance in redirecting the course of anatomical researches, although other contemporary influences were also converging in the same direction. However mistaken certain of his principles, Gall's attempt to relate the analysis of mental function to the structure of the brain (and the shape of the skull) advanced the importance of cerebral localization enormously and helped to establish it high among the priorities of future research. Gall's own accomplishments were also significant, particularly in his comparative psychology which related the development of intelligence and skills in men and animals to the parallel development of increasing complexity in the cerebral cortex. Combining comparative anatomy and psychology provided a sound basis for Gall's description of the brain as a highly differentiated apparatus with a plurality of independent centres or specific organs. This was a promising and fruitful advance, despite the naming of 'Faculties' such as 'amativeness', 'adhesiveness', and 'philoprogenitiveness'.

As regards medical psychology proper, the tenets and approaches of physiognomy, craniology, and phrenology were very widely influential; they were adopted, one must add, in many cases without explicit acknowledgement and in forms which their proponents would hardly have sanctioned. But the approaches which physiognomy, for example, represented had already entered the scientific culture implicitly, in a general form. The ground over which the different schools of inquiry into 'individual differences' contested one another became to a remarkable degree established as part of the terrain on which general study advanced; it was indeed absorbed as one of the bases of the broad research programme in psychology. However vociferous the disputing schools, the common ground of their positions had gained assent, albeit often silently.

Alexander Morison's *Outlines of Mental Diseases* was typical of the medical treatises in its eclectic approach. The treatise included a long discussion of the 'physiognomy' of insanity with a series of plates representing the species of madness in their specific lineaments. Morison commented on the plates in turn by adducing the views of different (competing) writers; he refrained from endorsing any specifically, to the exclusion of others. On the 'moveable physiognomy' of madness (by which he meant its pathognomy) he wrote simply:

'The appearance of the face, it is well known, is intimately connected with, and dependent upon, the state of the mind. The repetition of the same ideas and emotions, and the consequent repetition of the same movements of the muscles of the eyes, and of the face, give a peculiar expression, which, in the insane state, is a combination of wildness, abstraction, or vacancy, and of those predominating ideas and emotions which characterize the different species of mental disorder, as pride, anger, suspicion, love, fear, grief, etc.' (Morison 1824: 131–32)

The generality of this formulation was characteristic of medical treatises, and it suggests how widely the basic approach to physiognomy was itself diffused.

A few alienists were actively involved in the phrenological movement, most famously Sir William Charles Ellis who was medical superintendent at the West Riding County Lunatic Asylum and later at Hanwell. Ellis's open commitment was exceptional. From the side of phrenology, for their part both George and Andrew Combe produced works which were directly relevant to mental disorders and to the practices of medical psychology (see A. Combe, 1831, and G. Combe 1836). These works were widely diffused, and at least at times respectfully cited. The most important link between phrenology and medical psychology was, however, less specific. It had nothing to do with the contentious claims of phrenology to its own special 'scientific' status, but was rather simply the individual examination which was the phrenologists' principal tool. Like other approaches to 'individual differences', phrenology required actually observing closely – and indeed probing and prodding – the individual subject. Its very procedures were based on individualized observations. Andrew Combe hence advertised quite appropriately the benefits of phrenology for the practice of medical psychology when he described its applicability to the individual case:

'By unfolding to us what the primitive powers of the mind are, and the objects and relations connected with each; and further, by enabling us to distinguish with accuracy the natural dispositions and talents of the patient, or the proportionate strength in which every individual faculty is possessed, Phrenology gives us a power of acting, and of adopting external circumstances to the exigencies of the case, with a precision, confidence, and consistency, which it is impossible to obtain in any other way.' (Combe, A. 1831: 353–54; see also 219, 346, 359)

Apart from its specific rationales the use of phrenology in clinical examinations involved precisely the individual approach to particular cases (and to the 'exigencies of the case') which characterized moral treatment generally. Combe indeed suggested:

'Now, it gives the physician immense command over such [mental] patients, when by the examination of the head he can, as generally happens, discover the natural dispositions so accurately as to know what are the probable points of attack in the mental constitution . . . and what class of motives or line of mental discipline is likely to be attended with the best effects in subduing excitement, and promoting the return of reason.'   (Combe, A. 1831: 354)

What this passage best describes is the ideal of moral management, as it was advocated and practiced with or generally without benefit of phrenology. Although Ellis, and a number of other alienists tried to practice phrenology self-consciously, what was (perhaps) most significant in their work was the actual procedure of individual examination, where the physicians 'read heads', tried to diagnose particular patients' characters and propensities, and worked accordingly to prescribe a suitable regimen and 'course of moral treatment';[5] apart from the feeling of 'bumps', this was not a procedure limited to the phrenologically-inclined. As a 'science' of individual differences phrenology was of course a potent rationale for the approach to individual cases; but in this it merged with greater tendencies in the study and treatment of madness, which promoted the segregation and isolation of patients, and the moral management of their own specific disorders. Alienists of whatever persuasion were less involved in the treatment of disease, than of disordered individuals.

A natural history of the disordered individual

In the prevailing scientific climate alienists continued to produce, as had their predecessors, quasi-botanic classifications of the forms or 'species' of madness. There was indeed a flurry of new and quite elaborate 'tables' of madness, differentiating and defining the condition according to its characteristic types. In actual clinical cases, however, the alienists' approach was not on the whole 'ontological', or premissed on the treatment of specific disease entities. In the contemporary state of knowledge few 'specific disease entities' among the insanities were isolated; classification could thus hardly serve as a way of selecting a specific remedy appropriate to one or other underlying pathology. 'Madness' was represented more commonly as a diffuse complaint, with many manifestations, signs, and symptoms, and subject in its expression to many contingencies. There was no determinate uniform pathology in the insanities, and the very range and variations in their occurrence prompted alienists to concern themselves with individual case-histories and the particular circumstances, both predisposing and exciting, which surrounded outbreaks of madness. In their clinical work alienists were involved in treating 'disorder' as a phenomenon of the discrete individual; the treatment of madness could to this extent claim to work on a 'science of the individual'.

In its orientation, the medicine of insanity, and more especially the later medical psychology, differed radically from the practices founded on the notion of demonic possession. The logical structure of conceiving madness at the level of its myriad effects, without the positing in most cases of a specific disease entity, broke fundamentally from the notion of a morbid invading agent. The bad spirit or demon in theories of possession figured as a disease entity which invaded, took over, and literally 'possessed' an individual. By its structure this theory and its variants allowed a firm distinction between the individual and the invading agency responsible for the disorder or possession (see Temkin 1963: 631). The characteristic therapies of expulsion and exorcism were accordingly less a means of approaching the suffering individual than a ritualized procedure appropriate to the character of the disease itself (to the disease entity). In cases of 'possession' the individual's particular circumstances, even previous rectitude, were thus not pertinent to his condition, and did not modify its understanding or treatment. This at least was the case in principle.

In the medical psychology of the late eighteenth and early nineteenth century on the contrary 'madness' was conceived less 'ontologically', in terms of specific morbid agents or entities, than as the condition of disordered individuals. It was individuals who variously suffered the 'species' of madness, and in their own particular circumstances and through their own 'natural history'. The range of particular circumstances in which madness appeared was thus highly pertinent to its correct 'classification', diagnosis, and treatment. This is the basis for the close similarity of Cabanis's physiological researches to the emerging medical psychology. The 'Hippocratism' which Cabanis praised as the proper mode of understanding the physiology of the individual organism (by situating it among its myriad 'circumstances')[6] was equally characteristic of the medical psychology of Pinel. 'In spite of his classificatory tendencies', as Walther Riese has written, Pinel

'advocated the study of the undisturbed, i.e., natural course of disease. This was true Hippocratism. In fact, Hippocratic medicine had no use for disease entities and diagnoses. That Pinel, when facing the insane as an *individual*, deprived him temporarily of his diagnosis or his *nosologic*

152

stigma, was a masterstroke. He then experienced him simply as a human being in distress, excitement, anxiety, hostility, humiliation.'

(Riese 1951: 446)

Despite its humanistic overtones this is an accurate enough description of how moral treatment appeared in its characteristic approach to the disordered individual. The clinical contact of doctor and patient was not, *pace* the advocates of medical humanism, a 'simple human encounter' in which the one party brought all his humane sympathies and energies to bear on 'understanding' the other; the mode of contact between alienist and madman was in fact highly structured, both by the institutional context of the asylum (as a variety of 'total institution') and by the prevailing ideological notions of moral influence. But the mode of conduct in moral management was necessarily *individual*; the courses of treatment in moral management were not administered by the round of routine in which patients were bled, purged, and drugged collectively, virtually irrespective of their distinctive and particular disorders.

The theory and practice of medical psychology approached indeed a 'science of the individual'. Correct diagnosis and treatment of a clinical case required not simply pertinent observations of the signs and symptoms of disease that would allow a clinician to refer – and reduce – the particular case to an established syndrome or familiar constellation of symptoms. Diagnosis also required, moreover, judging the 'peculiar nature of each individual' and the 'exigencies of each case', in all the specificity of a 'physiological' analysis. Physicians of the physiological school opposed the routinized application of standard treatments. Disease, on their interpretation, was explicable as a process of life, within the continuum of variations in form and gradations of function. Hence the site of treatment as well as the object of treatment were the disordered individual, not the disease itself. The traditional 'art of healing' was accordingly revived in a particular form when clinicians tried to array before their 'regard médical' the great range of individual circumstances, moral and physical, which surrounded the expression of disease (see Foucault 1973, especially ch. 7, 'Seeing and Knowing'). The collection of such circumstances of course varied from patient to patient, as much as the individuals varied; and thus each collection of circumstances recorded in more and more elaborate casehistories was fitting and appropriate only to the individual case itself. As regards treatment, the courses of 'moral management' of the insane likewise were ideally highly particular to the individual, and based on a close evaluation of the state of his passions.

153

Of all complaints 'madness' required perhaps the greatest attention to 'moral' factors; on a broad view these included virtually all aspects of an individual's life and livelihood. Hence thorough attention to an individual madman would highlight the uniqueness of the case. This is not to suggest, however, that medical psychology constituted in the event a genuine science of the individual – whatever that term would mean. It was founded, on the contrary, on theories of general human nature, in which the survivals of mental philosophy, thinly-veiled moralisms, and rudimentary knowledge of anatomy and physiology played distinctive and active parts. The nature of mental and moral disease was thus grounded in the 'nature of man', as this was theorized, imagined, and constructed.

The conditions of asylum practice further were specifically endorsed for the opportunities they allowed of systematic observation and comparison of inmates. The ultimate promise of asylum confinement was that large numbers of inmates, carefully observed through the course of their disorders and compared on statistical measures, would provide finally the basis for a new science of mental disorders. The new science would be founded more securely on a more adequate set of inductions from 'natural history', in all its empirical variety.

Despite these hopes the actual conditions of study were nonetheless rooted at the individual bedside, in the lunatic cell and the examination room, where peculiarities and marked propensities received their inordinate attention. The manifold links and reciprocal influences between medical psychology and other contemporary approaches to the study of 'individual differences', were based on this shared interest in the extreme and particular in mental life which, paradoxically, were so important in the constitution of the new 'science of man'.

CONCLUSION

Ideas of influence

'That which we have learnt, or, at least, that which has been proved to us, in a clear and satisfactory manner, by our enquiry into the phenomena of mesmerism, is that – *man can act upon man*, at all times and almost by will, by striking his imaginations – that signs and gestures the most simple may produce the most powerful effects; that the action of man upon the imagination may be reduced to an art, and conducted after a certain method, when exercised upon patients who have faith in the proceedings.'

(Report of the Experiments on Animal Magnetism 1784)

Beyond an approach to disordered individuals, the 'Hippocratism' of medical psychology revived also the importance of the 'art of healing'. Moral management depended essentially upon a range of psychological techniques which engaged directly the powers of the physician's personality and magisterial presence in the work of curing. The proper qualifications for specialists treating the mentally disordered were accordingly less related to a background and training in the strictly medical interventions than to attributes of character. It was the moral qualities of alienists which in large measure enabled the courses of moral treatment. The special relationship of alienist to madman was based on influence and identification; and it was in this respect that medical psychology provides some echo of that other contemporary pseudo-science of mental phenomena, animal magnetism, which demonstrated so strikingly in its techniques the potentials of moral influence and the power of mind over mind.

As with the case of phrenology, some few medical practitioners and mental specialists became active proponents of animal magnetism. From the decade after Mesmer's death there were more or less continuous researches into the phenomena of 'magneticism' carried out in conjunction with clinical practices; these culminated eventually in the studies of hypnosis of James Braid (see 1843 and 1853), of Liebault and Bernheim, and in the work of Charcot, Janet, and Freud. In the greater field of medical

155

psychology such researches were at best marginal, and were often derided. But apart from the direct links there were broader and looser connections or affinities between animal magnetism in its vogue and the more sober, established practices of medical psychology. Although Mesmer's claims for the therapeutic powers of the universal 'magnetic fluid' were rejected decisively during his lifetime and many times afterwards, the actual effects of magnetic cures were beyond challenge. What produced the effects, and whether they were genuinely therapeutic, were the points at issue between the proponents of magnetism and their adversaries. The effects themselves, which demonstrated the power of mind over mind and body in striking fashion, were clearly of fundamental interest to specialists in the mental disorders; and regardless of their therapeutic potential, the mesmeric phenomena fascinated philosophers like Dugald Stewart. Thus, despite the sharp controversies around animal magnetism and its claims, the 'influence' which Mesmer and his followers had demonstrated was highly pertinent for orthodox healing as well, particularly in an era when specific moral treatments of the mentally disordered were rapidly supplanting routine physical remedies.

The mesmeric cure itself was indeed in certain respects a close reflection of the prevailing treatment practices within medical psychology; apart from the special nature of the relationship between 'magnetizer' and patient, with its overtones of 'healing' and its specially heightened emotionality, Mesmer and his followers also emphasized the therapeutic 'crisis', which recalled equally the conversion experiences of religious revivalism and the 'crises' which contemporary physicians provoked in order to resolve the disorders of nervous and insane patients.[1] In such respects the magnetic cure was in its structure in considerable accord with the prevailing medical theory and practice; more germanely, it was undoubtedly also a highly suggestive reminder of the deep resources and powers available through moral influence. Mesmerism and medical psychology both testified in their respective fashions to the contemporary fascination with moral force and influence which swept broadly as a cultural current.

The controversy which developed around mesmerism and other magnetic cures from the last decades of the eighteenth century concerned principally their relation to established medical practices. Mesmer regarded himself, far from being 'mystical', as a consistent materialist, but his practices were assimilated by physicians to those of other 'quacks' who preyed upon the weaknesses of the vulgar imagination and who as 'healers' constituted a threat to established medical practice.

The mysterious powers of the healer have been a consistent theme in the folklore surrounding illness and disorder, and in more sophisticated accounts of the *ars et scientia medica*, until the present day. 'Healers' have not necessarily been heterodox to established medicine, since to a degree all practice of the 'science' of medicine also depends upon its 'art' and thus invariably involves the person of the physician as healer. But the mode of influence in healing has not commonly been represented as 'medical' in itself. Although many healers who have claimed miraculous or strange powers have fully exploited the *res medica*, the efficacy of their healing has nonetheless often attached not to the techniques themselves so much as to their own person; the concoctions, potions, and charms employed by wizards and wise women were often drawn from among folk remedies, were likewise visible and palpable media of cure, but were not themselves sufficient explanation of the 'aura' of the healer. The most dramatic instances of healers, finally, have been those who have dispensed with all technical means of exercising their powers, and have cured by ritual laying-on of hands or simple stroking (see Lewis 1971). Despite the apparatus of the *bâquet* (the tub supposedly filled with magnetic fluid) and the metallic rods, Mesmer's cure was itself essentially a method of stroking or 'making passes' with the hands by way of stimulating the ebb and flow of the 'nervous fluid' in affected parts.

A moral medicine

In the several centuries before Mesmer the predominant explanation of such healing or influence – expressed with or without medical techniques or folk remedies – still drew on the terms of the ancient doctrine of sympathies. 'The Phancy of one Person', wrote the seventeenth-century physician Nehemiah Grew, 'may by some Subtile Intervening Fluid, bind the Phancy of another. Provided, that the Phancy of the Agent be strong, and the Reason of the Patient weak, and the distance between them not over-great' (Grew 1701: 63). In similar fashion, on the analogy between the macrocosm of the universe and man the microcosm, physicians attributed to the sun, moon, and other astral bodies, dominion over not only 'those Grand Fluids, the Sea and the Air', but also those within the body; thus the astrological significance of menstruation, and of supposedly periodic disorders like epilepsy and lunacy, or 'moon-madness'. The phenomena of 'hysterical conversion' were likewise referred to the operation of 'sympathy' between organs, which acted upon each other within the body, although they were apparently unconnected (see Ferriar 1792).

By the early nineteenth century few physicians or natural historians regarded the ancient doctrine of sympathies and antipathies as other than a pernicious curiosity, which suggests in part why Mesmer's talk of the 'ether' was so ill-received. Ironically, however, the notion of 'moral agency' was accorded in the same decades a remarkably wide and rarely questioned scope, in medicine and psychology alike. The influence of the mind over the body through the media of the emotions and the imagination, became indeed one of the principal topics of medical discussion and principal objects of investigation in the early research programme of physiology and psychology. Even sceptical physicians like John Haygarth, who conducted a series of experiments to debunk the patented Perkins 'Metallic Tractors' (for the treatment of disease by 'Galvanism, or Animal Electricity'), acknowledged the apparent efficacy of cure by 'tractors'; as Haygarth suggested, 'Such is the wonderful force of the Imagination!'

Dugald Stewart argued similarly in his *Elements of the Philosophy of the Human Mind* (1827) that the emotions, enhanced by the resources of imagination, were a means of influence and communication between people at once more primitive, direct, and powerful than language. He suggested indeed that all learning, and thus all growth in the mental powers, depended upon man's pre-verbal capacity for 'sympathetic imitation'. Mesmerism was one simple, albeit dramatic, illustration of the 'moral' influences which were fundamental in human interaction, and an illustration which suggested pointedly their therapeutic promise:

> 'the general conclusions established by Mesmer's practice, with respect to the physical effects of the principle of sympathetic Imitation and of the faculty of Imagination (more particularly in cases where they co-operate together,) are incomparably more curious, than if he had actually succeeded in ascertaining the existence of his boasted fluid: Nor can I see any good reason why a physician, who admits the efficacy of the *moral* agents employed by Mesmer, should, in the exercise of his profession, scruple to copy whatever processes are necessary for subjecting them to his command, any more than he would hestitate about employing a new *physical* agent.'   (Stewart 1827: III, 221–23)

Medicine indeed profited widely from the use of agents 'so peculiarly efficacious and overbearing', particularly in treating disorders (like so many of the insanities) in which moral causes were predominant.

The powers attributed to mad-doctors and alienists were often no less mysterious than those claimed by traditional healers, although they were described in rather more prosaic terms.[2] It was in the end on the diffusion of a high confidence in 'moral agency' that the success of 'moral medicine' rested.

Although the lunacy reformers of the early nineteenth century regarded themselves, justly, as humanitarian, it was the more complicated and elaborate ideological rationales, notably their faith and confidence in 'moral agency', which informed the programme for model asylums and which made medical psychology distinctive. Indeed, as this study has tried to argue, historians cannot adequately understand the lunacy reforms and their characteristic aims without a proper appreciation of the ideological elements and varieties of social thought with which the reform programme was articulated.

The severe strains on the system of confinement toward the end of the eighteenth century, which were the pretext for the building of separate lunatic asylums (and simultaneously for the general re-organization of the system of confinement), are incontrovertible. The reformers themselves left abundant evidence of the baleful consequences on inmates of institutional overcrowding, poor diet, and 'gaol fever'; they likewise had a sound impression at a time when insanity seemed greatly on the increase of the number of lunatics and idiots who languished in neglect or under secret custody.

The matter of the reforms which they proposed and in large measure accomplished is, however, more complicated. The criticisms which the reformers amassed did not in themselves suggest immediately a reform programme of the scope and ambitious character which philanthropists and alienists had undeniably conceived. The 'diagnosis' of madness in society on which the programme was ultimately grounded, was rather more complex and nuanced than the conclusions of Parliamentary investigations or 'fact-finding' missions alone would warrant. This study has tried to reconstruct certain of the elements from which the programme was formed and by which it was shaped.

Despite the energy with which the reformers conducted their inquiries, investigations, and inspections, they managed to leave in fact very little systematic and representative information on the 'insane' themselves. This naturally complicates, perhaps impossibly, the historians' task of assessing realistically the actual extent of the public health problems and individual disorder and malaise, which composed the contemporary category of 'madness' or 'insanity'. It is striking that philanthropists, alienists, and the moral statisticians alike compiled so few adequate

159

statistics of 'insanity' and sponsored virtually no epidemiological investigations of its incidence or social distribution. The medicine of insanity, however, developed through other procedures and styles of investigation.

What the philanthropists, alienists, and moral statisticians did leave behind in abundance were clinical studies and more diffuse writings on 'madness in society', often frankly speculative but not any the less interesting for that reason. It was such reflections on madness, frequently buttressed by clinical materials, which informed the programme for model asylums and grounded the techniques of moral treatment. These various reflections on madness and the mad, written from different vantages, expressed the contemporary 'perceptions' of madness, both as a social phenomenon and as a category of human experience.

The perceptions of madness, which this study has approached by way of certain widely-diffused cultural themes, did not together compose a system; on the contrary, far from being a rigorously derived set of propositions assembled into a uniform and coherent whole, they were inchoate, shifting, and in some ways apparently mutually exclusive or contradictory. They were, however, nonetheless suggestive and powerful images; and, as this study has tried to suggest further, they together composed the 'frame' through which the contemporary problem of 'madness' appeared and in which it was constituted. The characteristic approaches to the study and treatment of madness, and to the formulation of social policies toward the insane, were accordingly bounded or circumscribed by a cluster of perceptions which were themselves rarely examined or accessible to criticism. In similar fashion the discipline of medical psychology, and the asylum setting in which it was authoritatively installed, composed the 'field' where the concepts of the classical system of psychiatry were developed and deployed.

The various cultural themes – the 'problem of the irrational', 'universal reason and individual differences', ideas of 'influence' and 'moral agency', and the psychological differences and attributes of social classes – are perhaps too diffuse in form to allow any subtle appreciation of the social thought of an epoch. Yet, on the basis of a list of similar cultural themes or 'principles', Michel Foucault has tried recently in a persuasive essay to describe a general normative 'discipline' characteristic of bourgeois civilization, which he has discerned commonly in penal, medical, educational, and religious 'techniques'. The terms of his argument are cast as broadly (or indeed as universally) as Bentham's 'panoptism' or the 'inspection principle' (Foucault 1977).

There were many apparent links and similarities between, for instance, the moral management of the insane and the reformation of prisoners, as between the model asylum and the penitentiary. The distinctiveness of medical psychology lay in the application and adjustment of general principles of 'management' and moral agency to the specific characteristics of the 'insane'. How these characteristics appeared was in turn the result of the 'statements' that bounded madness and were most pertinent to its definition. They were by no means exclusively medical or technical.

Echoes of the relations between the classes in the early nineteenth century were pervasive, not only in their grossly prejudicial forms, but also in specific variants: the notion of 'moral insanity', the association of certain insanities with public drunkenness, the description of superstition as intellectual error and weakness, the special sympathies extended to 'refined' lunatics, the mode of representing the mind hierarchically, etc. Similarly the hopeful expectations of 'education', personal reform, and the power of example, were narrowed and focused into a conception of the social relations in the model asylum; these general themes were expressed through the techniques of associationist psychology and the revived Hippocratism of moral medicine. The notion of 'moral agency' was linked to the character and the person of the ideal asylum governor, to the powers of his 'eye', and to the ingeniously fashioned resources of the asylum building which so enhanced the governor's sanative influence. The study of individual differences was located at the individual bedside, or in the separate cell, which formed the basic unit in hospital and asylum architecture. And so as general practices of management were applied to the insane, the specific character of medical psychology and its setting progressively emerged.

NOTES

Part I

Chapter 1

1 The 1844 Report of the Metropolitan Commissioners in Lunacy set the total number of persons 'ascertained to be insane' in England and Wales on 1 January 1844, at 20,893 of whom 11,272 were officially recorded as resident in asylums. In 1890 there were 61,985 inmates in asylums; see the Annual Report of the Lunacy Commissioners for 1890, Appendix.

2 There is a large fund of legend surrounding the wandering 'Toms o' Bedlam', of whom John Aubrey wrote in 1691:

> 'Till the breaking out of the Civill Warres, Tom o' Bedlams did travell about the country. They had been poore distracted men that had been put into Bedlam, where, recovering to some sobernesse, they were licentiated to goe a-begging. . . . They wore about their necks a great horn of an oxe in a string or bawdric, which, when they came to an house for alms, they did wind.' (Aubrey 1969: 93)

3 For a discussion of the contemporary uses of 'bedlam' see Christopher Hill, 'The Island of Great Bedlam', in *The World Turned Upside Down* (1972). The Puritan divine Thomas Adams entitled a work of 1615, which took Bedlam as a metaphor for the whole of creation, *Mystical Bedlam, or the World of Mad-Men*.

4 Thomas Pennant described eighteenth-century Moorfields as 'the haunt of the most motley amusements' and a spot where there was every allurement to 'low gaming':

> 'Here the mountebanks set up their stages, and dispensed infallible medicines, for every species of disease, to the gaping gulls who surrounded them. Here, too, I lament to say, that religion set up its stage itinerant, beneath the shade of the trees; and here the pious, well-meaning *Whitefield* long preached so successfully, as to steal from a neighbouring Charlatan the greater part of his numerous admirers, in defiance of the eloquence of the doctor.' (Pennant 1791: 251–52)

5 In Quarter Sessions papers there are sometimes records of the petitions presented to Justices of the Peace asking the commitment of a dangerous

162

lunatic to the house of correction, which was apparently a common resort. Such detention was a matter for Quarter Sessions, and it is likely that the 1744 Vagrancy Act simply endorsed and legalized practices which were already long-standing. One study of the Lancashire Sessions Records discovered a striking decline in the number of references to lunatics in the papers, after about 1730. This was probably the result of orders being signed 'out of sessions', which may well have been the general trend. After the 1723 Workhouse Act parishes were more likely to send cases for relief directly to the workhouse, thus reducing the Justices' scope to intervene in the administration of poor relief. See Fessler (1956). The Webbs were almost certainly wrong in suggesting that 'right down to 1835, the typical method of dealing with pauper lunatics was to place them out under contract' (Webb and Webb 1927: 304).

6 See Walker 1968. Walker has noted for the years after 1755 a striking 'increase in the relative frequency with which lunatics and idiots appeared in the dock at the Old Bailey' (Walker 1968: 70).

7 As William Farr wrote, 'There are innumerable omissions in the returns of the insane poor made to Parliament; all agree in this: yet of 12,547 insane persons "ascertained, beyond all doubt as existing in England", by Sir Andrew Halliday (5741 idiots, 6806 lunatics), 11,000 were paupers' (Farr 1837a: 652).

8 The Commissioners' Report in 1844 noted the large and increasing numbers of 'incurable cases', without however trying to analyze or break down the group of incurables. The Report proposed building separate auxiliary, custodial asylums to receive idiots, the chronic and harmless insane, and other incurables, on the following rationale:

'the disease of Lunacy, it should be observed, is essentially different in its character from other maladies. In a certain proportion of cases, the Patient neither recovers nor dies, but remains an incurable lunatic, requiring little medical skill in respect to his mental disease, and frequently living many years. A Patient in this state requires a place of refuge; but his disease being beyond the reach of medical skill, it is quite evident that he should be removed from Asylums instituted for the cure of insanity, in order to make room for others whose cases have not yet become hopeless.'

(Official Papers 1844a)

9 Such practical designations of the insane ('harmless', 'dangerous', 'incurable', etc.) were of course common, and probably more important in the institutional practices than the medical classifications of insanity. The meaning of such practical designations was not, however, unequivocal. 'Incurable', for instance, was sometimes merely a practical means of describing an inmate still remaining in confinement after twelve months, or some other period arbitrarily defined as an administrative convenience. It is noteworthy that

'chronicity' developed as a practical category and a concept in theory particularly when asylums were increasingly organized as roughly self-sufficient colonies, with their own permanent labour requirements; see Lanteri-Laura 1972.

10 Some records of the so-called Chancery lunatics survive. See for example the papers relating to the case of Edmund Francklin (Bedford County Record Office, FN 1060–084) which provide details of the legal procedures under the Court of Wards for depriving a lunatic of the management of his affairs, and appointing a Committee of the Person to manage his estate. Francklin was found lunatic by inquisition, according to the procedures of investigation, in 1630. Two years later, after he had been 'violent and outrageous in his Carriage divers several times' and had also 'disturbed the Minister in the Church when he was preaching several times', Francklin was ordered to be put under restraint and committed to Bethlem.

11 The following table, compiled from Annual Reports of the Commissioners in Lunacy, represents the increase through the nineteenth century in the average occupancy of county asylums:

on 1 Jan.	no. county asylums	total patients	average no. patients
1827	9	1,046	116
1850	24	7,140	297
1860	41	15,845	386
1870	50	27,109	542
1900	77	74,004	961

A similar table appears in Jones 1972: 357.

Chapter 2

1 'The Retreat' was a name suggested by William Tuke's daughter-in-law 'to convey the idea of what such an institution should be, namely . . . a quiet haven in which the shattered bark might find the means of reparation or of safety' (Tuke, D. H. 1892: 20).

2 John Howard, who was concerned with all manner of irregularities in prisons, was especially agitated about the filth and poor ventilation in the places. He had abundant contemporary medical opinion to support his attack on the 'nastiness' of prisons, including notably the influential Dr Mead, whose *Discourse concerning Pestilential Contagion* he cited:

'Nothing approaches so near to the first original of *contagion*, as air pent up, loaded with damps, and corrupted with the filthiness that proceeds from *animal bodies*. Our common *prisons* afford us an instance of this, in which very few escape, what they call the gaol-fever, which is always attended with a degree of malignity in proportion to the *closeness* and *stench* of the place.' (Mead in Howard 1792: 31)

3 'Alienist': 'One who treats mental diseases; a mental pathologist; a "mad-doctor"' (OED). A term popularized in the nineteenth century, from the French *aliénation*.

Chapter 3

1 See French (1951: 37–8). An aquatint by Rowlandson in *The Microcosm of London* (1803) portrays the interior of the women's gallery; see the edition presented by Summerson (1947: 19).
2 See Huxley (1950). Piranesi's 'carceri' were not of course designs but in form more in the manner of imaginative and fantastic exaggerations of the theatrical backdrops and sketches of Roman ruins which he produced for a living.

Chapter 4

1 Henry de Bracton, *De Legibus et Conseutudinibus Angliae* (Woodbine edition, New Haven, 1915). See Nigel Walker's discussion of Bracton's text in *Crime and Insanity in England* (Walker 1968: 28). Walker has suggested that the medieval sense of *furiosus* probably described 'states of spectacular and obviously unreasoning violence', such as would occur in epilepsy and schizophrenia of the catatonic type. This is highly questionable, and in any case purely speculative. See the comments below on the problems inherent in such retrospective diagnoses. The categories of psychopathology, and the signs and symptoms of madness, have been notoriously relative, historically and across cultures, and do not easily translate into modern psychiatric classifications.

With regard to the so-called 'wild beast' test, the expression 'wild beast' ironically was probably a misrendering of *brutus* in Bracton's Latin text, which implied no more than 'insensible' or 'dumb'; the notion of 'wildness', however seemingly appropriate, was a later embellishment.
2 R v. M'Naghten, *State Trials*, New Series, ed. by J. MacDonnell, IV. The counsel was Alexander Cockburn, QC, who drew heavily in his arguments from a work of the American physician Isaac Ray, *A Treatise on the Medical Jurisprudence of Insanity* (1838).
3 The term 'monomania' was coined by Esquirol, but the concept was clearly anticipated by Cullen, and later popularized by Pinel and Chiarugi on the continent. As Cullen argued, in setting out the basis of his *Synopsis and Nosology*: 'Insanity consists in such false conceptions of the relations of things, as lead to irrational emotions and actions. Melancholy is partial insanity without indigestion – Mania is universal insanity'; the class 'partial insanity'

included as a sub-category derangement on one subject only. Chiarugi devised a class he called 'raving melancholy', which was attended with 'a fixed hatred towards some single object, to which at a later period, sallies of rage associate themselves' (Chiarugi cited in Beddoes 1803: III, 26ff.). In place of the ancient category melancholy used to describe 'partial delirium' and the like, Esquirol proposed 'monomania',

> 'a term which expresses the essential character of that form of insanity, in which the delirium is partial, permanent, gay or sad. . . . Monomania is of all maladies, that which presents to the observer, phenomena the most strange and varied, and which offers, for our consideration, subjects the most numerous and profound. It embraces all the mysterious anomalies of sensibility, all the phenomena of the human understanding, all the consequences of the perversion of our natural inclinations, and all the errors of our passions'. (Esquirol 1838: 199–200)

The vagueness of this formulation correctly reflects the breadth through which 'monomania' could be construed.

4 Kathleen Jones has suggested that the 1808 County Asylums Act was perhaps so permissive in its provisions since 'the total dimensions of the need could only be guessed at, and it was necessary for the scheme for county asylums to pass through an experimental stage' (Jones 1972: 58). The 'need' for asylums obviously depended, however, on to what uses state policies put asylums; the phenomena of insanity, their dimensions as 'social problems', and the 'needs' for institutional confinement, were hardly unequivocal.

5 The 1684 sermon was preached by George Hickes; the 1741 by Mattias Mawson; both were published in London under the title, A Sermon Preached before the Right Honourable, the Lord Mayor, the Alderman, Sherriffs, and Governors of the several Hospitals of the City of London.

Part II

Introduction

1 See, for instance, Howells and Osborn, 'The Incidence of Emotional Disorder in a Seventeenth-century Medical Practice' (1970).

2 Report of the Fourth Meeting of the Association, held in London, 1834. See also the text of a lecture delivered by Sir Alexander Morison before a meeting of the Society for Improving the Condition of the Insane, in 1844, entitled 'A Paper Suggesting the Propriety of the Study of the Nature, Causes and Treatment of Mental Disease, as Forming Part of the Curriculum of Medical Education'.

3 There was little formal instruction in medical psychology within the curricula of medical faculties until the 1850s. As early as 1753 William Battie had

secured permission from the Governors of St Luke's Hospital to take pupils informally, but the practice survived only a few years. Sir Alexander Morison delivered annual courses of private lectures in Edinburgh from 1823 and in London from 1826. In 1828 at the opening of the medical school for the new London University, Dr John Conolly delivered an inaugural lecture promising students of medicine 'for the first time in this country' opportunities 'of becoming familiar with the diversified aspects of this alarming malady', madness; however, he was unable to arrange visits for the interested students to any established asylum, and the project fell into neglect. Only in 1842 was Conolly himself able to invite some pupils from the London medical schools to lecture-demonstrations at the Hanwell Asylum.

4 Two earlier comprehensive works, Prichard's *A Treatise on Insanity* (1835) and Esquirol's *Maladies mentales* (1838) were however well-known among established practitioners.

Chapter 5

1 The anonymous review appeared in the number of *The Examiner* for 17 September 1809. It began: 'If beside the stupid and mad-brained political project of their rulers, the sane part of the people of England required fresh proof of the alarming increase of the effects of insanity, they will be too well convinced from its having lately spread into the hitherto sober region of art' (*The Examiner* 1809: 605). The piece continues similarly in a satiric vein, and yet manages serious comment on Blake's project to 'represent immateriality by bodily personifications of the soul', which it judges in measured tones as the conception and product of a disordered, fevered, or overexcited imagination. The suggestions of madness are thus not simply in the nature of rhetorical flourishes.

2 See Whyte, *The Unconscious before Freud* (1960) and Rank, 'Schopenhauer über den Wahnsinn' (1910).

Chapter 6

1 It is noteworthy that Prichard was equally famed as an ethnographer, and particularly as an exponent of the 'monogenist' view of the human species. Although his clinical reports were carefully constructed and painstakingly recorded in specific, observable detail, in his more general reflections Prichard betrayed some more fanciful leanings to assimilate the inmates with whom he worked to the primitive and ancient peoples he studied, in respect of their basic psychology. As a monogenist, Prichard asserted the unity, despite 'racial' variation, of the human species; and he thus rejected those explanations of diversity based on biological determinism alone. However backward or ignoble, the savage was biologically capable of becoming an Englishman, as Prichard suggested, given the proper 'moral environment'. The savage's

condition was the result of the forestalled or rudimentary development of his moral faculty, which the environment limited. This 'moral environmentalism' repeated the attitudes inherent in *The Philanthropist* articles with striking similarity. Within his own work Prichard unified two of the themes linked in the greater philanthropic programme for 'moral improvement'. The ethnographer who argued generously that savages, with proper education and moral training, could acquire a moral faculty (and thus begin to acquire civilization), as a medical psychologist argued in resonant terms that a perversion of the moral faculties constituted madness – which opened the victims of moral insanity to being described as savage.

2 Orwell noted in passing that Dickens's original idea for the novel was to have three escaped lunatics as the ring leaders of the riot (Orwell 1961: 38).

Chapter 7

1 See Manuel, 'From Equality to Organicism' (1972) for a representative treatment of the theme.

2 'In the hospitals of the nineteenth century it became possible to observe many cases of the same disease, clinically as well as anatomically, and thus to strengthen the diagnosis of "diseases". At the same time, it became possible to establish standards of what was normal, and to elaborate tests which expressed numerical agreement with, or deviation from the norm. The norm here was a value found in a smaller or greater number of healthy persons. Without this norm, measurements were of little avail. The ever lengthening chart of data accumulating in the course of medical examinations, from pulse rate and temperature curve, to X-ray pictures, chemical, physical, bacteriological and immunological tests, mirrors this development.' (Temkin 1963: 636)

See also Faber (1930) and Canguilhem (1966).

3 See Lavater (1789–98 and 1806). The thirteenth fragment in the *Essays on Physiognomy* depicts a complete 'vision of a madhouse', based on a drawing by Fuseli. The different physiognomies of the inmates represent on Lavater's interpretation 'Fury and force, an energy uniformly supported, and ever active' (Lavater 1789–98: 288).

4 Darwin's work *The Expression of the Emotions in Man and Animals* (1872), which refers respectfully throughout to Bell, develops this theme considerably. The insane were most usefully 'to be observed and closely studied' because their passions were 'unbridled' and appeared with particular force. Apart from numerous incidental references to the insane, who provided a large proportion of his illustrative examples, Darwin included a specific discussion on 'various strange animal-like traits in idiots' and madmen (Darwin 1872: 245ff.).

5 For Ellis's own views on phrenology see his letter to G. Combe in Hunter and Macalpine 1963: 819–20).

6 'Chez chaque malade, il se développe une série de phénomènes: ces phénomènes sont tout ce qu'il y a évident et de sensible dans les maladies. Hippocrate s'attache à les décrire par ces coups de pinceau frappans, ineffaçables, qui font mieux que reproduire la nature, car ils en rapprochent et distinguent fortement les caracteristiques. Chaque histoire forme un tableau particulier: le sexe, l'âge, le tempérament, le régime, la profession du malade, y sont notés avec soin. La situation du lieu, la nature de ses productions, les travaux de ses habitans, sa témperature, la manière dont le soleil le regarde, le temps de l'année, les changements que l'air a subis durant les saisons précédentes: telles sont les circonstances accessoires qu'il rassemble autour de ses tableaux.' (Cabanis Year VI: 54)

Conclusion

1 See Foucault (1973: ch. 10, 'Crisis in Fevers'): 'Fever is an excretory movement, purificatory in intention; and Stahl recalls an etymology: *februare* is to expel ritually from a house the shades of the dead' (Foucault 1973: 178–89). Physicians provoked or stimulated 'artificial' fevers likewise to expel disease.

2 'the medical personage, according to Pinel, had to act not as the result of an objective definition of the disease or a specific classifying diagnosis, but by relying upon that prestige which envelops the secrets of the Family, of Authority, of Punishment, and of Love; it is by bringing such powers into play, by wearing the mask of Father and of Judge, that the physician, by one of those abrupt short cuts that leave aside mere medical competence, became the almost magic perpetrator of the cure, and assumed the aspect of the Thaumaturge; it was enough that he observed and spoke, to cause secret faults to appear, insane presumptions to vanish, and madness at last to yield to reason. His presence and his words were gifted with that power of disalienation, which at one blow revealed the transgression and restored the order of morality.

It is a curious paradox to see medical practice enter the uncertain domain of the quasi-miraculous at the very moment when the knowledge of mental illness tries to assume a positive meaning.' (Foucault 1965: 273–74)

REFERENCES

A Description of Bedlam with an Account of its Present Inhabitants (1772).

Abel-Smith, B. (1964) *The Hospitals, 1800–1948: A Study in Social Administration in England and Wales*. Cambridge, Mass: Harvard University Press.

Ackerknecht, E. H. (1959) *A Short History of Psychiatry*. New York: Hafner Publishing Co.

—— (1967) *Medicine at the Paris Hospital, 1794–1848*. Baltimore: Johns Hopkins Press.

Adams, T. (1615) *Mystical Bedlam, or the World of Mad-Men*.

Aikin, J. (1771) *Thoughts on Hospitals*.

Allen, M. (1831) *Cases of Insanity, with Medical, Moral and Philosophical Observations upon Them*.

—— (1837) *Essays on the Classification of the Insane*.

Altschule, M. (1957) *Roots of Modern Psychiatry*. New York: Grune & Stratton (revised edition, 1965).

An Account of Several Workhouses in Great Britain (1732).

An Account of the Rise and Present Establishment of the Lunatic Asylum in Manchester (1771). Manchester.

Arlidge, J. (1859) *On the State of Lunacy and the Legal Provision for the Insane, with Observations on the Construction and Organization of Asylums*.

Arnold, T. (1782–86) *Observations on the Nature, Kinds, Causes, and Prevention of Insanity, Lunacy, or Madness*. Leicester.

—— (1809) *Observations on the Management of the Insane and Particularly on the Agency and Importance of Human and Kind Treatment in Effecting their Cure*.

Aubrey, J. (1969) *Natural History of Wiltshire*. First published 1691.

Bakewell, T. (1809) *The Domestic Guide in Cases of Insanity*. Newcastle.

Barlow, J. (1843) *Man's Power over Himself to Prevent or Control Insanity*.

Bastide, R. (1972) *The Sociology of Mental Disorders*. London: Routledge & Kegan Paul.

Bateman, F. and Rye, W. (1906) *The History of the Bethel Hospital at Norwich*. Norwich: Gibbs & Waller.

Bateman, T. (1819) *Reports on the Diseases of London*.

Bateson, G. (ed.) (1961) *Perceval's Narrative: A Patient's Account of His Psychosis, 1830–1832*. Palo Alto: Stanford University Press.

Battelle, M. (1845) *Rapport sur les établissements des aliénés d'Angleterre, et sur ceux de Bicêtre et de la Salpêtrière*. Paris.

Bayle, A. (1822) *Recherches sur les maladies mentales*. Paris.

Beddoes, T. (1803) *Hygeia; or, Essays Moral and Medical, on the Causes affecting the Personal State of our Middling and Affluent Classes.*

Bell, C. (1847) *The Anatomy and Philosophy of Expression*. First published 1806.

Bell, J. (1792) *The General and Particular Principles of Animal Magnetism.*

Bentham, J. (1791) *Panopticon; or, the Inspection-House.*

—— (1812) *Pauper Management Improved: Particularly by Means of an Application of the Panopticon Principle of Construction.*

—— (1843) *Works*, ed. Bowring, 11 vols. Edinburgh.

Bickerton, T. (1936) *A Medical History of Liverpool*. London: John Murray.

Black, W. (1788) *A Comparative View of the Mortality of the Human Species, and of the Diseases and Casualties by which They are Destroyed or Annoyed.*

—— (1810) *A Dissertation on Insanity, Illustrated with Tables, and Extracted from between Two and Three Thousand Cases in Bedlam.*

Blackstone, W. (1765–69) *Commentaries on the Laws of England.*

Blomfield, R. (1921) *A History of French Architecture*. London: G. Bell & Sons.

Boullée, E. L. (1968) *Architecture, essai sur l'art*. Textes réunis et présentés par Jean-Marie Pévouse de Monclos. Paris: Hermann.

Bowen, T. (1784) *An Historical Account of the Origin, Progress and Present State of Bethlem Hospital.*

—— (1797) *Thoughts on the Necessity of Moral Discipline in Prisons.*

Bracton, H. de (1915) *De Legibus et Consuetudinibus Angliae*. First published: Woodbine edition, New Haven, Conn.

Braid, J. (1843) *Neurypnology; or, the Rationale of Modern Nervous Sleep, Considered in relation with Animal Magnetism.*

—— (1853) *Hypnotic Therapeutics, Illustrated by Cases.*

Bramwell, J. (1903) *Hypnotism: its History, Practice and Theory*. London: Grant Richards.

Brockbank, E. (1934) *A Short History of the Cheadle Royal from its Foundation in 1766*. Manchester: Sherratt and Hughes.

Browne, W. A. F. (1837) *What Asylums Were, Are and Ought to Be*. Edinburgh.

Bru, P. (1890) *Histoire de Bicêtre*. Paris.

Bucknill, J. and Tuke, D. H. (1858) *A Manual of Psychological Medicine.*

Bumm, A. (1903) *Zur Geschichte der panoptischen Irrenanstalten*. Erlangen.

Burdett, H. C. (1891–93) *Hospitals and Asylums of the World*. London: J. & A. Churchill.

Burke, E. (1757) *A Philosophical Enquiry into the Origin of our Ideas of the Sublime and Beautiful.*

Burrow, J. W. (1966) *Evolution and Society: A Study in Victorian Social Theory*. London: Cambridge University Press.

Burrows, G. (1820) *An Inquiry into Certain Errors relative to Insanity.*

—— (1828) *Commentaries on the Causes, Forms, Symptoms and Treatment, Moral and Medical, of Insanity.*

171

Burton, R. (1621) *The Anatomy of Melancholy*.

Byrd, M. (1974) *Visits to Bedlam: Madness and Literature in the Eighteenth Century*. Columbia, S. Carolina: University of South Carolina Press.

Cabanis, P. (Year VI, 1797) *Considérations générales sur l'étude de l'homme, Mémoires de l'Institut National*, Classes des sciences morales et politique. Paris.

—— (1802) *Rapports du physique et du moral de l'homme*. Paris.

Canguilhem, G. (1966) *Le normal et le pathologique*. Paris.

Chaplin, A. (1919) *Medicine in England during the Reign of George III*.

Charcot, J. M. and Richer, P. (1887) *Les Démoniaques dans l'art*. Paris.

Charlesworth, E. P. (1828) *Considerations on the Moral Management of Insane Persons*.

Charters of the Royal Hospitals of Bridewell and Bethlem (1807).

Chenevix-Trench, C. (1964) *The Royal Malady*. New York: Harcourt, Brace and World.

Chevalier, L. (1973) *Labouring Classes and Dangerous Classes in Paris during the First Half of the Nineteenth Century*. New York: H. Fertig.

Cheyne, G. (1733) *The English Malady; or, a Treatise of Nervous Diseases of All Kinds, as Spleen, Vapours, Lowness of Spirits, Hypochondriacal, and Hysterical, Distempers*.

Cicero (1927) *Tusculan Disputations*. Loeb Classical Library. London: Heinemann.

Clay, R. M. (1909) *The Medieval Hospitals of England*. London: Methuen & Co.

Collinson, G. (1812) *Treatise on the Law concerning Idiots, Lunatics and Other Persons 'Non Compotes Mentis'*.

Combe, A. (1831) *Observations on Mental Derangement: being an Application of the Principles of Phrenology to the Elucidation of the Causes, Symptoms, Nature, and Treatment of Insanity*. Edinburgh.

Combe, G. (1836) *A System of Phrenology*. Edinburgh.

Condillac, E. Bonnot de (1754) *Traité des sensations*. Paris.

Condorcet, Marquis de (1795) *Outlines of an Historical View of the Progress of the Human Mind*.

Conolly, J. (1828) *An Introductory Lecture Delivered in the University of London*.

—— (1830) *An Inquiry concerning the Indications of Insanity*.

—— (1847) *The Construction and Government of Lunatic Asylums*.

—— (1850) *Familiar Views of Lunacy and Lunatic Life*.

—— (1856) *The Treatment of the Insane without Mechanical Restraints*.

Copeland, A. (1888) *Bridewell Royal Hospital, Past and Present*.

Coulter, J. (1973) *Approaches to Insanity: a Philosophical and Sociological Study*. New York: Wiley.

Cox, J. M. (1806) *Practical Observations on Insanity*.

Crichton, A. (1798) *An Inquiry into the Nature and Origin of Mental Derangement*.

Crowther, B. (1811) *Practical Remarks on Insanity*.

Cullen, W. (1784) *First Lines of the Practise of Physic*.

172

—— (1792) *Synopsis and Nosology*.

Dain, N. (1964) *Concepts of Insanity in the United States, 1789–1865*. New Brunswick, NJ: Rutgers University Press.

Dainton, C. (1961) *The Story of England's Hospitals*. London: Museum Press.

Darwin, C. (1872) *The Expression of the Emotions in Man and Animals*.

Defoe, D. (1700) *The True-Born Englishman*.

—— (1706) *A Review of the State of the English Nation*, vol. 3.

—— (1728) *Augusta Triumphans: or, the Way to Make London the Most Flourishing City in the Universe*.

Détails sur l'établissement du Docteur Willis, pour la guérison des aliénés (1796). *Bibliothèque Britannique*, Littérature, vol. 1.

Deutsch, A. (1948) *The Mentally Ill in America*. Garden City, NJ: Doubleday & Co.

Dickens, C. (1841) *Barnaby Rudge* (1883 edition).

—— (1851–52) The Treatment of the Insane. *Household Words* **76, 115**.

Doerner, K. (1969) *Buerger und Irre*. Frankfurt am Main: Europäische Verlagsanstalt.

Driver, E. (1972) *The Sociology and Anthropology of Mental Illness: A Reference Guide*. Amherst, Mass.: University of Massachusetts Press.

Dudley, E. and Novack, M. (eds) (1974) *The Wild Man Within: an Image in Western Thought from the Renaissance to Romanticism*. Pittsburgh, Pa.: University of Pittsburgh Press.

Duncan, A. (1809) *Observations on the Structure of Hospitals for the Treatment of Lunatics*. Edinburgh.

Duncan, A., Jr (1809) *Observations on the General Treatment of Lunatics as a Branch of Medical Police*. Edinburgh.

Earle, P. (1837) *Of the Causes, Duration, Termination and Moral Treatment of Insanity*. Philadelphia, Pa.

—— (1841) *A Visit to Thirteen Asylums for the Insane in Europe*. Philadelphia, Pa.

Eaton, J. and Weil, R. (1955) *Culture and Mental Disorders*. Glencoe, Ill.: Free Press.

Eden, F. (1797) *The State of the Poor*.

Ellenberger, H. (1970) *The Discovery of the Unconscious: The History and Evolution of Dynamic Psychiatry*. London: Allen Lane.

Ellis, W. C. (1815) *Considerations on the Necessity of Proper Places being Provided by the Legislature for the Reception of All Insane Persons*. Hull.

—— (1838) *A Treatise on the Nature, Causes, Symptoms and Treatment of Insanity*.

Esquirol, J. E. D. (1805) *Des Passions considerées comme causes, symptômes, et moyens curatifs de l'aliénation mentale*. Paris.

—— (1819) *Des Etablissements consacrés aux aliénés en France*. Paris.

—— (1838) *Maladies mentales*. Paris. English translation 1845, Philadelphia, Pa.

Evans, R. (1971) Bentham's Panopticon: an Incident in the Social History of Architecture. *Architectural Association Quarterly* **3** (2).

Faber, K. (1930) *Nosography*. New York: P. B. Hoeber.

Falconer, W. (1791) *A Dissertation on the Influence of the Passions upon Disorders of the Body*.

Farr, W. (1835) *Statistics of English Lunatic Asylums*.

—— (1837a) Statistics of Insanity. *British Annals of Medicine*, 1: 648–53, 679–83, 744–48, 811–14; 2: 137–40, 171–74, 204–07, 235–39.

—— (1837b) Vital Statistics. In J. McCulloch (ed.) *A Statistical Account of the British Empire*.

—— (1841) Report upon the Mortality of Lunatics. *Journal of the Statistical Society* 4: 17–33.

Ferriar, J. (1792) *Medical Histories and Reflections*.

Fessler, A. (1956) The Management of Lunacy in Seventeenth-Century England: An Investigation of Quarter Sessions Records. *Proceedings of the Royal Society of Medicine* 49: 901–07.

Foucault, M. (1956) *Maladie mentale et psychologie*. Paris: Press Univérsitaires, de France (third edition, 1966).

—— (1961) *Folie et déraison; histoire de la folie à l'âge classique*. Paris (revised edition, 1972).

—— (1965) *Madness and Civilization*. New York: Pantheon Books.

—— (1972) *The Archaeology of Knowledge*. London: Tavistock Publications.

—— (1973) *The Birth of the Clinic*. London: Tavistock Publications.

—— (1977) *Discipline and Punish*. London: Allen Lane.

Frankel, C. (1948) *The Faith of Reason*. New York: King's Crown Press.

Franklin, B., *et al.* (1785) *Report of Dr Benjamin Franklin and Other Commissioners, Charged by the King of France with the Examination of the Animal Magnetism, as now Practised in Paris*.

French, C. (1951) *The Story of St Luke's Hospital*.

Fussell, P. (1965) *The Rhetorical World of Augustan Humanism*. Oxford: Clarendon Press.

Gall, F. (1825) *Sur les fonctions du cerveau et sur celles de chacune de ses parties*. Paris.

Gentis, R. (1971) *Guérir la vie*. Paris.

George, M. D. (1967) *Hogarth to Cruikshank: Social Change in Graphic Satire*. London: Allen Lane.

Giustino, D. (1975) *Conquest of Mind: Phrenology and Victorian Social Thought*. London: Croom Helm.

Graunt, J. (1662) *Natural and Political Observations Made upon the Bills of Mortality*.

Greenblatt, M., York, R., and Brown, E. (1955) *From Custodial to Therapeutic Patient Care in Mental Hospitals*. New York: Russell Sage Foundation.

Grew, N. (1701) *Cosmologia Sacra; or, a Discourse of the Universe as it is the Creature and Kingdom of God*.

Grey, J. (1815) *History of the York Lunatic Asylum*. York.

Grob, G. (1966) *The State and the Mentally Ill: A History of Worcester State Hospital in Massachusetts*. Chapel Hill, N. Carolina: University of North Carolina Press.

—— (1973) *Mental Institutions in America: Social Policy to 1875.* New York: Free Press.

Grosley, P. J. (1772) *A Tour to London.*

Guillain, G. and Mathieu, P. (1925) *La Salpêtrière.* Paris.

Halévy, E. (1955) *The Growth of Philosophic Radicalism.* Boston, Mass.: Beacon Press.

Hall, J. (1767) *A Narrative of the Proceedings relative to the Establishment of St Luke's House.* Newcastle upon Tyne.

Hallaran, W. (1810) *An Inquiry into the Causes Producing the Extraordinary Addition to the Numbers of the Insane.* Cork.

Halliday, A. (1806) *On the Present State of Lunatic Asylums in Great Britain.* Edinburgh.

—— (1828) *A General View of the Present State of Lunatics and Lunatic Asylums in Great Britain and Ireland.*

Hamilton, B. (1951–52) The Medical Professions in the Eighteenth Century. *Economic History Review* **4**: 141–69.

Hammond, J. L. and Hammond, B. (1933) Poverty, Crime, Philanthropy. In A. Turberville (ed.) *Johnson's England.* Oxford: Clarendon Press.

—— (1936) *Lord Shaftesbury.* London: Longman & Co.

Hanway, J. (1775) *The Defects of Police.*

Hare, E. H. (1959) The Origin and Spread of Dementia Paralytica. *Journal of Mental Science* **105**: 594–626.

—— (1962) Masturbational Insanity: the History of an Idea. *Journal of Mental Science* **108**: 1–26.

Harper, A. (1789) *A Treatise on the Real Cause and Cure of Insanity.*

Harrison, B. (1966) Philanthropy and the Victorians. *Victorian Studies* **9**: 353–77.

Hartley, D. (1749) *Observations on Man.*

Haslam, J. (1809) *Observations on Insanity.* First published 1798.

—— (1810) *Illustrations of Madness.*

—— (1817) *Considerations on the Moral Management of Insane Persons.*

Haygarth, J. (1800) *Of the Imagination, as a Cause and as a Cure of Disorders of the Body; Exemplified by Fictitious Tractors, and Epidemical Convulsions.* Bath.

Heasman, K. (1962) *Evangelicals in Action.* London: G. Bles.

Helvétius, C. A. (1818) *De l'homme.* Paris. First published 1775.

Henry, M. (1922) *La Salpêtrière sous l'Ancien Régime.* Paris.

Highmore, A. (1810) *Pietas Londinensis: the History, Design, and Present State of the Various Public Charities in and near London.*

Hill, C. (1962) Clarissa Harlowe and her Times. In *Puritanism and Revolution.* London: Secker & Warburg.

—— (1965) 'Reason' and 'Reasonableness' in Seventeenth-Century England. *British Journal of Sociology* **20**: 235–52.

—— (1972) *The World Turned Upside Down: Radical Ideas during the English Revolution.* London: Temple Smith.

Hill, R. G. (1839) *Total Abolition of Personal Restraint in the Treatment of the Insane.*

—— (1857) *The Non-Restraint System of Treatment in Lunacy.*

Himmelfarb, G. (1968) The Haunted House of Jeremy Bentham. In *Victorian Minds.* New York: Knopf.

Hodgkinson, R. (1966) Provision for Pauper Lunatics, 1834–1871. *Medical History* **10**: 138–54.

Hoeldtke, R. (1967) The History of Associationism and British Medical Psychology. *Medical History* **11**: 46–65.

Holdsworth, W. (1903) *A History of English Law.*

Howard, J. (1789) *An Account of the Principal Lazarettos in Europe.*

—— (1792) *The State of the Prisons in England and Wales.* First published 1777, Warrington.

Howells, J. and Osborn, M. (1970) The Incidence of Emotional Disorder in a Seventeenth-Century Medical Practice. *Medical History* **14**: 192–98.

Howse, E. (1952) *Saints in Politics.* London: Allen & Unwin.

Hunt, H. C. (1932) *A Retired Habitation: A History of the Retreat.* London: H. K. Lewis.

Hunter, R. A. and Macalpine, I. (eds) (1963) *Three Hundred Years of Psychiatry, 1535–1860: A History Presented in Selected English Texts.* Oxford: Oxford University Press.

Hunter, R. A. and Macalpine, I. (1969) *George III and the Mad-Business.* London: Allen Lane.

—— (1974) *Psychiatry for the Poor.* Folkestone: Dawsons of Pall Mall.

Huxley, A. (1950) Variations on 'The Prisons'. In *Themes and Variations.* London: Chatto & Windus.

Ireland, J. (1791–98) *Hogarth Illustrated.*

Ireland, W. (1885) *The Blot upon the Brain.* Edinburgh.

Ives, G. (1910) *A History of Penal Methods: Criminals, Witches, Lunatics.* Edinburgh: printed privately.

Jacobi, M. (1841) *On the Construction and Management of Hospitals for the Insane.*

Jarvis, E. (1851–52) On the Supposed Increase of Insanity. *American Journal of Insanity* **8**: 333–64.

Jaspers, K. (1962) *General Psychopathology.* Manchester: Manchester University Press.

Jetter, D. (1962a) Das ideale Irrenhaus im Spiegel historischer Bauplaene. *Confinia Psychiatrica* **5**: 1–30.

—— (1962b) Ursprung und Gestalt panoptischer Irrenhaeuser in England und Schottland. *Suddhoffs Archiv.* **46**: 27–44.

Jones, K. (1972) *A History of the Mental Health Services.* London: Routledge & Kegan Paul.

Johnson, S. (1887) *Rasselas, The Prince of Abissinia.* Oxford. First published 1759.

Kiev, A. (1972) *Transcultural Psychiatry.* New York: Free Press.

King, A. (1966) Hospital Planning: Revised Thoughts on the Origin of the Pavilion Principle in England. *Medical History* **10**: 360–73.

King, L. (1971) *The Medical World of the Eighteenth Century*. Huntington, NY: R. E. Krieger.

Klein, D. B. (1970) *A History of Scientific Psychology*. New York: Basic Books.

Klibansky, R., Panofsky, E., and Saxl, F. (1964) *Saturn and Melancholy: Studies in the History of Natural Philosophy, Religion and Art*. London: Nelson.

Kraepelin, E. (1918) *Hundert Jahre Psychiatrie*. Berlin.

Lanteri-Laura, G. (1972) La chronicité dans la psychiatrie moderne. *Annales* **27**: 548–68.

Lasch, C. (1973) Origins of the Asylum. In *The World of Nations*. New York: Knopf.

Lavater, J. C. (1789–98) *Essays on Physiognomy*.

—— (1806) *L'Art de connaitre les hommes par la physionomie*. Paris.

Lavoisier, A. (1865) *Oeuvres*, vol. 3. Paris.

Lecky, W. E. H. (1865) *History of the Rise and Influence of the Spirit of Rationalism in Europe*.

Leibbrand, W. and Wettley, A. (1961) *Der Wahnsinn: Geschichte der abendlaendischen Psychopathologie*. Munich.

Leigh, D. (1961) *The Historical Development of British Psychiatry*. Oxford: Pergamon Press.

Leistikow, D. (1967) *Ten Centuries of European Hospital Buildings*. Ingleheim.

Lewis, I. (1971) *Ecstatic Religion: An Anthropological Study of Spirit Possession and Shamanism*. Harmondsworth: Penguin Books.

Lichtenberg, G. C. (1966) *Commentaries on Hogarth's Engravings*. Boston, Mass.: Houghton Mifflin.

Locke, J. (1690) *An Essay concerning Human Understanding*.

—— (1698) *Two Treatises on Government*. Cambridge: Cambridge University Press, 1963.

Lowe, L. (1883) *The Bastilles of England; or, the Lunacy Laws at Work*.

Lumley, W. (1845) *The New Lunacy Acts*.

Mack, M. (1962) *Jeremy Bentham: an Odyssey of Ideas, 1748–1792*. London: Heinemann.

Mackenzie, I. (1935) *Social Activities of the English Friends in the First Half of the Nineteenth Century*. New York: printed privately.

Manchester Royal Lunatic Hospital (1791) *Rules for the Government of the Lunatic Hospital and Asylum*. Manchester.

Manuel, F. (1972) From Equality to Organicism. In *Freedom from History and Other Untimely Essays*. New York: New York University Press.

Markus, T. (1954) The Pattern of the Law. *Architectural Review* **106**: 251–56.

Marshall, J. D. (1961) The Nottinghamshire Reformers and their Contribution to the New Poor Law. *Economic History Review* **13**: 382–96.

Marx, O. (1967) Descriptions of Psychiatric Care in Some Hospitals during the

177

First Half of the Nineteenth Century. *Bulletin of the History of Medicine* **41**: 208–14.

Marx, O. (1970) Nineteenth-Century Medical Psychology. *Isis* **61**: 355–70.

Maudsley, H. (1879) *The Pathology of Mind.*

Mayhew, H. and Mayhew, A. (1849) *The Magic of Kindness.*

Menninger, K. and Pruyser, P. (1963) *The Vital Balance.* New York: Viking Press.

Mesmer, F. A. (1779) *Mémoire sur la découverte du magnetisme animal.* Paris.

Millar, J. (1859) *A Plea in Favour of the Insane Poor.*

Mora, G. (1965) The History of Psychiatry: A Cultural and Bibliographical Survey. *Psychoanalytic Review* **52** (2): 154–84.

Morel, B. (1857) *Traité des dégénérescences physiques, intellectuelles, et morales de l'espèce humaine.* Paris.

Morison, A. (1824) *Outlines of Mental Diseases.* Edinburgh.

—— (1844) *A Paper Suggesting the Propriety of the Study of the Nature, Causes and Treatment of Mental Disease, as Forming Part of the Curriculum of Medical Education.* London: for the Society for Improving the Condition of the Insane.

Neild, J. (1802) *An Account of the Various Prisons of England and Wales.*

Neuberger, M. (1913) *Johann Christian Reil.* Stuttgart.

Nobel, D. (1853) *Elements of Psychological Medicine: An Introduction to the Practical Study of Insanity.*

O'Donoghue, E. (1914) *The Story of Bethlehem Hospital.* London: T. Fisher Unwin.

Oesterreich, T. K. (1930) *Possession, Demoniacal and Other.* New York: R. R. Smith.

Official Publications

(1763) Report of the Select Committee Appointed to Enquire into the State of Private Madhouses.

(1788–89) Report from the Committee Appointed to Examine the Physicians who have Attended His Majesty.

(1807) Report from the Select Committee on the State of Criminal and Pauper Lunatics and the Laws Relating thereto.

(1815–16) Reports from the Select Committee on the Better Regulation of Madhouses in England.

(1819) Return of the Number of Lunatics Confined in the Different Gaols, Hospitals, and Lunatic asylums.

(1824) Return of Counties in which there are Lunatic Asylums.

(1827) Report from the Select Committee on the State of Pauper Lunatics.

(1831) Returns of the Number of Public and Private Lunatic Asylums in England and Wales.

(1837) Returns of the Number of Pauper Lunatics and Idiots in Each County in England and Wales; and of Criminal Lunatics, with Their Places of Confinement.

(1841) Annual Reports (1835–41) made by the Metropolitan Commissioners in Lunacy.

(1844a) Report of the Metropolitan Commissioners in Lunacy.

(1844b) Tenth Annual Report of the Poor Law Commissioners.

(1862) Return of the Number of Lunatics in Lunatic Asylums of England and Wales.

(1845–   ) Annual Reports of the Commissioners in Lunacy.

Opler, M. (1959) *Culture and Mental Health: Cross-Cultural Studies.* New York: Macmillan.

Orwell, G. (1961) *Collected Essays.* London: Secker & Warburg.

Parchappe de Vinay, J. B. (1839) *Recherches statistiques sur les causes de l'aliénation mentale.* Rouen.

Pargeter, W. (1792) *Observations on Maniacal Disorders.* Reading.

Parkinson, J. (1811) *Mad-houses: Observations on the Act for Regulating Madhouses.*

Parrish, J. (1805) *Influence of the Passions on the Body.*

Parry-Jones, W. (1972) *The Trade in Lunacy.* London: Routledge & Kegan Paul.

Partridge, R. (1953) *Broadmoor: A History of Criminal Lunacy.* London: Chatto & Windus.

Paternoster, R. (1841) *The Madhouse System.*

Paul, G. O. (1806) *Suggestions of Sir G. O. Paul to Earl Spencer.*

—— (1812) *Observations on the Subject of Lunatic Asylums.* Gloucester.

Pennant, T. (1791) *Some Account of London.*

Perceval, J. (1838, 1840) *A Narrative of the Treatment Experienced by a Gentleman, during a State of Mental Derangement.*

Perfect, W. (1779) *Cases of Insanity.* Rochester.

—— (1805) *Annals of Insanity: Comprising a Large Selection of Curious and Interesting Cases, with the Medical and Moral Treatment of Each.*

Pinel, P. (1806) *A Treatise on Insanity.* Sheffield.

—— (1818) *Nosographie philosophique.* Paris.

Pinker, R. (1966) *English Hospital Statistics, 1861–1938.* London: Heinemann.

Platt, A. and Diamond, B. (1965) The Origins and Development of the 'Wild Beast' Concept of Mental Illness and its Relation to Theories of Criminal Responsibility. *Journal of the History of the Behavioral Sciences* 1: 355–67.

Plumb, J. (1972) Bedlam. In *In the Light of History.* London: Allen Lane.

Powell, R. (1813) Observations on the Comparative Prevalence of Insanity at Different Periods. *Medical Transactions of the College of Physicians* 4: 131–59.

Poynter, F. N. L. (1962) *The Evolution of Hospitals in Britain.*

Prichard, J. C. (1835) *A Treatise on Insanity.*

—— (1842) *The Different Forms of Insanity in relation to Jurisprudence.*

—— (1843) *The Natural History of Man: Comprising Inquiries into the Modifying Influence of Physical and Moral Agencies of the Different Tribes of the Human Family.*

Pugh, R. B. (1968) *Imprisonment in Medieval England*. London: Cambridge University Press.

Quen, J. (1968) An Historical View of the M'Naghten Trial. *Bulletin of the History of Medicine* **42**: 43–51.

Quetelet, L. (1827) *Recherches sur la population*. Brussells.

—— (1830) *Recherches sur le penchant au crime aux différens âges*. Brussells.

Quinlan, M. (1941) *Victorian Prelude: A History of English Manners 1700–1830*. New York: Columbia University Press.

Rank, O. (1910) Schopenhauer über den Wahnsinn. *Zentralblatt fuer Psychoanalyse* **1**: 69–71.

Rather, L. J. (1965) *Mind and Body in Eighteenth-Century Medicine: A Study Based on Jerome Gaub's 'De Regemine Mentis'*. London: Wellcome Institute.

Ray, I. (1838) *A Treatise on the Medical Jurisprudence of Insanity*. Boston, Mass.

Reasons for the Establishing and Further Encouragement of St Luke's Hospital for Lunatics (1772).

Reed, R. (1952) *Bedlam on the Jacobean Stage*. Cambridge, Mass.: Harvard University Press.

Rees, T. P. (1957) Back to Moral Treatment and Community Care. *Journal of Mental Science* **103**: 303–13.

Reid, J. (1808) Report of Diseases. *The Monthly Magazine* **25**.

—— (1816) *Essays on Insanity*.

Reid, T. (1764) *An Inquiry into the Human Mind, on the Principles of Common Sense*.

Reil, J. C. (1803) *Rhapsodien über die Anwendung der psychischen Cur-Methode auf Geisteszerruettungen*. Halle.

Report of the Experiments on Animal Magnetism, Made by a Committee of the Medical Section of the French Royal Academy of Sciences (1784).

Richard, E. (1889) *Histoire de l'Hôpital de Bicêtre*. Paris.

Riese, W. (1945) History and Principles of Classification of Nervous Diseases. *Bulletin of the History of Medicine* **18**: 465–512.

—— (1951) An Outline of a History of Ideas in Psychotherapy. *Bulletin of the History of Medicine* **25**: 442–56.

—— (1967) *The Legacy of Pinel*. New York: Springer Publishing Co.

Rive, C. G. de la (1798) *Lettre sur un nouvel établissement pour la guérison des aliénés*. Geneva.

Roberton, J. (1812) *Medical Police; or, the Causes of Disease, with Means of Prevention*.

Roberts, N. (1967) *Cheadle Royal Hospital*. Altrincham: Sherratt.

Robertson, C. (1867) The Care and Treatment of the Insane Poor. *Journal of Mental Science* **13**: 289–306.

Rogers, J. (1816) *A Statement of the Cruelties, and Frauds which are Practised in Madhouses*.

Rose, G. (1805) *Observations on the Poor Laws and on the Management of the Poor*.

Rosen, G. (1946) The Philosophy of Ideology and the Emergence of Modern Medicine in France. *Bulletin of the History of Medicine* **20**: 328–39.

—— (1953) Cameralism and the Concept of Medical Police. *Bulletin of the History of Medicine* **27**: 21–42.

—— (1968) *Madness in Society: Chapters in the Historical Sociology of Mental Illness*. London: Routledge & Kegan Paul.

Rosenau, H. (1970) *Social Purpose in Architecture: Paris and London Compared, 1760–1800*. London: Studio Vista.

Rothman, D. (1971) *The Discovery of the Asylum*. Boston: Little, Brown & Co.

Rowley, W. (1790) *Truth Vindicated; or, the Specific Differences of Mental Diseases Ascertained*.

Rules and Orders of the Public Infirmary at Liverpool (1803). Liverpool.

Rusche, G. and Kirchheimer, O. (1939) *Punishment and Social Structure*. New York: Columbia University Press.

Rush, B. (1830) *Medical Inquiries and Observations*. First published 1789. Philadelphia, Pa.

Sarbin, T. and Juhasz, J. (1967) The Historical Background to the Concept of Hallucination. *Journal of the History of the Behavioural Sciences* **3**: 339–58.

Scull, A. (1979) *Museums of Madness: The Social Organization of Insanity in Nineteenth-Century England*. London: Allen Lane.

—— (ed.) (1981) *Madhouses, Mad-doctors, and Madmen: The Social History of Psychiatry in the Victorian Era*. Philadelphia, Pa.: University of Pennsylvania Press.

Séguin, E. (1846) *Traitement moral, hygiène et éducation des idiots*. Paris.

Select Committee on Madhouses (1815–16) *Minutes of Evidence*.

Semelaigne, R. (1912) *Aliénistes et Philanthropes: Les Pinel et Les Tuke*. Paris.

Sharma, S. (1970) An Historical Background to the Development of Nosology in Psychiatry and Psychology. *American Psychologist* **25**: 248–53.

Shryock, R. (1936) *The Development of Modern Medicine: An Interpretation of the Social and Scientific Factors Involved*. Philadelphia, Pa.: University of Pennsylvania Press.

Silvette, H. (1938) On Insanity in Seventeenth-Century England. *Bulletin of the History of Medicine* **6**: 22–33.

Sketches in Bedlam (1823).

Skultans, V. (ed.) (1975) *Madness and Morals: Ideas on Insanity in the Nineteenth Century*. London: Routledge & Kegan Paul.

Smith, T. S. (1836–37) *The Philosophy of Health*.

Spurzheim, J. G. (1815) *Physiognomical System of Drs Gall & Spurzheim*.

—— (1817) *Observations on the Deranged Manifestations of the Mind, or Insanity*.

Standing Rules and Orders for the Government of the Royal Hospitals of Bridewell and Bethlem, with the Duty of the Governors (1792).

Stark, W. (1807) *Remarks on the Construction of Public Hospitals for the Cure of Mental Derangement*. Edinburgh.

Starobinski, J. (1960) Histoire du traitement de la mélancolie des origines à 1900. *Acta Psychosomatica* **4**.

Stearns, S. (1791) *The History of Animal Magnetism*.

Stewart, D. (1827) *Elements of the Philosophy of the Human Mind.*
Strype, J. (1720) *A Survey of the Cities of London and Westminster.*
Summerson, J. (ed.) (1947) *The Microcosm of London.* Harmondsworth: Penguin Books.
Taylor, N. (1973) The Awful Sublimity of the Victorian City. In H. Dyos and M. Wolff (eds) *The Victorian City,* vol. 2. London: Routledge & Kegan Paul.
Temkin, O. (1946) Gall and the Phrenological Movement. *Bulletin of the History of Medicine* **20**: 10–35.
—— (1963) The Scientific Approach to Disease: Specific Entity and Individual Sickness. In A. Crombie (ed.) *Scientific Change.* London: Heinemann.
Tempest, J. (1830) *Narrative of Treatment Experienced by John Tempest, Esq. during Fourteen Months Solitary Confinement under a False Imputation of Lunacy.*
Tenon, J. R. (1788) *Mémoires sur les hôpitaux de Paris.* Paris.
Thackrah, C. (1831) *The Effects of Arts, Trades, and Professions, and of Civil States and Habits of Living, on Health and Longevity.*
Thelwall, J. (1810) *On Imperfect Developments of the Faculties, Mental and Moral, as well as Constitutional and Organic.*
Thomas, K. (1971) *Religion and the Decline of Magic.* London: Weidenfield & Nicolson.
Thomas, V. (1827) *An Account of the Origin, Nature and Objects of the Asylum on Headington Hill, near Oxford.* Oxford.
Thompson, J. and Goldin, G. (1975) *The Hospital: A Social and Architectural History.* New Haven, Conn.: Yale University Press.
Thurnam, J. (1841) *The Statistics of the Retreat.* York.
—— (1845) *Observations and Essays on the Statistics of Insanity.*
Tissot, S. (1781) *Traité des nerfs et de leurs maladies.* Paris.
Townsend, J. (1786) *A Dissertation on the Poor Laws.*
Townshend, C. (1840) *Facts in Mesmerism.*
Trenchard, J. (1709) *The Natural History of Superstition.*
Trotter, T. (1804) *An Essay, Medical, Philosophical, and Chemical, on Drunkenness.*
Trusler, J. (1768) *Hogarth Moralized.*
Tuke, D. H. (1878) *Insanity in Ancient and Modern Life.*
—— (1882) *Chapters in the History of the Insane in the British Isles.*
—— (1892) *Reform in the Treatment of the Insane: Early History of the Retreat.* York.
Tuke, S. (1813) *Description of the Retreat.* York.
—— (1815) *Practical Hints on the Construction and Economy of Pauper Lunatic Asylums.*
Tuveson, E. (1960) *The Imagination as a Means of Grace.* Berkeley, Calif.: University of California Press.
Uwins, D. (1833) *A Treatise on those Disorders of the Brain and Nervous System, which are usually Considered and Called Moral.*
Vallery-Radot, R. (1947) *Paris d'autrefois, ses vieux hôpitaux.* Paris.

Veith, I. (1965) *Hysteria: The History of a Disease*. Chicago, Ill.: University of Chicago Press.

Venturi, F. (1971) *Utopia and Reform in the Enlightenment*. Cambridge: Cambridge University Press.

Vilain XIV, Count (1775) *Mémoires sur les moyens de corriger les Malfaiteurs et Fainéants à leur propre avantage et les rendre utiles à L'État*. Ghent.

Vinchon, J. (1936) *Mesmer et son secret*. Paris: A. Legrand.

Voisin, F. (1826) *Des causes morales et physiques des maladies mentales*. Paris.

―― (1847) *Du traitement intelligent de la folie et application de quelques uns de ses principes à la reforme des criminels*. Paris.

Voltaire (1835) *Oeuvres*, vol. 7. Paris.

Walk, A. (1954) Some Aspects of the 'Moral Treatment' of the Insane up to 1854. *Journal of Mental Science* **100**: 807–37.

Walker, N. (1968) *Crime and Insanity in England*, vol. 1. Edinburgh: Edinburgh University Press.

Waserman, M. (1972) Benjamin Rush on Government and the Harmony and Derangement of the Mind. *Journal of the History of Ideas* **33**: 639–42.

Webb, S. and Webb, B. (1922) *English Prisons under Local Government*. London: Longmans, Green & Co.

―― (1927) *English Poor Law History*, vol. 1. London: Longmans, Green & Co.

Welsford, E. (1935) *The Fool: His Social and Literary History*. London: Faber & Faber.

Westermarck, E. (1906) *The Origin and Development of the Moral Ideas*. London: Macmillan.

Wheatley, H. (1891) *London Past and Present*.

Whyte, L. (1960) *The Unconscious before Freud*. New York: Basic Books.

Whyte, W. (1916) Reil's Rhapsodien. *Journal of Nervous and Mental Diseases* **43**: 1–22.

Williamson, G. (1933) The Restoration Revolt against Enthusiasm. *Studies in Philology* **30**.

Willis, F. (1823) *A Treatise on Mental Derangement*.

Woods, E. and Carlson, E. (1961) The Psychiatry of Philippe Pinel. *Bulletin of the History of Medicine* **35**: 14–25.

Woodward, J. (1974) *To Do the Sick no Harm: A Study of the British Voluntary Hospital System to 1875*. London: Routledge & Kegan Paul.

Wright, T. (1850) *Cholera in the Asylum*.

Yap, P. M. (1974) *Comparative Psychiatry: A Theoretical Framework*. Toronto: University of Toronto Press.

Young, R. (1970) *Mind, Brain and Adaptation in the Nineteenth Century*. Oxford: Clarendon Press.

Zilboorg, G. (1941) *A History of Medical Psychology*. New York: Norton.

Zweig, S. (1933) *Mental Healers*. New York: Viking Press.

NAME INDEX

SUBJECT INDEX

Acts: lunacy and asylums, eighteenth century 10, 12, 19–20, 25, 79, 166; lunacy and asylums, nineteenth century 3, 12, 15, 17, 20–3, 26–7, 81–3, 166; Poor Laws 11, 13, 15, 23, 28; vagrancy 11, 69, 163; workhouse 163
age of insane 89
airiness 30–4
alcoholism 93, 135, 137, 161
alienists see doctors, mad-
Allgemeines Krankenhaus, Vienna 61
amentia 70
America 90, 128
anachronisms ix
Anatomy of Melancholy, The 125, 130
animal magnetism 155–58
apothecaries 41
appropriateness, architectural 53
architecture: of confinement 48–67, 165; segregation and 39–40, 56, 65
architecture parlante 54, 56
articles and books on insanity 19, 43, 65, 71, 92, 104–31 passim, 139–49 passim, 155, 158, 167–68; see also literature; Reports
'artificial' insanity 71
Association of Medical Officers of Asylums and Hospitals for Insane 104, 166
'associationist' psychology 111–13
asylum: architecture of 39–40, 48–67, 165; 'discovery' of viii; representations of 30–47, 164–65;

see also Acts; Bethlem; funding; madhouses; provincial; Retreat; St Luke's
attraction, public, Bethlem as 45
Augustan moralists 127–28; see also Reason
Austria 61
'awakening', as therapy 113–14, 116–18

barbarism see savagery
Barnaby Rudge 140–41, 168
Bedford Asylum 24, 81
'bedlam' 162; see also Bethlem
Bethel Hospital, Norwich 7
Bethlem: as attraction 45; case-histories in 85, 91–2; costs 90; cures in 84; in early days 3–7, 11, 18, 20; forms of insanity in 72, 77, 147; Hogarth and 31, 36, 40–1, 46, 122; investigations of 5, 24, 34–6; mortality in 78, 84, 86; numbers in 4, 78, 84, 86; rebuilding of 12, 50–2; restraint in 4, 36, 45, 51; segregation, lack of 38
Bicêtre, Paris 34, 58
'birth of the clinic' 56
'birth of psychiatry' viii–ix
'Black Sessions' (1750) 32–3
brain 148–49
Bridewell Hospital 5
Bristol 13, 137
British Association for Advancement of Science 104

187